A. S. MATHER

LAND
USE

LONGMAN
LONDON AND NEW YORK

LONGMAN GROUP U.K. LIMITED
Longman House, Burnt Mill, Harlow
Essex CM20 2JE, England
Associated companies throughout the world

*Published in the United States of America
by Longman Inc., New York*

First published 1986

BRITISH LIBRARY CATALOGUING IN PUBLICATION DATA
Mather, A.S.
  Land use
    1. Land use
    I. Title
    333.73'13   HD111
  ISBN 0-582-30131-9

LIBRARY OF CONGRESS CATALOGING IN PUBLICATION DATA
Mather, Alexanders S. (Alexander Smith)
  Land use.

  Bibliography: p.
    includes index.
    1. Land use.   I. Title.
HD111.M36 1986   333.73'13   85-12920
ISBN 0-582-30131-9

Set in 10pt Linotron Sabon
Produced by Longman Group (FE) Limited
Printed in Hong Kong

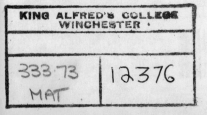

Contents

List of figures

List of tables

Preface

Land use is the concern of many disciplines and the preserve of none. Its principles are largely those of economics and ecology, but it is the product of human decisions operating within social, political and legal frameworks. It is all too easy to regard land use from single viewpoints such as ecology, economics or law, and to forget that it is a multi-faceted subject. The aim of this book is to view it as such. The underlying theme is that individuals and groups decide how to use and manage land. At times this theme is explicit, as, for example, in Chapter 2, and at times it is implicit, as in Chapter 6 which shows that both choice of land use and choice of land management affect the natural environment.

No single textbook can hope to present a comprehensive treatment of the philosophy, economics, sociology, politics and ecology of land use, and this work makes no attempt to do so. What it does attempt is to show something of the complexity of land use and the diversity of influences that act on it and effects that stem from it. This complexity and diversity are reflected in a set of references that, it is hoped, can offer a starting point for the student who wishes to pursue specific themes and aspects of land use.

Sincere thanks are due to all who have helped in the preparation of this book. Many students, postgraduates and undergraduates, have contributed, knowingly or unknowingly, to the approach adopted and the ideas expressed. Jimmy Coull, Richard Jackson, Eric Naylor, John Smith and Nick Williams made helpful comments and offered useful suggestions on drafts of various chapters, but neither they nor anyone other than the author are responsible for errors and omissions. Jane Calder typed the manuscript with an exemplary speed, accuracy and efficiency that highlighted to the author his slowness, carelessness and general inefficiency in preparing it.

Acknowledgements

We are grateful to the following for permission to reproduce copyright material:

Association of American Geographers for fig. 5.4 from fig 8 p 80 (Sinclair 1967) & adapted diagram (Boal 1970), table 2.5 from table 7 p 34 (Kollmorgen & Jenks 1958); Cambridge University Press for data in table 1.2 from tables 9.1, 9.2 (Bayliss–Smith 1982); Canadian Association of Geographers for fig 8.4 from fig 1 p 194 (Furuseth & Pierce 1982); Countryside Commission for table 5.1 from table 1 p 9 (Hall 1976); the author, Dr R W Edwards and Academic Press Inc (London) Ltd for fig 6.3 from p 83 Copyright 1977 by Academic Press Inc (London) Ltd (Scotter et al 1977); the editors for fig 6.1 from fig 8 (Davis 1976) & (Wolman 1967); the author, Dr R Gasson and the Agricultural Economics Society for tables 2.2, 2.3 from pp 534, 527 (Gasson 1973); the Controller, Her Majesty's Stationery Office for data in fig 1.3 (Northfield, Lord 1979); the author, Dr A R Hill and Academic Press Inc (London) Ltd for fig 6.2 from p 253 Copyright Academic Press Inc (London) Ltd (Hill 1976); the author, Dr G E Jones and the Agricultural Economics Society for fig 2.3 from figs 1, 2 pp 389–90 (Jones 1963); the author, Professor G E Likens and the American Association for the Advancement of Science for fig 6.4 redrawn from fig 1 Copyright 1978 by AAAS (Likens et al 1978); Longman Group Ltd for fig 3.2 from fig 1.1 (Bowler 1979); the Macaulay Institute for Soil Research and the authors for data in fig 8.2; the Nature Conservancy Council for table 6.2 from table 2 (Nature Conservancy Council 1977); the editor for figs 5.5a from fig 8 p 42 (Troughton 1976) & 5.5b from fig 3a p 76 (Bryant 1976); Organisation for Economic Co-operation & Development for figs

4.1, 4.3 from diagram A, F (OECD 1976); Oxford University Press Inc for fig 5.3 from fig 1 Copyright (c) 1982 by Oxford University Press Inc., Pergamon Press Ltd for data in table 1.4 from table 3.6 p 70 (Darin-Drabkin 1977); the author, Professor D Pimentel and the American Association for the Advancement of Science for table 6.1 from pp 149–155 Copyright 1976 by AAAS (Pimentel 1976); Rothamsted Experimental Station for data in table 1.3 (Spoor & Muckle 1974); the editor for fig 8.3 from fig 6 p 235 (Linton 1968); Soil Science of America for fig 8.1 (Hockensmith & Steele 1949); the author, Dr J S Steinhart and the American Association for the Advancement of Science for fig 1.1 redrawn from fig 5; the author Professor G Wall for fig 6.5 from fig 10 (Wall & Wright 1977) and Eyre and Spottiswoode (Publishers) Ltd, Her Majesty's Printers London for extracts from the *Authorized King James Version of the Bible* which is Crown Copyright in the United Kingdom.

1

Land and its use

It has often been said that land is the basic natural resource. Over the span of human history, man has drawn most of his sustenance and much of his fuel, clothing and shelter from the land. Land has been man's habitat and living space; land has been a matter of life and death, of survival or starvation. That the use of land should have been of major importance to man is, therefore, not surprising. What is more surprising is that man's attachment to land and his concern for it have persisted into the industrial (and post-industrial) age. In the developed west, and increasingly in other parts of the world, man has become separated from the land, in terms of his sustenance at least, if not of his living space. His food comes from the supermarket rather than directly from the soil. Much of his clothing is of synthetic fibre. In place of firewood he uses fossil fuels from deep below the land surface. Days, weeks or months may pass when his only landscape is townscape. Yet he is still concerned about the use of the land from which he has become largely separated. Should farmland around the edges of a town be built over? Should open moorland be afforested? Should native wood-land be cut over? How should commercial and residential land uses relate to each other within the city? The number of people directly involved in land-use issues such as these is small, but the controversies that surround them may be both fierce and sustained. Man may live in the city, but he has a general concern for the use of both rural and urban land. The use of most natural resources – minerals, fossil fuels, water power – invariably evokes concern, but the use of land seems to stand out in attracting special attention. Perhaps even urban man remembers that he is a terrestrial creature, and that his roots reach back to the land. No clearer identification between man and land is expressed than in the Hebrew language; man is *adam* and land is *adama*.

CONCEPTS OF LAND

In 1 Kings 21, we read of an encounter between Ahab and Naboth that illustrates a fundamental contrast in attitudes to land. Ahab, in coveting Naboth's vineyard, sees land simply as a commodity that can be bought and sold (v.2): 'Give me thy vineyard, that I may have it for a garden of herbs because it is near unto my house: and I will give thee for it a better vineyard, or if it seem good to thee, I will give thee the worth of it in money.' But to Naboth, land is not just a tradable commodity (v.3): 'The Lord forbid it me, that I should give the inheritance of my father unto thee.' Land to Naboth is an inheritance over which he has stewardship. He has temporary rights of use, but no permanent right of disposal.

This encounter encapsulates two of the most enduring concepts of land. On the one hand, land is simply a form of property that may be traded at will. On the other, land is much more than just personal private property, and its possession is not (just) a matter for market forces to determine. In this second concept, a sense of stewardship attaches, and land is a form of common property, either in the sense of succeeding generations or, by extension, in the wider sense that the community has an interest in it. This basic contrast in attitudes is of fundamental importance, and it lies at the root of many issues and conflicts in the use of land. It underlies public controls or constraints on the extent to which the individual may use land as he pleases, and it may have a bearing on how he manages the land under his control. (For discussion of the relationship between concepts of land and controls on land use, see, for example, Andrews 1979 and Chassagne 1979a. For a review of the philosophical issues arising from the concept of land as property, see Clark 1982b.)

The literature on land ownership and its origins and evolution is enormous, and no thumb-nail sketch can avoid the dangers of over-simplification (for a fuller outline, see, for example, Bryant 1972). In very general terms, it is possible to discern a cycle in which an ancient pattern of communal control or ownership of land gave way to individual private property rights. More recently, individual rights in land have become subject to increasing influence from central and local government, reflecting a growing community concern about land and a changing attitude towards it. This cyclical model, as outlined by Jacoby (1971), is crude and over-generalised. As the case of Naboth's vineyard illustrates, the concept of marketable private property rights in land was not unknown in the ancient world, and the model also over-simplifies by reducing the issue to one of public or private control of land. Nevertheless, in spite of these and other failings, the model does seem to have at least partial validity, and is attractive by virtue of its simplicity in a field of such great complexity.

In pre-agricultural times, the modern concept of land ownership would not have been very meaningful. If the population were sparse and ample land were available, land might be regarded as a 'free good' like water or air. The territory of a tribe or group of families might be defended against other groups if populations grew and competed for land, but there would be no concept of individual ownership of parcels of land. In time, however, this communal 'ownership' was usually replaced by a system of individual ownership. Communal land gradually became vested in the hands of the chief or leader of the group. The chief or leader may have held the land on behalf of the group, and in this role may have felt strong responsibilities and obligations towards his people. These feelings usually faded as time went by, and in effect a system of individual ownership became established.

The passage from communal to individual ownership and the emergence of a concept of private property rights and their sale and exchange is by no means a simple, linear story. Different rates and courses of development have applied in different parts of the world. In feudal times, for example, land was not a marketable commodity. It could be received from the king or acquired through marriage, but with it was linked territorial administration and political and social authority. Later, under the mercantilist concept, the land belonged to him who paid most for it, and ownership was technically dissociated from political power and administration. In practice, however, some of the earlier connotations of land ownership with power and authority survived through the heydays of the burgeoning mercantilist views of recent centuries.

In Victorian Britain, private property rights in land were almost completely untrammelled. The concepts of land as the inheritance and property of the group, and of stewardship and social responsibility in the use of land, had faded. But the failings of the *laissez-faire* system were soon recognised, and with their recognition, curbs were imposed on some land owners and some land was acquired by the state for social (communal) purposes. In 1886, the Crofters' Holdings Act constrained the freedom of the land owner to evict his tenants and re-organise his land as he pleased in parts of north and west Scotland. At around the same time, the supply of timber from privately owned land was being perceived as inadequate for national needs. Eventually in 1919, the Forestry

Commission was set up as a state forestry service with powers to acquire land to be held by the state for purposes of forestry: the system of *laissez-faire* and of purely private land ownership was now acknowledged to have been at odds with the perceived welfare of the nation.

Since then in Britain and in most other western countries, the state has intervened by acquiring land for national or community purposes, by providing increased security for tenants, and by imposing curbs and constraints on the use of land by private owners. In several European countries, there are now restrictions on who may own land and on how land may be used. Ownership may be restricted to certain types or classes, and various curbs and checks may be imposed in an effort to ensure that the use of land is in accordance with the perceived well-being of the country as a whole.

The pendulum which had swung so far in the direction of private property rights has now begun to swing back in the opposite direction. The rate of swing has not been constant, and its distance varies from country to country, but the swing is sufficiently clearly defined to give some credibility to Jacoby's model, and to suggest that the view of land *merely* as private marketable property is no longer generally accepted or acceptable in most of the western world. The conclusion that may be drawn is that man is unwilling to see land as subject to unrestricted private property rights. The ownership and use of land, it seems, are too important to be seen solely in terms of private property rights.

On the other hand, it can be argued that there has been a quantitative extension of private property rights in land in countries such as Britain, with the great increase that has occurred in owner-occupation during the twentieth century. The fact that the number of private land owners has greatly increased seems to be at odds with the Jacoby model, and is only partly reconciled with it by the realisation that state action (especially through fiscal policy) was a powerful driving force behind it. At the same time, a strong and for the most part effective defence of private property rights has been offered: land ownership in Britain is still largely shrouded in secrecy, and government has shown a marked reluctance even to compile ownership inventories. The continued concentration of land ownership in a relatively few hands, together with the persistence of the concept of land as private property, has given rise to a number of radical or Marxist interpretations such as those of Massey and Catalano (1978) in relation to Britain as a whole and of Newby *et al.* (1978) in relation to farmland in East Anglia.

If in the past private interests overwhelmed those of the group or community, there are clear signs that communal interests have begun to re-assert themselves in recent decades. What is less clear is whether there is any real emergence of the concept of stewardship, although the emergence of national conservation services and international conservation groups might be seen in this light. If it is true that 'we abuse land because we regard it as a commodity belonging to use' (Leopold 1949), a mere shift of view from private commodity to common property is unlikely to prevent such abuse. Perhaps man's continuing emotional or psychological attachment to land indicates that we should not just view land as property, either private or common, but rather that we should view it with a sense of stewardship or responsibility.

Naboth's attitude to his vineyard reflects a sense of stewardship and a concept of land *given* to Israel: the land was given for use but not for sale (Leviticus 25: 23–24). (Perhaps a survival of this view can be seen in the fact that 90 per cent of the land of modern (pre-1967) Israel is owned by the state (Strong 1979).) Land was allocated to individual family groups, according to their size and need. Every 50 years, in the year of Jubilee, it was to revert to the original possessors, so that it would not be permanently and progressively concentrated in a few hands. Similarly, it was to be rested from cultivation every seven years (the year of Sabbath) so that its fertility could be maintained and so that at least some food would be available on the fallow land for its users and for wildlife alike. As it transpired, these rules or guidelines were not heeded, to the detriment of both the community and the land. More recent examples of the social and ecological problems resulting from systems of land tenure and land management, and ultimately from the concept of land merely as private property, are not difficult to find.

THE USEFULNESS OF LAND

Perhaps man's biological links with land may explain part of his emotional attachment to it, but it is doubtful whether they can adequately account for his continuing interest in land-use issues. Part of the explanation probably lies in the diversity of land. Land itself is diverse, and even in countries such as Britain and France, it ranges from barren mountain tundra or alpine snowfield to well-watered lowlands and rich woodland. The uses to which land may be put are equally diverse: the growing of food or timber; housing; airports; golf courses or playing fields; manufacturing industry, and a myriad of other uses that reflect the complexities of modern life. Like the sea, the land is useful in many different ways: it is perhaps better regarded as a resource base rather than a resource in itself.

The resource base of land has a number of aspects or facets of usefulness. One potential land user may seek to utilise its ecological potential by raising crops or grazing animals on natural or sown pastures. Another may have little interest in the nature of soil or its fertility. He may be interested in land only in so far as it provides him with space on which to build his house or factory. The ways in which land users proceed to make use of land will also have effects on their neighbours, in the broadest sense, because they will have effects on the landscape. While land may not be materially *used* as landscape, it is certainly *valued* for aesthetic reasons, and it can be argued that tourism and recreation are sometimes based on the resource of land in much the same way that agriculture is based on the soil. In a wider sense, landscape is the setting for human life, and so it is understandable that people should be concerned about its appearance. Many of the major controversies surrounding rural land use in western countries in recent decades have involved the concept of land as landscape.

Thus in thinking about land use we have to consider a number of aspects or attributes of land. We have to consider its physical and biological nature and its productivity in the ecological sense. We have to see it as space on which a house, shop or office may be located, and we must be mindful of its appearance as landscape. Those aspects of land are obviously not mutually exclusive: land as ecosystem is set in space and has definite physical dimensions, and the use of both land as space and land as ecosystem has definite consequences on land as landscape. But many land-use conflicts and controversies involve two or more of these aspects; conflicts may arise between people who value different attributes of land. An understanding of land use therefore involves both an understanding of the values of these individual attributes of land, and an awareness of the different standpoints from which land use may be considered.

Land as ecosystem

An ecosystem consists of a set of organisms and the physical environment in which they live. Since it is a system, it involves dynamic relationships between the organisms and their environment, and indeed one of its characteristics is the interaction between its various parts. Ecosystems exist at a wide range of scales, from a drop of pond water at one end to the whole planet at the other. Any piece of land (unless sterilised and isolated) may support whole ecosystems and at the same time be part of other very extensive ecosystems. The soil ecosystem and its microorganisms are sustained by the fall of plant litter and droppings, while animals graze the vegetation on its surface and migratory birds may visit it and so integrate it into a continental or global-scale ecosystem. Regardless of its scale, the ecosystem has a throughput of energy. Solar energy is converted by photosynthesis into plant material. Plant material is then consumed by grazing animals or soil organisms. Eventually it is returned to the soil in animal carcases or droppings. Energy flows through the ecosystem, and ultimately it is the means by which the physical life of man (whether peasant or urban dweller) is sustained. He comes at the end of the food chain, consuming directly in the form of vegetable products such as potatoes or wheat or rice, or in the form of meat or milk produced by animals fed on vegetable material.

At each stage in the food chain, energy is converted from one form to another, and there is a big energy loss on conversion. Green plants usually fix only a very small proportion of the energy incident upon them, of the order of 1 per cent. Energy may be converted from vegetation to animals slightly more efficiently, but there is again a very large loss on conversion.

The energy content of food produced can be calculated in relation to input of solar energy and to area of land. If this is done in relation to units of 100,000 mcal of solar radiation and hectares of land, cereal systems in Britain are found to produce 200–250 mcal and 2,000 mcal respectively, while the corresponding figures for cereal-fed livestock systems are 15–30 and 180–340 (Duckham and Masefield 1970 (mcal = 1,000 kcal)). The energy contents as percentages of annual solar radiation are around 0.16 for cereal systems, 0.03 and 0.01 for pigmeat and lamb, and 0.05 for milk. In ecological terms, it is clearly more efficient for man to consume wheat or rice than meat or milk. As a further consequence, it follows that if man consumes much of his food in the form of meat and milk, then a larger area of land is required to feed him than if he consumed vegetable products.

In using land (as ecosystem), man seeks to manipulate these ecological processes in such a way that as much as possible of the ecological potential and energy flow are channelled into plants or animals perceived as valuable or useful to man for food, clothing or timber. Man intervenes to act as manager of the ecosystem, removing those components which he regards as useless 'sinks' of energy, and promoting or fostering those other components which he views more positively. In using land, he almost invariably simplifies the ecosystem by removing or suppressing the components for which he has no use. In place of mixed woodland, for example, he may impose a single-species plantation forest or a field of barley.

In the natural ecosystem, there is usually an almost closed cycle of nutrients or biogeochemicals. These are taken up from the soil by plants, and are returned to it again in plant debris or animal droppings or carcases. In the manipulated ecosystem, this cycle is opened and extended. The nutrients taken up by a crop of wheat, for example, are not returned directly to the soil, but may be transported over thousands of miles to the point of consumption. If further crops are to be grown, and if the soil is not to be depleted, a return of nutrients must be made in the form of artificial fertilisers. Furthermore, by providing in artificial fertilisers the nutrients which are one of the limiting factors in plant growth, the land user may boost the productivity of the ecosystem.

The productivity of an ecosystem is an important characteristic in relation to land use. It is influenced both by external environmental factors (such as climate), and by its internal structure. Net primary production (NPP) is the increment of plant material over time. Of the major natural ecosystems, tropical rain forests have the highest NPPs and deserts and tundra the lowest (Table 1.1). A characteristic of manipulated ecosystems or land-use systems is that their NPPs are usually lower than those of the natural ecosystems that they displace. As Table 1.1 shows, the NPP of sugar cane is high compared both with most other crops and with natural ecosystems. It is an exception. Even the figures given for wheat, potatoes and rice in Table 1.1 are misleadingly high, because crops such as these are usually grown only on better land, and hence are not strictly comparable with natural ecosystems. Eyre (1978) estimates that the average NPP of cropland and grazing land in North Carolina, for example, is only ⅕th of what it was under natural vegetation some centuries ago. Man's intervention as a manipulator of the ecosystem usually results in a change of product rather than an increase in production. He seeks to produce material that he perceives to be valuable or useful, at the expense of some loss of total production.

Table 1.1 also fails to make the point that even the relatively low NPPs of crops such as wheat and potatoes are to some extent 'bought' by the input or expenditure of energy into the manipulated ecosystem. Farming systems in western countries usually rely heavily on artificial fertilisers. Nitrogenous fertilisers are one major input. Large quantities of natural gas are used in their manufacture. Fossil-fuel energy is also expended in the driving of tractors and other implements of cultivation, and indeed in the manufacture of farm machinery. Energy inputs vary enormously, according to the nature of the farming system. For example, Slesser (1976) estimates inputs of 0.6 GJ/hectare (ha) in extensive hill farming in Scotland,

Table 1.1   Mean net primary production

	g/m²/year dry matter
Tropical rain forest	2,200
Deciduous temperate forest	1,200
Boreal forest	800
Savanna	900
Temperate grassland	600
Tundra and alpine	140
Wheat (world average)	430
Rice (world average)	760
Sugar cane (world average)	1,726

Sources: Compiled from data in: Whittaker, R. H. and Likens, G. E. (1975). 'The biosphere and man', in H. Lieth and R. H. Whittaker (eds) *Primary productivity of the biosphere*. Berlin, Heidelberg and New York: Springer-Verlag Ecological Studies 14, 305–28; Odum, E. P. (1971) *Fundamentals of ecology*. Philadelphia: Saunders.

5 GJ/ha in open-range beef farming in New Zealand, and 12–15, 15–20 and 40 GJ/ha respectively for mixed farming, intensive crop production and feed-lot animal production in developed countries (GJ = giga-joule, or 239,000 kcal: the energy content of 5 imperial gallons (23 litres) of refined oil is roughly equivalent to 1GJ).

Output per unit area rises, of course, as energy inputs are increased: increases in yield or output are 'bought' by inputs of energy. By comparing energy inputs with the energy content of the food produced, a measure of the efficiency of the system may be obtained. By this measure, most western forms of agriculture are extremely inefficient, and have become more so as traditional practices such as transhumance have fallen into disuse (e.g. Gómez-Ibáñez 1977). In contrast, many more primitive forms of cultivation are more efficient. Leach (1976) has calculated the energy ratios (or the energy content of a crop in relation to the energy inputs in its cultivation) for a range of farming systems.

Tropical subsistence crops have ratios typically in the range between 13 and 38 (i.e. the energy content is 13–38 times the energy inputs), while those for barley and wheat grown in Britain are around three. Overall energy ratios for national agricultural food production systems are listed by Wood (1981) in an interesting review as 0.5 in the United Kingdom, 0.6 in the Netherlands, 0.7 in the USA and 2.8 in Australia.

The inefficiency of western agriculture, again by this limited measure, is further emphasised by the importance placed on the

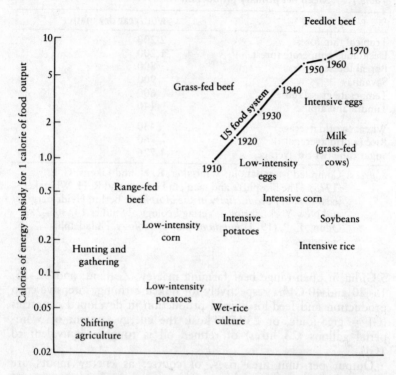

Fig. 1.1 Energy subsidies for various land-use systems. The energy history of the US food system is shown for comparison. Note that the scale is logarithmic.

Source: Modified after Steinhart, J.S. and Steinhart, C.E. (1975). Energy history of the US food system, *Science*, **184**, 307–15.

production of meat and milk. The energy ratios for milk and broiler poultry produced in Britain are around 0.4 and 0.1 respectively (Leach 1976), illustrating the point that in some animal farming systems, the input of energy greatly exceeds the outputs in the form of food.

Figure 1.1 shows how the energy cost or subsidy varies according to the nature of the food production system, and how it has increased over the last few decades in the American food system. The increase over a longer period is even more dramatic. Bayliss-Smith (1982) has shown that the energy ratios of farming systems in the south of England fell from around 40 to around two between 1826 and 1971. During that time, energy inputs per unit area increased by more than one hundredfold. The contribution of fossil

Table 1.2 Annual energy budgets for selected agricultural systems

	Energy input MJ/ha	Percentage from fossil fuel	Energy output MJ/ha	Energy ratio (output/ input)
Pre-industrial				
New Guinea	103	0	1,460	14.2
Wiltshire 1826	183	2	7,390	40.3
Semi-industrial				
Ontong Java	1,079	54	14,760	14.2
South India 1955	3,255	58	42,280	13.0
South India 1975	6,878	77	66,460	9.7
Industrial				
Moscow collective	6,145	96	8,060	1.3
South England 1971	21,870	99	44,890	2.1

Source: Compiled from data in T. P. Bayliss-Smith (1982).

fuels to energy inputs was negligible in 1826: more recently it stands at over 99 per cent (Table 1.2).

The view of land use as the manipulation of natural ecosystems in order to produce materials useful to man offers a helpful framework for viewing some aspects of land use. It provides a means of assessing efficiency in terms of energy, and it is also useful in a number of other ways. If material is cropped (whether in the form of vegetable matter or animal carcases), then nutrients that would otherwise be returned to the soil for uptake in subsequent cycles are removed from the area entirely. If this nutrient loss is significant in relation to the nutrient budget, and if it is not compensated for by applying artificial fertilisers, then the productivity of the system will decline. In other words, some forms of land use can be extractive of nutrients and may result in damage to the ecosystem. In a similar way, some land-use processes such as grazing on open rangeland may cause vegetation changes or shifts in the structure of the ecosystem, which again may have implications for productivity. This concept of environment damage from land-use practices is a prominent theme in land-use studies, and is considered further in Chapter 6.

While its internal structure is one of the key characteristics of an ecosystem, the other crucial feature is the environment in which it is set. Climate is obviously a major factor, determining the amount of solar energy available to drive the ecosystem. Different types of ecosystem (natural and manipulated) are found in different climates. Banana plantations, for example, are not found in Britain, nor are coconut palms. Vines grow successfully in southern England but not in Scotland. Most plants have definite climatic, and hence geographical, limits beyond which they will not grow successfully. These limits are not necessarily permanent or rigid. Crop breeding has successfully extended the range of wheat, for example, by producing early-maturing varieties that suit the short growing seasons of northern latitudes. Andreae (1981) describes how the introduction of the *Marquis* variety of wheat in Canada in 1909 helped to push the polar boundary of wheat cultivation some 300 km to the north. Important as these successes are, though, it may be tentatively concluded that their impact on limits of cultivation at the global scale is usually restricted. It is also true that artificial climates can be created to suit the needs of the most demanding crops. Bananas, for example, could probably be grown quite successfully in Britain if sufficient heating were supplied. The British climate, therefore, may not completely preclude the growing of bananas, but the cost of overcoming the difficulties of climate by providing heated glasshouses would be so high that, in a free market, no British banana grower could compete with his Jamaican counterpart.

Various other environmental factors exert similar influences. Some soils are better drained and richer in nutrients than others. While the poorer soils may be artificially drained and fertilised, they will remain at a disadvantage, in economic if not in purely physical terms, compared with the richer ones. In one sense it is true that advances in technology may help to even out differences in climate or soil by providing the means whereby artificial climates or soils may be produced, but in another sense modern technology in the form of cheap and efficient transport systems allows even subtle differences in soil or climate to be exploited. Whereas in bygone days, a city's vegetables had to be grown in its vicinity because of poor and expensive transport, now its vegetables can be readily freighted in from an area perhaps hundreds of miles distant, where environmental conditions are more suitable and allow cheaper production, even allowing for additional transfer costs.

The same trend may operate in relation to slope angles. When harvesting was by sickle and scythe, cereals could be grown on flat and sloping ground alike. When the reaper/binder replaced the sickle, the steeper land could not be harvested, and when the combine harvester was introduced, another new evaluation of croppable land was required. Each piece of farm machinery will operate only within certain slope limits (Table 1.3): land beyond these limits will tend to pass out of cultivation, or be transferred to other uses.

Hence the influence of the physical environment on land use

remains strong even today and it may indeed have strengthened rather than weakened in recent decades. Perhaps there is no clearer reflection of its significance than the evolving pattern of agriculture in Britain. Since the 1950s, the drier and sunnier south and east of the country has emerged as a major cereal-growing area, while the damper west has increasingly concentrated on livestock. Elsewhere, Dumanski *et al.* (1982) have commented on the close correlations between land-based agriculture and soil and climatic types in Canada, and Manning and McCuaig (1981) have found that the correlation coefficients between the area in improved agricultural use and potential cropland, as indicated by land capability (i.e. environmental) classification, have risen, indicating growing conformity. Similarly, Moran and Mason (1981) have found that dairying in New Zealand has, since the 1920s, become increasingly localised in environmentally advantaged areas, while Hart (1978a) concludes that cropland in the American South has increasingly been concentrated on areas of high land quality.

Table 1.3 Slope angle and the use of machinery

Implement	Slope limit (°)
Standard wheeled tractor (upslope)	13
Combine harvester	10–12
Forage harvester/trailer	8½
Fertiliser distributor	10
Precision seeder (cross slope)	4

Source: Based on Spoor and Muckle (1974).

While it is true that many environmental constraints can be overcome at a cost, it is equally true that some environments and some types of land offer much wider ranges of possible land uses than others. A warm, sunny, well-watered lowland with rich soils, for example, may be eminently suitable for numerous farm crops and animals, the growing of fruit or vegetables or timber, and a wide range of other land uses such as housing, factories or airports. As slope angle increases and climate worsens, then some of the crops and other land uses would be no longer feasible in practical terms. The cost of constructing glasshouses or of levelling the land for an airport would be prohibitive. On still poorer land, with steep slopes and adverse climate, the number of physically and economically feasible land uses might dwindle to a mere handful such as forestry or rough grazing. In practice, the effective range of choice of land uses is usually much narrower than those physically

possible, as will be discussed in Chapter 2, but the principle remains
that some types of land are more flexible as well as more productive
than others.

Land as space

Farmland and forest are useful because they yield physical or
ecological products sought by man, but urban land or land used for
recreation is valuable because of the space it provides. All land
obviously has a spatial extent, but this is the attribute of land which
is of particular importance in relation to land uses such as housing,
manufacturing, commerce, transport and recreation. Ecological
properties are of a correspondingly lesser importance in relation to
these land uses. Part of the distinctiveness of land as a natural
resource stems from its usefulness in providing space or standing
room. In its ecological sense, land may be regarded as a renewable
or 'flow' resource. Crops can be taken from the same area of land
year after year if the land is appropriately husbanded. In this
respect a 'flow' of goods can be produced indefinitely – land is a
resource like water power or wind or solar energy. But land in the
sense of space is rather different. The surface of the earth is of
finite, limited extent, and the land surface is even more limited.
Over a given time period, if space is used, it is inevitably 'used up'
just as a coal deposit, for example, begins to be depleted as soon as
it is exploited. The extent of land is limited, and so land as space in
some respects resembles a non-renewable or 'stock' or 'fund' resource like coal or oil.

But this distinction between 'ecological' land as a flow resource
and 'spatial' land as a fund resource is an over-simplification. The
cropping of a piece of land can be carried out in such a way that
future crops are impaired or precluded. In this case, the 'ecological'
use of land depletes the resource. Crop yields will fall if land
continues to be used in this way, because the resource is not being
conserved. Use in this form will mean that the land cannot be
viewed as a renewable or flow resource. Instead, it will function as
a fund or stock resource. Furthermore, the use of land in the spatial
sense means that land is used up (within a given time period), but it
is not consumed in the sense of being permanently destroyed. It is
true that the inexorable physical processes of erosion and accretion
ensure that the land area is not constant and unchanging, but for
practical purposes we can regard it as static and indestructible.
Thus while the use of 'spatial' land depletes the fund resource of
land in the short term, in another sense 'spatial' land is a renewable
resource if considered in the very long term. A deposit of coal is
consumed as mining proceeds, and in the course of use the coal is

irrevocably changed into smoke, ash and gas. Land as space is not exhausted or consumed in this way, since it can subsequently be redeveloped and re-used.

Land therefore does not fit neatly into the conventional classification of natural resources. It shares some of the characteristics of both flow and fund resources. Further complications arise when land is considered as the resource of landscape.

Land as landscape

The majority of people in western countries do not work on the land and do not own or occupy significant areas of land. Yet they have an interest in land that does not stem from the production of food or other crops. Part of this interest probably derives from a purely emotional or psychological attachment which stems from man's biological dependence on land, but part of it probably arises from man's aesthetic appreciation of landscape. Land in the sense of landscape can be an ambient resource, just like the atmosphere, for example, or like water. In this sense no material use is made of the resource, and it is not used in the sense of being consumed, although it may be modified as a result of man's activities. Its value lies in amenity rather than in physical material. Man may be a creature of the city, but land is still his habitat, and he values its scenic beauty as well as its fruits. He has an awareness and appreciation of the aesthetic qualities of land as well as of its physical qualities. This awareness is not confined to land under his direct control or ownership, but extends to the much wider landscape. Increasingly, man is asserting what he regards as a right to be heard in debates about how land should be used, even if he does not own or control the land in question. This growing public interest arises at least partly from a growing appreciation of landscape, or land as an ambient resource. In Britain, extensive tracts of land have been designated as Areas of Outstanding Natural Beauty (England and Wales) and National Scenic Areas (Scotland), and planning policies towards land-use change in these designated areas are supposed to protect the character and quality of their landscapes. The aesthetic consequences of proposed developments are now required to be considered because land is valued by the public (or its representatives) as landscape, irrespective of how the proposed developer values it as ecosystem or space.

LAND USE AS AN ECONOMIC ACTIVITY

Economics is usually an important factor in land use, and is a major influence in competition between potential land users for the use of land. A key concept is that of economic rent. Numerous definitions of economic rent have been offered over the last two centuries, with varying degrees of purity and clarity. At its simplest, the concept of economic rent refers to the net value of the returns arising from the use of land in a given period of time (Found 1971). It is similar to net income in that it is the balance remaining after production costs are subtracted from gross income, but it differs from net income in that all costs of production, including opportunity costs, are calculated at their full economic values. Economic rent is not necessarily the same as the actual or contract rent paid for the use of land, but there will usually be at least some relationship between the two concepts.

Gross income depends on the volume of production and the unit-price that the product commands. This price in turn depends on the relationship of supply and demand. For many agricultural products, demand is fairly inelastic. By this we mean that consumption of basic commodities such as wheat and potatoes is fairly constant, and does not rise or fall greatly as the price varies. If production is increased, then prices fall rapidly, and as gross income to the producer falls, production becomes no longer economic. On the other hand, demand for fruit, salad vegetables and meat is more elastic. Consumption tends to increase as prices decrease, but total demand for some of these more specialised products is small. For example, a city's demand for rhubarb can be met by a few hectares. If more were to be grown, the price would fall steeply and production would become uneconomic.

If we may assume for the moment that the land user seeks to maximise his net income (and this doubtful assumption is considered in Chapter 2), then he is likely to choose the land use yielding the highest economic rent. The land use with the highest economic rent will therefore prevail, at least in theory. In practice all sorts of complications arise. One complication is social and political constraints on the land user and his decisions. The time scale of assessment is another – how can a 50-year forest rotation, for example, be compared with an annual crop of potatoes? But despite these and many other complications, this basic idea, that the land use with the highest economic rent will prevail, is a useful starting point in the understanding of patterns of land use.

As a broad and sweeping generalisation, commercial land uses usually have the highest economic rents, followed by industry and housing, cropland and improved grazing, and then forest and rough grazing or rangeland. This gradation is obviously related in part to what was said previously about land quality and the range of possible land uses on a given type of land, and is depicted in Fig. 1.2.

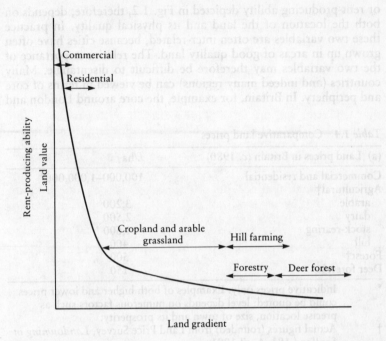

Fig. 1.2 Rent-producing ability, land value and land gradient. (See also Table 1.4, and text for definition of land gradient).

The land gradient on the horizontal axis of the graph refers not to the slope angle of the ground, but rather to two separate although perhaps inter-related characteristics of land. One is location. The attractiveness or usefulness of land as space depends on its location. As is well known, land in the middle of a city is much more valuable than land in a remote rural area, because there is a premium on accessibility. Shopkeepers seek to locate in an area accessible to large numbers of potential customers, and there is usually a stronger demand for housing in the city than in the country. If a farmer looks towards a local city to sell his produce, it is obviously in his interests to locate close to the city so that his transport costs are minimised. Therefore a gradient in economic rent emerges between the more accessible land and the remoter areas.

At the same time there is also another gradient, between more fertile land and less fertile land. Other things being equal, the more fertile land will produce a higher economic rent, since it offers higher yields for a given level of input. The level of economic rent or rent-producing ability depicted in Fig. 1.2, therefore, depends on both the location of the land and its physical quality. In practice these two variables are often inter-related, because cities have often grown up in areas of good quality land. The relative importance of the two variables may therefore be difficult to disentangle. Many countries (and indeed many regions) can be viewed in terms of core and periphery. In Britain, for example, the core around London and

Table 1.4 Comparative land prices

(a) Land prices in Britain (*c.* 1980)	£/ha
Commercial and residential	100,000–1,000,000*
Agricultural†	
arable	3,200
dairy	2,500
stock-rearing	1,600
hill	400
Forest‡	500
Deer forest§	150

*	Indicative prices only. Examples of both higher and lower prices could be quoted: level depends on numerous factors such as precise location, size of town and its prosperity.
†	Actual figures (rounded) from Land Price Survey, *Landowning in Scotland 183*, April 1981.
‡	Farm land for afforestation. From *Economic Report on Scottish Agriculture*, 1981, Edinburgh, DAFS.
§	Deer forest is mainly open moorland, used for deer stalking. This figure is illustrative only: prices vary according to factors such as number of shootable stags, anglings, nature and condition of lodges.

(b) Relative land prices around Milan (1962)	Index of land prices per m² (city centre = 100)
City	
Central business district	100
Peripheral zone	58.2
Exterior zone (edge of built-up area)	14.9
Metropolitan area (beyond built-up area)	
Zone 1	3.6
Zone 2	1.3
Zone 3	0.5
Zone 4	0.4
(30 km from city centre)	

Source: Indices calculated from data in Darin-Drabkin (1977).

the south-east has much of the country's area of urban and intensively used crop land, while the periphery towards the north and west has most of the forests and moorland grazings. Corresponding patterns can be seen in numerous other countries such as Norway, Canada and Australia. Both location and land quality are partly responsible for the contrasts in land use between the core and the periphery, and each is related (at least historically) to the other. Early cities (at least in pre-industrial times) tended to grow up in the richer, more fertile lowlands where population was greater than in the less fertile areas. But while it may be difficult to disentangle the relative effects of location and land quality, it is usually the case in particular instances that the steeper section of the graph in Fig. 1.2 is related to variations in location and the gentler parts to land quality.

Economic rent is a major influence on land value, and indeed at first sight may be expected to determine it. Both variables are shown on the vertical axis of Fig. 1.2, and some examples of variations in land prices are presented in Table 1.4.

Land capable of producing a high economic rent may be expected to be more valuable than less fertile or less well located land which will produce a lower rent. One way of measuring the present value of land (in relation to the output from it) is to sum all future incomes or economic rents which the land is expected to yield. This sum is finite, because the present value of incomes expected in the future is less than their future face value, and if they are expected in the distant future, then their present value is low. For example, an income of say £100 expected next year may be worth only £95 today, and a similar income expected 50 years hence will be worth no more than a very few pounds. Exactly how much it will be worth will depend on the discount rate employed to reduce its value to the present-day level, and on the length of period concerned. The formula for calculating the present value of land is:

$$v = \frac{a}{(1 + r)} + \frac{a}{(1 + r)^2} + \frac{a}{(1 + r)^3} + \ldots\ldots + \frac{a}{(1 + r)^n}$$

$$\text{(year 1)} \qquad \text{(year 2)} \qquad \text{(year 3)} \qquad\qquad \text{(year n)}$$

where a is the expected annual rent and r is the annual interest rate. The sum tends to a limit as n tends towards infinity, and the expression can be reduced to $v = a/r$. The interest rate employed in the calculation will depend on the prevailing interest rates and the degree of risk involved in deriving future incomes from land. Obviously the higher r is, the lower v will be.

While this is one method of assessing land value, actual market

19

value or land price can be quite different. Market value depends on several factors other than capitalised value. It depends to some extent on the amount of land or the number of properties on the market. It also depends on the extent to which potential buyers are interested in seeking goals other than purely economic ones from land ownership. Some people buy land for the prestige or social status they consider that it affords, and they may be prepared to pay prices well above the capitalised value of the land. The fact that they are prepared to pay such prices reflects something of the peculiar attachment that man (or at least some men) feel towards land. Other people or institutions may wish to buy land because they feel that it offers a secure investment and a hedge against inflation (Munton 1976). After all, land is an unusual commodity, which is available in fixed quantity. To paraphrase Mark Twain, no more land is being made. Figure 1.3 shows how trends in agricultural land prices have outstripped inflation in Britain in recent years.

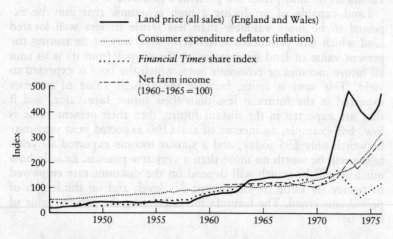

Fig. 1.3 Agricultural land prices (all sales) and comparative indicators (1960–65 = 100).
Source: Northfield, Lord (1979).

In short, land may be purchased not only in order to produce an annual income or rent, but also from a variety of other motives.

The purchaser's motives in acquiring and using land may be complex, and he may have several objectives in mind. These are examined further in Chapter 2, but we should note at this stage that there is a two-way relationship between land use and land price. If land is to be owned commercially, rather than for non-economic reasons (such as prestige), then the price to be paid will be geared to the economic rents generated by actual or potential land uses. The economic rent from agriculture will not justify the paying of urban land prices. The growing of potatoes, yielding say £100/ha, would be highly incongruous in city centre commercial land costing over £1 million/ha. In less extreme terms, Table 1.5 shows how much could be paid for potential forest land in the light of stated assumptions about tree growth rates and economic performance.

Table 1.5　Land purchase for afforestation

The value of a parcel of land for forestry depends on the cost of establishing and maintaining the tree crop and the value of the revenue expected from the produce. Total revenues and total costs must be discounted back to the beginning of the rotation. Revenues depend on the unit price of timber and on the amount of timber produced per unit area, which in turn will be related to the nature of the land, the species selected and the management regime.

Estimates of discounted revenue expected from the type of land under consideration can be obtained from tables, as can estimates of discounted costs of establishment and management. Let us assume that discounted revenues and costs are, respectively, £479 and £274 ha over a 50-year rotation. In this case, up to £205 ha (i.e. £479–274) could be paid for the parcel of land under consideration, and the proposed use would still be economically viable (although other uses might be more attractive). In actual fact, a little more could be paid, since a 'residual' value of the land and roads on it will remain at the end of the 50-year period. In practice, the discounted value over 50 years is small (the discount factor for 50 years at 5 per cent is 0.087–i.e. the present value is the future value multiplied by 0.087), but the values of these 'residuals' could if wished be incorporated into the calculation.

Source:　Example simplified from Busby and Grayson (1981).

If a land user can only obtain land by paying a price higher than that merited by the economic rent from the present type of land use, then he may have to adjust the present land use into a form which will produce a higher economic rent. Here we again enter the difficult and confused area of the motives of land owners and their inter-relationships with land prices and land use. Further complications may be added by the nature of the prevailing arrangements for the taxation of income derived from the land, and of its capital value. In addition, the subject may be further confused by differences between the values of public and private benefits arising from the use of land resources.

Land is by definition a basic ingredient of land use, but it is not the only ingredient. As soon as natural ecosystems are manipulated, and as soon as space is utilised by man for his buildings or playgrounds, capital and labour are applied to land. The amounts of labour and capital vary tremendously from one type of land use to another. The grazing of rangeland, for example, requires little input of capital or labour. The use of land for commercial purposes or housing, on the other hand, requires much greater inputs. *Intensity* of land use refers to the amount of inputs of capital and labour per unit area. Intensive land use is characterised by large inputs, whereas non-intensive (or extensive) uses have low inputs. Within agriculture, for example, the growing of vegetables or cereals is a more intensive form of land use than the rearing of sheep on open rangeland or rough grazings. Vegetables and cereals, in turn, may be grown at various intensities, depending on the level of inputs such as fertilisers. The land user must decide the intensity at which he is to use his land. One obvious way in which intensity may be varied is in the application of fertilisers. This is a form of capital input into the land-use system. Similarly, labour inputs may be varied according to how much labour the land user is prepared to devote to his crop. Leaving aside for the moment the complication that capital and labour may be interchangeable (for example, more machinery may be acquired so that fewer workers are needed), the crucial question becomes the level of inputs to be used. If the grower increases his inputs, he will expect an increased level of output or marketable crop. This relationship between inputs and output is subject to the law of diminishing returns. If successive increases of input are supplied, a point is reached when the additional (or marginal) output or product achieved for each unit of input decreases. In fact, output will probably eventually decrease. For example, if additional units of fertiliser are supplied, the output will at first rise steeply, but then it will level off and ultimately it will begin to fall. The grower has to decide at what point he will supply no further fertiliser. Obviously his decision will depend on the cost of the fertiliser and the price he expects to obtain per unit of output.

Thus the land user has to select a level of intensity which is appropriate to his circumstances (these will include the price at which he has purchased the land). He must also decide on how best to combine his inputs. If labour is expensive, he may seek to substitute capital by investing in machinery. There are, of course, three factors of production – land as well as capital and labour – and the decision maker has to consider all three inputs. Some inputs may be more flexible and more easily adjusted than others. For example, in a densely settled agricultural country where additional land is not readily available for purchase or renting, the land user with limited reserves of capital may have no choice but to intensify his labour inputs if he wishes to increase production. For practical purposes, his 'input' of land is fixed. On the other hand, a rancher in a lightly settled country could, at least in colonial days, spread his activities over an ever increasing area of land while his capital (in the form of his herd or flock) and his labour supply were fixed. Eventually a point would be reached beyond which he added nothing to total production by grazing more land.

Some inputs such as fertiliser may be supplied in units or quantities of any size, but other factors such as machinery and labour are less easily divisible. It may be possible to obtain part-time or contract labour if the required labour input does not correspond to a full-time worker, but the labour input cannot be adjusted in a continuous fashion. Nor can half a tractor or half a combine harvester always be provided easily, although again contracting services may sometimes be available. Each piece of equipment has an optimal area for efficient use. Thus the farmer may seek to increase his land input by purchasing or renting more land, in order that the efficiency of use of his equipment is increased and that he can enjoy increased economies of scale. The price he is prepared to pay for additional land in these circumstances may well be higher than that which would be expected from the economic rent arising from use by another farmer in other circumstances.

This is one (but only one) of the reasons for the escalation of land prices in many countries, and as land prices rise, land use is usually intensified. Rural land use in the western world has been characterised during the twentieth century by rapidly increasing intensity of capital inputs and decreasing labour inputs. High capital intensity, large inputs of fertilisers and farm chemicals, together with the intensive use of machinery have increased yields enormously, but they have had significant effects on the physical environment as well as on rural employment and population. There are now signs that intensification is being questioned, in the light both of overproduction of some farm products and of environmental consequences. Future trends in the direction of increasing capital inputs will probably be slower and less pronounced than during the last few decades. Indeed an increasing amount of attention is being paid to 'organic' systems of farming, with lower yields and capital inputs, but perhaps higher labour intensities (e.g. Klepper *et al.* 1977).

The nature of land use in an area is a function of the factors of land production within the prevailing social and political constraints. Land use is influenced by the physical nature of land and its location, by available capital and its distribution, and by the availability and cost of labour. It is also influenced by the social and political climate in which they operate. Libby (1974) talks of land-use patterns as a physical expression or template of the pressures inherent in modern society. Any change in these factors, or in the climate, will have repercussions throughout the land-use system. It may be met by a response that seeks to adjust the combination or mix of outputs. It may result in a change in the intensity with which the land is used, or it may give rise to a change in type of land use.

One factor that has been of fundamental importance in triggering land-use change is transport. Transport costs have often been major items in total production costs, and hence in economic rents. With improvements in transport and reductions in real transport costs, areas which previously were far too remote from the main centres of land for economic use to be made of land can be brought into use and their physical advantages exploited. During the nineteenth century, huge areas of land in North America and Australia were brought into use in this way, and the land-use consequences extended back to land in the Old World. With the development of transport linkages, frontier zones could specialise on a cash crop such as wheat for the European or international market. In the Mid-West of America, for example, specialisation eventually resulted in declining yields due to soil exhaustion or disease, and hence to a trend towards diversification. But diversification offered no lasting solution, because all regions are not equally suited to all crops, and so a new specialisation, perhaps more closely adjusted to local environmental conditions, emerged (Conzen 1971). Transport clearly played a major role in allowing both the initial and subsequent specialisation to develop. Transport companies sometimes also played active roles by promoting new land uses so that traffic and revenues were thereby fostered (e.g. Scott 1979).

Transport is (and has been) an important influence in land-use economics, and economics is an important influence on type and intensity of land use. But man may regard land as *more* than just a factor of production or a marketable commodity, and all decisions about land use cannot be understood in terms of economics alone. Furthermore, land use is the product of human decision, and not of blind and impersonal economic forces. The subject of land-use decisions is considered in the next chapter.

FURTHER READING

Andrews, R. N. L. (1979) *Land in America : commodity or natural resource?*
Barlowe, R. (1978) *Land resource economics.*
Bayliss-Smith, T. P. (1982) *The ecology of agricultural systems.*
Bryant, R. W. G. (1972) *Land : private property, public control.*
Ely, R. T. and **Wehrwein, G. S.** (1964) *Land economics.*
Found, W. C. (1971) *A theoretical approach to rural land use patterns.*
Leach, G. (1976) *Energy and food production.*

Land use and decision-making

Many attempts have been made to explain patterns of land use on the basis of one of two approaches. One emphasises the role of the physical environment. In its extreme form, this approach assumes that land use is determined by the nature of the physical environment in the same way that natural vegetation is related to climate. The other approach is based on the assumption that land use is an economic activity, and that it is determined by economic forces. Over the last two or three decades, the obvious point that land use is the product of human decision has been given more recognition. This recognition, of course, does not deny that environment and economics exert strong influences on land use, but it acknowledges that these influences are mediated through the land user, and that they do not operate in a direct or automatic fashion.

Environment and economics can, at the most, 'explain' only part of the variation in land use from place to place, and the failure of traditional economic models of land use to correspond to reality was a potent force leading to an acceptance that other factors are involved. Simple and elegant economic or environmental explanations have been sought by numerous exponents of land-use studies, but the harsh realities are that human choice and decision are involved. If patterns of land use are to be understood, then the human dimension must be considered and the making of decisions examined. In this respect, the question of control and occupancy of land becomes vital. Generally, the person, company or agency owning or occupying the land is able to decide how the land is to be used, but this control is subject to various legal and cultural constraints, which themselves may be significant factors in the process of decision-making.

Decisions about the use of land involve a multiplicity of factors:

the objectives of the land user; the process or means by which he reaches a decision, and the background factors that consciously or unconsciously influence his decision. These include both intrinsic personal and psychological factors, and also external influences stemming from the nature of the land unit and its wider setting. A schematic model showing the relationship of these groups of factors is illustrated in Fig. 2.1. Three major components are indicated – processes, objectives and factors. Discussion in the remainder of the chapter is organised under these headings.

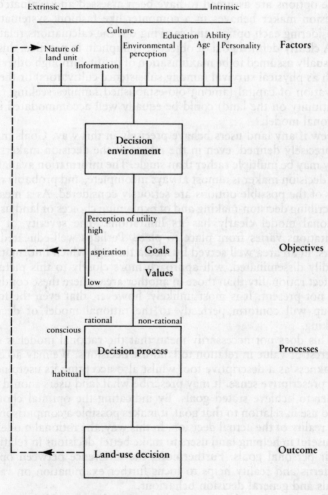

Fig. 2.1 Decision-making in land use.

PROCESSES OF DECISION-MAKING

The rational model

In classical economic theory of land use, many assumptions are made about the behaviour of the decision maker and the setting of his decision. He is assumed to have access to a complete set of information relating to a decision, including perfect knowledge of all costs and prices, and he is also assumed to be able to carry out the processing necessary in order to reach an optimal decision. All possible options are assumed to have been assessed and evaluated; the decision maker behaves in a computer-like fashion, systematically considering each option and carrying out the calculations related to it. A clearly-defined goal or objective is implicit. In practice, this goal is usually assumed to be maximisation of profit, although other goals such as physical survival (among subsistence cultivators) or the conservation of capital (among old-established families seeking family continuity on the land) could be equally well accommodated in the rational model.

Few if any land users behave precisely in this way. Goals may be imprecisely defined, even in the minds of the decision makers, and they may be multiple rather than single. The information available to the decision maker is almost always incomplete, and probably only a few of the possible options are seriously considered. As a means of describing decision-making and of explaining choices of land use, the rational model clearly has its limitations. The severity of these limitations varies from place to place. Perhaps well-educated land users, in an area well served by media through which information is readily disseminated, will approach more closely to this picture of perfect rationality than those in another area where these conditions are not present. It is most unlikely, however, that even the former group will conform perfectly to the rational model of decision-making.

This does not necessarily mean that the rational model is of no interest or value in relation to land-use decisions. We may accept its weakness as a descriptive tool whilst also accepting its usefulness in the prescriptive sense. It may prescribe what land users should do in order to achieve stated goals. By indicating the optimal choice of land use in relation to that goal, it makes possible a comparison with the reality of the actual decision. In this way, the rational model may be useful in helping land users to make better decisions in relation to their personal goals. Furthermore, the difference between optimal patterns and reality helps to focus further examination on varying goals and general decision behaviour.

The rational model assumes that a complete set of information is available to the decision maker. One of the characteristics of decision-making about land use is that a complete set of information is seldom available. Prices at the time of harvest, which may be several months (or in the case of tree crops, several years) ahead, cannot be known with certainty, nor is there any sure knowledge of weather conditions. The decision maker cannot know in advance what these conditions will be like, and he must rely on estimates or assessments of likely conditions. In some cases these estimates will be his own; in other cases he may be assisted by 'expert' forecasts or assessments. Past experience may help him to assess weather conditions, for example, and provide him with a basis for estimating probabilities of wet or dry seasons. In other cases, past experience is of little help – for example, in predicting future price trends or levels of government support – and a state of uncertainty prevails. Decisions are therefore made under risk and uncertainty rather than with full knowledge of all conditions. This fact obviously complicates the reaching of decisions by purely rational processes, but it in itself does not necessarily or completely invalidate the concept of rational decision-making. Rational decisions can still be made within defined assumptions and expectations of events or conditions.

As an example, let us suppose that a farmer can use his land for either potatoes or wheat. In this simple example, other crops or land uses are not permitted, nor are combinations. Five types of weather may be expected: average conditions in four years out of 10, wet and dry conditions in two years each, and very wet and very dry conditions each once in 10 years. The incomes expected from each crop under each type of weather conditions is shown in Table 2.1.

Table 2.1 Weather types and crop incomes

Weather type	Very dry	Dry	Average	Wet	Very wet
Probability	0.10	0.20	0.40	0.20	0.10
Net income per hectare	(£)	(£)	(£)	(£)	(£)
Wheat	200	300	250	200	150
Potatoes	100	200	300	400	200

Under 'average' conditions, potatoes offer the higher income, but these conditions occur only in two years out of five. In wet and very wet years, potatoes are also superior, and would thus have an advantage in seven years out of 10. Under more complicated conditions and with more realistic assumptions, the selection of the better crop could be assisted by calculating which alternative would offer the higher expected income. This could be done simply by multiplying the probabilities and incomes, and summing the products. The expected income for wheat would thus be 200 × 0.1 + 300 × 0.2 + 250 × 0.4 + 200 × 0.2 + 150 × 0.1 = £235/ha, while the corresponding figure for potatoes would be £270. By this criterion, potatoes again would be the better alternative. If, however, the farmer wishes to achieve the maximum *minimum* income, then he should opt for wheat. In other words, different objectives may be defined, such as maximum income in average years, maximum expected income, or maximum income under the worst expected conditions, and the land user can attempt by rational means to optimise in any of the directions. In practice, it is much more difficult to identify the optimal choice than our simple example suggests: yields and hence incomes vary continuously with weather conditions; there may be uncertainty about prices, and the costs of production of one crop, and hence the income derived from it, may depend on the scale of operation or the area devoted to it. The farmer may also try to protect himself against the possibility of both poor prices and poor weather conditions by spreading the risk and aiming for a diversified pattern of cropping. Such a system is a common adaptation in areas prone to drought, for example. An enormous literature on decision-making under risk and uncertainty has developed in recent decades. Found (1971) offers one introduction to it.

Incrementalism or 'muddling through'

Decision-making in the rational model is a systematic and rigorous process. In the real world, it is evident that all decision-making does not conform to this model, and it is doubtful if any land-use decisions conform to it perfectly. In reacting against the assumptions of rationalism, Lindblom (1959) suggested the alternative model of incrementalism, which is also described more vividly as 'muddling through'. In the incremental model, decisions are neither systematic nor rigorous. They take the form of small or gradual adjustments (increments) to existing policies. Proponents of the incremental model recognise that there are limitations to the abilities of decision makers in considering the options open to them, and in assessing the consequences of various possible decisions. They also recognise that there are very real limitations on the information available to the decision makers. Decision makers, therefore, they argue, 'muddle through' by making numerous small adaptations or adjustments to their policy in relation to changing circumstances, for example in response to pressure groups or persistent labour problems. Decisions are not likely to be radical, since they concentrate on adjusting existing policies rather than formulating new ones. The process of decision-making is piecemeal and evolutionary rather than comprehensive and revolutionary.

This incremental view of decision-making appears at first sight to be irrational and completely unsatisfactory. There is no certainty that a gradual, 'muddling through' approach will lead to satisfactory or efficient decisions about land use. Slight adjustments to previously unsatisfactory decisions may exacerbate rather than ameliorate the ensuing problems: incrementalism may seem to offer a zig-zag course, as likely to lead to disaster as to success. We may view the incremental process as irrational (or at least non-rational), but it is Lindblom's contention that we are adversely disposed towards the process for intuitive reasons rather than because it has been demonstrated to give worse results than alternative processes. Furthermore, it is difficult to see how some corporate decision makers such as public agencies, which are expected to be responsive to changing public opinions and political pressures, can avoid at least an element of incrementalism in their decision processes. The concept of incrementalism may have originated in the fields of politics and public administration, but it seems to tally with at least some observations of evolving decisions, and conforms well with the inertia evident in some aspects of land use. If decisions are reached incrementally, then major swings or radical changes are unlikely to result. Since incrementalism is closely associated with political activity (e.g. O'Riordan 1982), it follows that radical shifts are unlikely in the decisions of public agencies about land use. Nevertheless, such shifts are not unknown, and if perceived problems become severe and acute, major changes may well be made. For example, under the stress of conditions during the First World War, the British Government set up a state forestry service with powers to acquire and manage land, while during the Second World War objectives of increasing self-sufficiency in agricultural production became established and have persisted to the present day.

While incrementalism seems to describe many land-use decisions fairly accurately, it fails to account for more radical decisions leading to major changes in land use. For these, other decision models are required.

Mixed scanning

A third model has been suggested by Etzioni (1967). He rejects rationalistic models as failing to offer an effective means of describing or analysing decisions, and concludes that incrementalism can account for some decisions but not for others. Mixed scanning, he asserts, avoids the basic defects of both of these models. Mixed scanning, according to Etzioni, distinguishes fundamental decisions from 'bit' or item decisions. Basic or fundamental decisions are made through an exploration of the main options identified by the decision maker in relation to his defined goals. In contrast to what full rationality would imply, details are omitted so that overviews are feasible. 'Bit' decisions are made incrementally, but within the contexts set by fundamental decisions. The two elements complement each other. Bit incrementalism overcomes the unrealistic aspects of comprehensive rationalism by limiting it to fundamental decisions, and the application of rationalism in major decisions helps to offset the conservative bias of incrementalism. This third approach, according to Etzioni, is more realistic and more radical than its two elements individually. It is neither so unrealistic as full rationalism nor so pragmatic as undiluted incrementalism.

The mixed-scanning model may be attractive, and it may faithfully describe how some decisions are taken. But at the operational level, this model fails to give a clear indication of how major and minor decisions are to be defined. In practice a gradation probably exists, and fundamental and 'bit' decisions may be difficult to distinguish. Nevertheless, once initiated, a major policy may be subject to numerous minor adjustments, before major pressures build up and eventually lead to radical re-orientations and a renewal of the cycle.

The contrast between the rational and incremental models hints at another contrast in processes of decision-making. On the one hand, decision-making may be a conscious, deliberate process involving some reflection on the part of the individual. On the other hand, the decision or choice may be habitual (Kates 1962), and the individual resorts to traditional or repetitive behaviour. Perhaps having made a conscious decision initially and having found that the outcome was satisfactory, the decision maker simply implements the same decision again, without conscious evaluation or consideration of the alternatives. This tendency towards routine or habitual behaviour is readily understandable. The decision maker may have difficulty in assembling all the information required for a fully rational, deliberate decision, and in any case he probably has little appetite for the effort required even to assess the information readily available to him. Simon (1957) suggests that the combination of this inability and this lack of appetite helps to simplify decision-making. To a greater or lesser extent, depending on the aptitude and ability of the land user, conscious decision-making can be avoided. The decision maker, knowingly or otherwise, compromises between his decision effort and the extent to which he achieves his goals. This form of habitual decision-making may continue until a jolt such as crop failure or market slump encourages him once more to return to a more rigorous and conscious choice.

Both individual and corporate decision makers such as public agencies may avoid rigorous, conscious decision-making. On the one hand, the effort involved in such a process may be the deterrent. On the other hand, the decision maker may consciously avoid embarking on a rigorous decision process. Government institutions, for example, may limit the scope of actual decision-making to safe and uncontroversial issues (Bachrach and Baratz 1962), and hence land use and land management may be the product of 'non-decision' rather than of conscious decision. In some circumstances such as sudden crises, full deliberation between alternative policies may be practically impossible, and only one course of action remains. In such cases, governmental decision-making becomes the process of *not* making genuine decisions, since there are no choices available (Clark 1982a).

THE OBJECTIVES OF LAND USERS

The basic objective of the land user is *utility*. It is difficult to improve on an old definition of the concept: utility is 'that property in any object, whereby it tends to produce benefit, advantage, pleasure, good or happiness . . . to the party whose interest is considered' (Burns and Hart 1970: 12). This definition draws attention to non-material benefits, and it also emphasises the personal, objective element. Utility may mean different things to different people, and the individual will be guided in his expectation of utility by past experiences and by other personal and psychological factors.

Traditionally, it has been assumed that the land user is a sub-species of Economic Man who seeks to maximise or optimise his profit or income from his land enterprise. Two important points are involved in this assumption, firstly that the land user optimises, and secondly that he does so in the direction of the single goal of profit. Both these assumptions are doubtful. Simon (1957) argues that it is beyond both the abilities and the desires of an individual to examine all the possibilities open to him, and hence the individual accepts and adopts the first *satisfactory* decision that he reaches. He may seek to *optimise* but in practice he *satisfices*. In accepting the first satisfactory solution, he avoids the cost and effort of searching further for an even better result. (In the limited sense of this cost and effort, he could be said to be optimising in his search for solutions). The significance of this view of the decision maker is obvious. Actual land-use choices cannot be expected to conform fully with the land-use patterns predicted or prescribed by economic theory and assumptions of profit maximisation. This does not mean that decision-making is completely irrational nor that land-use choices are chaotic and incapable of explanation. Rather it means that the rationality of the decision maker is confined within certain limits. It is subjective or bounded rationality rather than full rationality.

33

In an important and well-known paper, Wolpert (1964) showed that a large sample of farmers in Sweden did not achieve maximum profit, and that their goals were not directed solely towards that objective. The concept of the satisficer applied more accurately to these Swedish farmers than that of the optimiser. Moreover, clear regional patterns were apparent in the *extent* to which profit maximisation was obtained. In general terms, such discrepancies between the actual and the optimal can arise either because the land-use decision makers are operating with imperfect information, which constrains their decision behaviour and their identification of optima, or alternatively because goals other than profit maximisation are significant. In the case of the latter alternative and in satisficing behaviour generally, the level of aspiration becomes important. Levels of aspiration vary from individual to individual and from area to area. The definition of a 'satisfactory' level of profit varies accordingly; the threshold of acceptability is higher in some places and in some individuals than in others. In a study set in Manitoba, Pemberton and Craddock (1979) showed that high-income farmers had higher levels of aspiration than low-income farmers. If it is assumed that high aspirations lead to high incomes (rather than the converse), then as a corollary, level of aspiration may be a significant constraint on the performance and economic achievement of low-income farmers, whose perception of a satis-factory profit is lower than that of their counterparts. In short, land use may vary from place to place because some land users have higher economic goals than others.

The other part of Simon's argument concerns the nature of the decision maker's objectives. Rarely, he contends, does man seek a single objective such as maximum profit. Instead, he is more likely to seek several objectives concurrently. For example, he may wish to combine an acceptable standard of living with an adequate amount of leisure time and an opportunity to devote attention to enterprises or activities in which he has a particular interest. The relative weights of these and other considerations vary tremendously: many public agencies with interests in land have clearly expressed multiple objectives, for example. But objectives are often multi-faceted even in the case of the individual, and they often occur in broad groups or clusters rather than in the form of narrowly defined single goals. Both immediate, specific goals and the broader values which lie behind them combine together in broad orientations. Gasson (1973) suggests a classification of values and value orientations that may apply to farmers (Table 2.2). Some of these values resemble goals in their specificity, and clearly there is some blurring between the concepts of goals and values.

Table 2.2   Values in farming

Instrumental
  Making maximum income
  Making a satisfactory income
  Safeguarding an income from the future
  Expanding the business
  Providing congenial working conditions – hours, security, surroundings

Social
  Gaining recognition, prestige as a farmer
  Belonging to the farming community
  Continuing the family tradition
  Working with other members of the family

Expressive
  Feeling pride of ownership
  Gaining self-respect for doing a worthwhile job
  Exercising special abilities and aptitudes
  Chance to be creative and original
  Meeting a challenge, achieving an objective, personal growth

Intrinsic
  Enjoyment of work tasks
  Preference for a healthy, outdoor, farming life
  Purposeful activity, value in hard work
  Independence – freedom from supervision and able to organise own time
    control

Source: Based on Gasson (1973).

Gasson reports several interesting findings from her series of investigations into the values held by farmers in eastern England. In these studies, intrinsic values are repeatedly revealed to be dominant,

Table 2.3   Importance of attributes of farming to Cambridgeshire farmers

	Size of farm business	
	Smaller (smd 600–950)	Larger (smd 1,300)
	Score	
Intrinsic	59	59
Expressive	35	50
Instrumental		
Income	38	46
Conditions	22	33
Social		
Belonging	39	23
Prestige	23	32
(Scores for smaller farmers differ significantly from larger (P<0.01)		

Source: Gasson (1973).

and special importance is placed on independence. A summary of the value orientations of a sample of Cambridgeshire farmers is shown in Table 2.3.

Instrumental values are relegated to a position subsidiary to both intrinsic and expressive values. Other work in areas such as south-west Scotland, the West Midlands and south-west England has reached similar conclusions (Gordon 1978; Ilbery 1983; Casebow 1980). Farmers are rarely motivated only by economic factors, but the extent to which they emphasise economic factors varies considerably. These variations may be related in part to farm size. An example of a contrast in value orientations between smaller and larger farmers is shown in Table 2.3. Although both sets of farmers emphasised intrinsic values and accorded less significance to instrumental values, farmers with large businesses appeared to lay more stress on economic considerations, while smaller farmers placed more emphasis on factors such as independence. Newby *et al.* (1978) report similar conclusions from work in East Anglia. These findings are in broad agreement with those of work in other parts of the world. Among small farmers in study areas in New Mexico and Oklahoma/Texas, family quality of life was ranked above profit, and agricultural activities met a non-monetary need first and an income need second (Harper and Eastman, 1980). Similarly, in the wheat – sheep zone of Western Australia, farming has been shown to be especially valued as a way of life by smaller and older farmers (Kerridge 1978).

The practical significance of such findings is obvious, even though the detailed relationships between values, goals and actual decisions about land use are not always clear. (Values and broad motivations may simply set the scene for decisions, and do not necessarily determine them directly.) Smaller farmers, if they place less emphasis on instrumental values, may be less responsive to economic forces and incentives than their larger counterparts. They may wish to avoid the indebtedness that would result if they borrowed capital for farm improvements, for example, and they may not be readily responsive to government policies and financial incentives to give up farming in order to allow their land to be amalgamated with larger units. Similarly, if they place a strong value on independence, they may be reluctant to enter into co-operative schemes, which are sometimes advocated as a way forward for small farming. Farmers who value independence highly may also be reluctant to enter into contract-farming agreements, even though contracts (for example, with vegetable processors) would give access to specialised knowledge and secure markets (Hart 1978b).

While a broad relationship may exist between the values held by a farmer and the size of his farm business, it would be misleading to suggest that this relationship is rigid. As in the case of many other aspects of decision-making, various other factors intervene to complicate the relationship. Size of unit is unlikely to be the only variable involved. Nevertheless, on the basis of comparing data in Gasson (1973) and Denman (1957), it seems that the owners of large rural estates in England place greater emphasis on expressive and social values than commercial farmers with smaller, purely agricultural properties; within the farming sector itself, however, instrumental values may be more prominent in the larger units, as has already been suggested.

The relationship between goals and values is a complex one. Goals are more specific and immediate, and are likely to exert strong influences on actual decisions about how to use and manage land. They are capable of being attained and satisfied, often in the fairly short term. Values, on the other hand, are more permanent and long-term, and are less capable of being satisfied. Goals may change while the values that lie behind them remain constant. For example, a young farmer may engage in intensive cropping for a few years in order to build up capital to allow him to develop livestock enterprises. His values may lead him to seek a well-balanced mixed farming system, but in the short term he may pursue goals that seem to be at odds with his values. Goals may well change during his career, and the relationship between goals and values is therefore not necessarily a constant one. This may be one reason for the relative lack of progress in understanding the ways in which values are related to land-use decisions.

Many other questions remain to be answered about goals and values. Do farmers develop distinctive value orientations because they are farmers, or do they become farmers in response to particular value orientations? The truth probably lies somewhere between these alternatives. Some individuals make conscious decisions to acquire land and to develop land-use enterprises. Others, such as some farmers' sons, may simply succeed to the parental farm, perhaps without making a conscious decision. Farmers follow in their fathers' footsteps to a much higher degree than other self-employed proprietors who also receive bequests of physical assets (Laband and Lentz 1983), and the great majority of farmers are farmers' sons. Penn (1979) reports that about 80 per cent of farmers in the United States are the children of farmers; in Wisconsin 75 per cent of farmers come from farming families (Lancelle and Rodefield 1980). In Ireland, 80 per cent of all transfers of agricultural land are by inheritance (usually father-son), and only 20 per cent are on the open market (Sheehy 1982). In a study in Buckinghamshire, England, Harrison (1972) found that between 70 and 80 per cent of farmers had farming fathers. Differences in earnings between follower-farmers and non-followers have been interpreted by Laband and Lentz (1983) as indicators of the value of transferred human capital, in the form of knowledge and experience passed on to sons.

Although there is a strong element of continuity of land ownership from generation to generation, there is some evidence that demand for rural properties from non-traditional owners has increased in recent years. In the United States, this demand has pushed up land prices and has resulted in the sub-divisions of timberland and marginal cropland for residential properties (Healy and Short 1979). The emergence of this 'non-traditional' demand, therefore, can have a general effect on land use by leading to higher land prices, and it can have a particular impact in the land-use sector in which it is concentrated.

An interesting field of enquiry is the possible existence of differences in the motivations of those who make conscious decisions to control land and those who merely succeed to it. This field is as yet largely untilled. We may speculate that the land-use decisions made by someone who is strongly motivated to own land will differ from those of someone who has merely inherited it without conscious decision. Similar differences may exist between those who have inherited land and who wish in turn to pass it on to the next generation of the family, and those who see it merely as a factor of production along with labour and capital. The former may wish to own and retain land for its own sake ('land ownership as such' in the words of Massey and Catalano 1978), while the latter see the ownership (or at least the control) of land as a pre-requisite for farming or some other form of economic activity.

Economic objectives

Although economic goals have perhaps been sometimes over-rated in importance in traditional land-use theory, they may at the same time be of greater and more widespread significance today than in the past. An economic dimension is present in the great majority of land-use decisions. A satisfactory level of income is likely to be a priority, and only after it has been achieved will other factors such as personal preference become significant in choice of land use. In his study of farmers in Oxfordshire, Ilbery (1979) attempted to rank the factors of importance in decision behaviour. He found that the first three factors were of an economic nature, relating to profit and stability of income. Only thereafter did social and personal consider-ations assume importance. Ilbery worked in an area of prosperous and largely commercial farming, and it is possible that economic objectives might be accorded rather less emphasis in some other areas. Nevertheless, the general tenor of his findings is probably applicable among farmers in much of the western world.

Income or profit is only one of several economic objectives that a land user may pursue. Long-term capital appreciation may be of equal or greater importance, especially at a time when land prices are rising faster than inflation rates and other forms of investment. In recent years, for example, the prospects of long-term appreciation have been one of the factors attracting financial institutions into the ownership of farm land (Munton 1977). In some cases, the ownership of land may become an economic objective in its own right, irrespective of how the land is actually used. In extreme forms, the goal of capital appreciation can take the form of sheer speculation, with scant regard for land use or land management. Land speculation is sometimes encountered around the outskirts of expanding cities, where land may be purchased in the hope of large capital gains if and when it is used as building land. The objectives of landowners seeking capital appreciation are usually more modest and longer term, however, and are usually more directly linked to the use of land. Land may be seen as an effective means of conserving capital in a family, and decisions about its use may revolve around this long-term objective. There is evidence that this is an important objective among many land owners in the Scottish Highlands, for example (Armstrong and Mather 1983). Short-term profit or income under these conditions is subordinated to long-term appreciation or conservation of capital. Risky enterprises are avoided, and the decision maker selects what he regards as well-tried land uses that do not endanger his capital. This distinction between annual profit and capital growth serves to highlight the importance of time-scales in relation to decisions about land use.

As well as these obvious economic goals of profit or growth of capital, there may also be less obvious ones relating to taxation. Tax regulations may apply more favourably to some land uses than to others, and changes in these regulations can have significant effects on land-use decisions. For example, tax changes in the United States in 1969 made livestock breeding and citrus and almond orchards less attractive (Carman 1972). On the broader scale, federal tax policies have contributed significantly to structural change in American agriculture, and have been one of the most important forces in recent years (Penn 1979). Tax regulations are extremely important in relation to forestry in Britain, and indeed favourable tax regulations are one of the means by which the British Government encourages an expansion of the forest area. This example of the effects of a government's fiscal policy is discussed further in Chapter 3.

Fiscal benefits arising from land-use choices apply unevenly in that they depend on the financial circumstances of the individual rather than on any inherent characteristics of land use. A struggling small farmer, with a low income and limited capital, will be unresponsive to them, while a large land owner with income from commercial or industrial sources and a potentially heavy liability for capital taxation when his assets are transferred to his successor, will probably consider them much more carefully before reaching a decision about land use.

Economic objectives may also operate in another indirect fashion, through the structure of land ownership. Some industrial companies seek to achieve a vertical integration in which the production of a commodity is geared to its processing. The company may acquire and use land to ensure security and continuity of supply of raw material, rather than for a direct economic return on the land use itself. This type of industrial ownership of rural land is not common in Britain, but is more widespread in some other countries such as Sweden and the United States. Paper-mill companies, for example, have sought to acquire land for afforestation in the south of the United States, while neighbouring small farmers have replaced low-grade forest with more intensive forms of land use (Prunty 1952). Thus, two contrasting trends in land use are associated with two different types of ownership.

In short, a wide range of economic objectives may be pursued in land use. Furthermore, they may be pursued with different intensities. In a study of 72 woodland estate owners in England and Wales, Nicholls (1969) found that only two were not interested in either annual profit or appreciation in capital value. The remaining 70 all sought some economic benefit, in appreciation of capital value or in estate-duty advantages or tax concessions. Many of these owners, however, simultaneously sought to improve the general amenity of their estates. An interesting point was that none of the 70 owners had calculated precisely the likely returns from their woodland enterprises, although they were anxious that their woodland management should be profitable in general terms.

Social and personal objectives

Social objectives in land use are perhaps exemplified more clearly by the activities of public agencies and similar owners. A wide range of agencies is involved in land ownership in western countries (Chapter 3), and their involvement directly reflects the pursuit of social objectives. These objectives are of various types. One common goal is to provide employment in rural areas, by selecting land uses with appropriate labour requirements. One of the objectives of the Forestry Commission in Britain at its inception in 1919 was to provide rural employment and thus help to stem the drift of population to the towns and cities. This objective was emphasised during the 1930s when programmes of afforestation were launched around some of the severely depressed industrial regions such as South Wales and Tyneside, and again during the 1960s and 1970s when the provision of employment in upland rural areas became a prominent part of British forestry policy (Mather 1978a).

In recent decades, many public agencies have responded to the growth in demand for outdoor recreation by acquiring and managing land for this purpose. The forerunner of this trend in Britain was legislation in the second half of the nineteenth century, which empowered councils to set up public parks in and around cities. In the United States, the first national park was established at Yellowstone in 1872. Since then, the trend has been strengthened, and parks and other facilities for outdoor recreation have been provided in large numbers.

While recreation and other social objectives are closely associated with public ownership, they are by no means confined to that sector. Private individuals also pursue social goals, as has already been suggested by reference to Gasson's work in eastern England. Prestige and status are sought by many land owners, and especially by large land owners. The relative importance of these objectives is difficult to measure, since the land owner may be reluctant to report them among his objectives, even if he consciously recognises them. But land ownership is undoubtedly an objective in itself in some cases (RICS 1977), in all sorts of holdings from the large estates of the Scottish Highlands to the small farms of Ireland. In such cases the actual use of land is often of secondary importance to its possession. Prestige and status are probably not the only factors involved in this respect. In some countries, there has been a long struggle for the occupancy of land, and once possessed, land is retained most tenaciously. In Ireland, for example, the long struggle against the landlords, together with the devastating effect of the Famine of 1848, has engrained on the folk consciousness an intense desire to own land: in hard times a family with land would not starve (Colbert and O'Brien 1975).

The practical consequences of these psychological objectives may be profound. If an individual owns land for its own sake rather than for what the land produces, then his decisions about land use may well differ from those of another owner occupying land for purely economic reasons. If land ownership *per se* is an important objective, then the land may be under-used in the economic sense. This may attract attention at the national level, and may be even more noticeable at the regional or local level. In the early 1970s, for example, it was estimated that livestock production in Ireland was only about 60 per cent of its estimated potential (Diamond and Lee 1972–3). Several reasons may have contributed to this low level, but the motives and psychological characteristics of the land owners, in

41

the context of the troubled land history of the country, are likely to have been a major one. Land may be retained by people who are unwilling or unable to work it, and hence may pass out of use or be used only at low intensities. At the same time, people who want to work the land have great difficulty in gaining access to it, such is the tenacity with which it is retained by its traditional owners. A similar tendency for land to pass out of use has been reported from countries such as Germany, where small farmers have been attracted by urban employment opportunities and no longer have the time (or the motivation) to continue to farm their land, although they continue to own it and to reside on it. The term 'social fallow' has been coined to describe this phenomenon (Hartke 1956; Kunnecke 1974).

Low intensities of management and low levels of production are also a common feature of some types of ownership of forest land. In the United States, for example, one reason for low levels of production in some private forests is lack of economic or commercial motives on the part of their owners (Dana and Fairfax 1980). In response to the same phenomenon, recently introduced legislation in Sweden requires private forest owners to disclose working plans and to undertake thinning operations as well as fellings in mature stands (Wunder 1983). These measures have resulted from a wish to increase timber production and so avoid under-utilisation in the mainly publicly-owned forest-products industries.

Prestige, status and a feeling of security are three possible social elements in the range of objectives of land users. Others may include simple preferences for the lifestyles that farming or landholding may offer, the satisfaction that may result from working on the land, and from the knowledge that a challenging occupation such as farming is being fulfilled with technical efficiency. Preferences for particular crops or livestock are often apparent in this respect, and the farmer may derive much satisfaction from the technical achievement of breeding pedigree livestock, for example. In many cases, this achievement may be sought only after a secure economic base has been established. It follows that land-use decisions on a single land unit may be motivated by different considerations. The growing of barley, for example, could constitute the farm's economic base while part of the farm's area is given over to the rearing of pedigree stock. On the other hand, an individual might have a simple preference for livestock over cropping, and might be prepared to forego a certain amount of income for the sake of that preference.

The relative importance of personal and social objectives, compared with each other and with economic objectives, varies from place to place and from individual to individual. But if any confirmation is required that land users are not concerned only with economic objectives, then it should be remembered that rural land prices are often far in excess of the net present worth of the land in relation to potential land uses. In many instances, the land user could increase his income by selling his land and investing his capital elsewhere. Prospects of long-term growth of capital may be one factor discouraging him from doing so. The extent to which he can achieve various social objectives, consciously or otherwise, is another major factor binding him to the land.

Finally, there are two further aspects of objectives that need to be considered. The first of these is that objectives may change but land-use decisions remain the same, while the second is that the land user may apparently have no objectives at all.

During the last few decades, there have been several changes in the defined objectives of state forestry in Britain; the objective of building up a strategic reserve of standing timber has faded, while those of economic strategy and the provision of employment have become stronger. Yet the policy of continuing to afforest has re-mained the same, albeit with differing rates and intensities (e.g. Clark 1982a; Mather 1978a). Similarly, O'Laughlin and Ellefson (1982) have shown that the objectives of forest-owning companies in the United States changed between 1969 and 1978, with financial re-turns receiving less emphasis and security of supply more pro-minence. This change, however, was not accompanied by a change in actual land-use decisions: objectives changed but land use remained the same.

The absence of clearly defined objectives is well illustrated by forest owners in Pennsylvania and Maryland. One-third of the forest owners in these two states were found by Birch and Dennis (1980) and Kingsley and Birch (1980) respectively to have apparently no firm objectives in mind and apparently no planned use for the land. This proportion contrasted with the 9–15 per cent of owners who listed land investment as their main objective and the 1–2 per cent who held land primarily for timber production.

FACTORS IN DECISION-MAKING

The process of decision-making about land use is exceedingly com-plex. Decisions have to be made about type of use, intensity of use, and form of management (different systems of tillage, for example, could be employed within the same type and intensity of use). These decisions depend partly on the objectives or goals of the land user, and on the decision process that he employs. A whole range of other factors can also exert an influence. Some of these are intrinsic or personal to the individual – his age, personality and ability, for example – and some are more extrinsic, such as the nature of his land unit and the economic and social climates in which it is set (Fig. 2.1).

Type of ownership and occupancy

Type of ownership and occupancy is one of a large number of factors (many of which are at least partly inter-related) that exert an influence on decision-making about land use. In most western-type countries, there is a range of different types of ownership of land, including corporate and public forms as well as private. In many countries, controls are imposed by the state on the ownership of land, and there may be curbs on land ownership by aliens, for example, or on corporate ownership (Chapter 3). State intervention in the land market in this way is usually motivated largely by social considerations, but also by the belief or suspicion that some forms of land ownership have undesirable characteristics. The true nature of the relationship between land ownership and land use is extremely difficult to establish, not least because it operates in both directions. Some types of land-use régime are conducive to the establishing of corporate forms of ownership, so that fiscal benefits (for example) may be reaped or levels of liability limited. On the other hand, the nature of ownership can exert a strong influence on the type of decision taken. For example, considerations of prestige or status are more likely to be significant to a private land owner than to a tenant or a large corporation or financial institution, although the latter type of owner is not immune from such considerations. Nevertheless, the belief that corporate and individual ownership differ in their characteristics of land use is perhaps more widespread than the evidence on which it is based. Complications arise from different sizes of holdings and different types of land, and it is often difficult to isolate the effects of types of ownership on land-use decisions from those of other factors. But it has been established, for example, that significant differences in rates of soil erosion are related, at least in some parts of the United States, to different types of ownership (Lee 1980).

On a more general level, it is sometimes assumed or asserted that absentee land occupiers differ from residents in their land-use régimes. Differences may exist in general attitudes to land and in types of use, intensity and management. A major study in the US Census of Agriculture as long ago as 1900 showed that size of farm increased steadily with the distance between farm and its owner, and at the same time, intensity of use decreased as size of farm increased (Gaffney 1977). Gaffney also concluded that absentee owners tended to be weak in conservation measures. Duffield *et al.* (1983) have concluded from studies in California, Iowa and Mississippi that clear differences in type of land use exist between owner operators on the one hand, and absentees on the other: a higher proportion of owner operators maintain livestock facilities and they grow more forage crops. At the local level, differences between resident and absentee owners of land in the Blue Ridge Mountains of the USA have been reported by Wunderlich (1975). These differences are illustrated in Table 2.4 and apply especially in the cases of woodland and grazing.

Table 2.4   Land use by residence of owner, Rappahannock County, 1973

	Resident	Non-resident
	(Percentage of area)	
Cropland	14	19
Pasture, grazing, permanent hayland	49	23
Woodland, timber	27	41
Brushland, waste	7	14
Other	4	3

Source: Based on Wunderlich (1975).

Further west, contrasts between absentee urban land occupiers and residents in the Flint Hills – Bluestem Pastures of Kansas have been documented by Kollmorgen and Simonett (1965). The urban-based land owners showed a definite preference for using land for grazing rather than cropping. Cropping requires closer attention to matters such as crop allotments (Chapter 3), and is perhaps altogether less suited to absenteeism in the local context. At a deeper level, grazing and cropping in this area are associated with different values and reasons for land ownership. The absentee group are more strongly motivated by the status value and recreational opportunities arising from land ownership.

Differences between absentees and residents are even more clearly illustrated in parts of the Great Plains. Table 2.5 shows contrasts in the use of cropland held by local and 'suitcase' farmers in South Dakota: the residences of suitcase farmers are sufficiently far from the land in question for a suitcase to be required when the land is attended (in practice more than about 50 km). In this case, wheat-growing fits much better into the farmers' régime than livestock feeding, which requires frequent and regular attention. In parts of the Great Plains, recurring drought and crop failure result in recurring decreases in land values. Absentees may then buy land, and move in with machines to extend wheat farming when conditions again become favourable. In bad times, non-residents can withdraw or cut back their operations more rapidly than local farmers (Hewes 1972). In other words, a relationship is established between type of ownership and type of land.

Table 2.5 Contrasts in cropland use between suitcase and resident farmers, Sully County, South Dakota

	Suitcase farmer	Local farmer
	(Percentage of cropland)	
Cash crops		
Wheat	67.5	34.0
Flax	2.0	1.7
Total	69.5	35.7
Feed crops		
Total	24.8	60.9
Fallow and idle	5.7	3.4
	100	100

Source: Based on Kollmorgen and Jenks (1958).

In several western countries, there has been a flow of 'city' money into rural land, and one of the consequences is that decision-making about land use may take place far from the land in question. Little is known about the effects of this flow (Brubaker 1977). Some effects may be invigorating and may include injections of capital and initiative. On the other hand, land may be idle or under-used because of this 'remote' ownership, and feelings of alienation may emerge because of differences in outlook and in motives between the owners and local residents. For example, Howell (1978) reports that in nineteenth-century Wales, an inflow of 'newcomer' estate owners with commercial and sporting objectives contributed to agrarian unrest, whereas the more traditional estate owners had less commercial objectives and a more harmonious relationship with their tenants.

Size of unit is another aspect of land occupancy that can exert a strong influence on decisions about land use. Because size is often inter-related with other variables such as type of land, tenure and personality of occupier, its precise role is often difficult to isolate. In general terms, however, an inverse relationship often exists between size and intensity. As size increases, intensity decreases. If land is the limiting factor of production, it may be used intensively, but if capital or labour is the limiting factor then land may be used less intensively. Empirical support to the idea of an inverse relationship between size and intensity, and to the corollary that output per unit area is greater on small units, is given by Dorner (1972) in his world-wide review of land reform. He concludes that the evidence is quite clear that small farms have a better record of performance of output per unit of land than large estates. Many small farms, in many parts of the world, are given over to intensive crops such as vegetables, while larger units are often devoted to more extensive forms of land use such as ranching. On the other hand, some farms are too small to permit the efficient use of machinery, and hence may be used for purposes not requiring high levels of input in this sense. Their operators may therefore seek alternative crops, perhaps requiring greater levels of labour intensity, or else they may seek to enlarge their land area by purchase or rental. In a climate of high prices, enlargement may take the form of renting rather than purchase, and the rented farmland area in the United States, for example, has increased recently as farmers have struggled to enlarge their farms in order to maintain viability (e.g. Johnson 1974). Both rental and purchase may lead to a pattern of fragmented farms. Land may not be available contiguous to the home unit, but only at some distance from it. This tendency for fragmentation to increase with increasing farm size has been noted in parts of the United States and New Zealand, for example (e.g. Smith 1975), and may carry with it other implications for land-use decisions. The outlying portions of land may be used in such a way that travel and the movement of farm machinery is minimised, and the detached portions of land take on some of the features associated with absentee ownership. In parts of South Australia, for example, cropping is the preferred use of detached portions of farms because wheat is less likely to be stolen than livestock, and requires fewer visits for checking (Smith and Smith 1977).

Another influence of size of unit may be exerted indirectly through the generally easier access to credit and information that is enjoyed by many larger farmers and other land owners. This may enable them to implement new techniques which allow them to produce new crops or to lower the costs for existing crops. Smaller farmers may find difficulty in competing, and eventually farm amalgamation may result (Just *et al.* 1979).

Size of unit may also be related to the land-holding objectives of the occupier. In recent decades, hobby farming has become a feature around many towns and cities in Europe and North America. These farms are usually small, and are operated by their occupiers for reasons other than livelihood. The primary objective on many part-time farms around London was found by Gasson (1966) to be technical efficiency rather than economic efficiency; the occupiers seek to achieve high technical standards of farming rather than maximum economic advantage. It may well be the case that technical efficiency is an objective on many commercial farms also, but its relative importance is probably greater on hobby units. Many hobby farms are not run commercially, and indeed are scarcely agricultural units at all. On some, the owner seeks recreational goals, and keeps horses or ponies for both business and pleasure. On others, he merely seeks a place of residence in attractive surroundings, which he may further seek to enhance by tree planting or landscaping. Areas of attractive scenery, which often coincide with rather poor land quality, may be especially preferred by hobby farmers, and the combination of the characteristics of the land and of its occupiers gives rise to a distinctiveness of land use in the local area. Even if the occupier is involved in commercial farming, time is likely to be a constraint that limits his choice of use, and enterprises such as dairying or tobacco growing, which are demanding of time, may be avoided (Gasson 1966; Layton 1978).

The significance of size of land unit is by no means confined to agricultural land use. One of the factors underlying the lack of productivity and inefficiency of management of the so-called non-industrial private forests (NIPFs) of the United States (compared with commercially owned and national forests) is their small average size. Diseconomies of scale and difficulties of access to credit hinder many NIPF owners from active forest management, and in any case many of the owners, as has already been suggested, are not motivated by economic goals (Dana and Fairfax 1980). This is one example of the complex inter-relationship that can exist between size of land unit, nature of land ownership and land-use characteristics.

Land tenure is another aspect of land occupancy that can influence

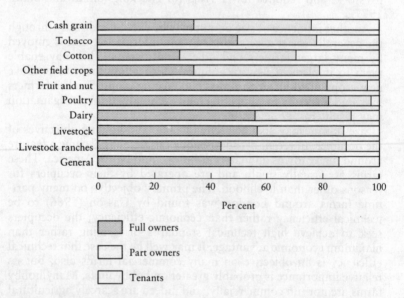

Fig. 2.2 Tenure characteristics by type of farm: USA, 1969 (48 states).
Source: Johnson (1974) (USDA).

the nature of decisions about land use. The inter-relationship between tenure and variables such as size of farm, age of farmer and other factors is complex, and it is difficult to isolate the influence of tenure on choice of land use.

Figure 2.2, however, suggests that differences do exist between tenure and type of farm in the United States. Generalisation is perhaps unwise because of the complexity of types of tenure, and because of the possible complications arising from other factors, but it would appear from the diagram that tenant status is more closely associated with land uses such as cash-grain cropping which require relatively little long-term investment, and is less associated with enterprises such as fruit and nut growing or poultry farming where more investment is required.

Tenant status takes many different forms. In some cases, the tenant is able to exercise a large measure of control and independence of decision. In other cases, he has almost no freedom of choice. In Britain, tenant farmers now enjoy firm security of tenure protected by legislation, and land use on tenanted units is similar to that on neighbouring owner-occupied farms. If tenure is less secure, however, some types of land use are likely to be discouraged. If confined to short periods, there will be a strong disincentive to practise types of land use that require an initial investment (for example, in land improvement or drainage) which will be recouped only over a period of years. Insecure tenure is often associated with exploitative forms of land use, in which the occupier seeks to reap as much as he can from the land irrespective of possibly harmful effects. An example may be quoted from New Zealand in the nineteenth century: insecure tenure of land in the interior of South Island was one of the factors inhibiting improvement of land and encouraging over-stocking with sheep, with the result that the carrying capacity of the rangeland deteriorated rapidly towards the end of the century (Mather 1983).

An extreme form of short-term tenure is the conacre system of Ireland, under which parcels of land are rented for periods of 11 months. This short period encourages the occupier to take as much as he can from the land, and the conacre system has been held responsible for the deterioration of much of the land on which it applies (Gillmore 1979). A related feature of this form of tenure is the lower level of fertiliser use on conacre pasture land compared with similar land under different tenure (Cox 1976). However, the fact that Cox found no significant difference between the levels of fertiliser use on crop-land under conacre and other forms of tenure serves as a reminder that generalisation is unwise. Relatively little research on the relationship between land tenure, land management and land use has been carried out, and some of it is conflicting. For example, Ironside (1979) found no significant correlation between land tenure and farm commodity in southern Ontario, and concluded that in contrast to the American experience, there was little difference in the relative care of owned and rented land.

Some letting agreements include conditions that restrict the range of choice open to the occupier. The land owner may, for example, require that certain crops be grown, certain crops avoided, or certain rotations followed. In extreme cases, the tenant may be a share cropper who is obliged to produce a certain crop and to turn over a substantial part of it to the land owner. In nineteenth-century Argentina, tenant farmers were the means by which the native pampas grasses were replaced by alfalfa and other forage crops after the advent of refrigerated shipping made beef production a profitable enterprise. Term contracts were given to tenant farmers (mainly Italians) to grow wheat for a specified number of years and thereafter to leave the land sown with alfalfa. Up to 30 per cent of the harvest came from a share-cropping system, in which the tenant supplied only labour. After the specified period, he moved on, and repeated the process elsewhere (Scobie 1964).

Communal tenure is now relatively unusual in the western world, although it is found in various areas such as parts of the Alps, as well as in the kibbutzim of Israel (see Paran 1970). It is often associated with low-capacity mountain land in temperate humid areas, and much communal land is under extensive grazing. Communal tenure has sometimes been regarded as undesirable, because the more progressive members of the communal group can be thwarted by their more conservative counterparts, and land improvement and selective animal breeding inhibited. On the other hand, it has been suggested by Pearce (1979) that the existence of communal land in parts of the French Alps has helped to make possible the integrated development of ski resorts, combining uphill facilities and accommodation. These have often been split between the state and private sectors in countries such as the United States and New Zealand.

Perception of the environment

A key factor in decision making is how the individual sees his surroundings. Each individual has his own perception of his environment, which differs from the real or objective environment by a greater or lesser degree. Decisions are made in the context of this perceived environment, and differences may exist between perceived and real, both in relation to the potential of the environment and to its hazards or limitations to the range of land uses that might be feasible in a given area and to hazards such as floods or hailstorms that threaten these uses. One of the most influential pieces of research in this field was carried out by Saarinen (1966) in the Great Plains of the United States, where drought is a major hazard faced by grain farmers. Saarinen discovered that drought frequency was consistently under-estimated by farmers, and that good years and the size of crops in these years were over-estimated. Estimates improved with increasing age (at least up to around 60 years) and experience in the area. But although the main hazard was under-estimated, and an apparently rosy view of the environment was thus taken, at the same time most farmers perceived the local environment as being suitable only for a very narrow range of land uses. Almost half of the farmers interviewed felt that their present operation was the only one open to them. This proportion decreased with increasing age and drought experience. It seems likely that as one grows older, the possibility of major switches of land use becomes less.

Perception also influences how the individual manages his land, as well as the use to which he puts it. Mumford (1981) has shown that farmers' decisions about pest control in the growing of sugar beet in eastern England depend on their subjective perception of the pest hazard, on the range of controls recognised to be available to them, and on their subjective estimate of their net effect. Buys (1975) has reported a significant disparity between ranchers' beliefs in heavy predation on livestock in New Mexico and current research evidence to the contrary. They continue to use poisons in an effort to control predation, even if they are both unnecessary, in view of the research evidence, and illegal.

The perception of environmental hazards, which is affected by a range of personal factors such as age and personality, is clearly related to attitudes to risk and uncertainty in land enterprises. The way in which the land user perceives his environment, and his subjective view of actual or potential hazards, will strongly condition his choice of use and form of management.

Information

The decision maker obviously has to operate within the limitations of the information available to him. Having access to information on technology, marketing and other matters is becoming more important in determining success in farming than the traditional agricultural knowledge about crops and animal husbandry (Brunn and Raitz 1978). The decision environment is constantly changing. New ideas or practices or crops are devised, and these new ideas become new inputs into the individual's decision environment. The receptivity of a set of land users to new ideas, and their readiness to adopt innovations for their own use then become important variables in decision-making. Numerous studies in many different

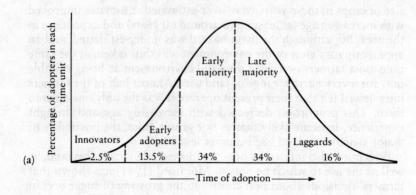

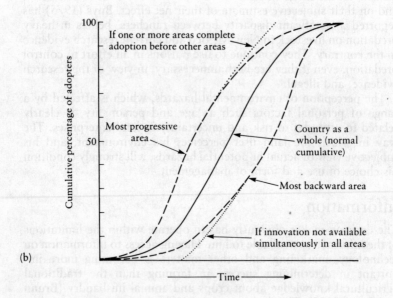

Fig. 2.3 Patterns of adoption of innovations.
    (a) Distribution of adopters by time of adoption
    (b) The national diffusion curve and possible regional variations.
Source: Jones (1963).

settings have suggested that the adoption of an idea or practice among a set of individuals follows a consistent pattern (Jones 1963). At first, only a few individuals adopt the idea. Then the number steadily grows until the majority have adopted, and thereafter the rate of uptake falls off as only the laggards remain. Figure 2.3 illustrates this pattern.

Within a group, some members will eagerly accept new information and perhaps may even seek it out for themselves. Others are most conservative, and will perhaps only accept a new idea after it has been tried out by a neighbour. A few will be more resistant, and keep doggedly to the old way rather than accept a new-fangled idea. The nature of the response to new ideas depends on personal factors such as age and level of education but, as Fig. 2.3b suggests, there may be regional dimensions in the shape of the national diffusion curve. Some parts of the country may be more ready to accept the innovation than others, depending on the sociological composition of the potential adopters as well as on the suitability of the innovation in relation to local conditions. A relationship will also exist with the type and motivation of the land user: a well-educated commercial land user is likely to be more responsive to the possible economic advantages of a new land-use practice, for example, than one who lays greater stress on non-economic goals or values, or one who is less accustomed to receiving new ideas.

This contrast may extend to differences in farm size: for example, Lee and Stewart (1983) have found lower adoption rates of minimum-tillage systems on smaller holdings in the United States in recent years than on larger farms. Lionberger (1960) in his review concludes more generally that adoption rates usually increase with farm income and farm size, with the biggest increases occurring between small and medium-sized farms. He also concludes that elderly farmers are less inclined to adopt new practices.

Information flows along several different channels, and different sources of information may be employed at different stages in the adoption of a new idea or practice. Some land users may actively seek out new ideas from research stations, whilst others are more passive and simply accept information as it is disseminated in bulletins, magazines or television programmes. Others again may be prepared to accept information and to adopt innovations only after direct contact with successful users.

An innovation is likely to be adopted first by skilled and experimenting individuals, and thereafter it diffuses down the scale of skills. If the innovation affects the supply of a commodity, prices may fall and thus profits will decline. The early adopters may then give up production of the affected commodity, and seek an alternative crop. This innovation cycle has been recognised in relation to winter vegetables, sugar beet and cut flowers in Israel, for example (Kislev and Shchori-Bachrach 1973).

Different sources of information may also be used for different types of decision. For example, Eisgruber (1973) has shown how farmers in Illinois and Indiana used farm magazines as a major source in making management decisions about planting width, depth and spacing, but made little use of them in deciding on whether and how to borrow money. The volume of information and the development of the media through which the information is disseminated are vastly greater now than in the past. As a consequence, it may perhaps be expected that rates of change of land use and land management will be faster in the future than they have been in the past, and that the whole decision environment will be more dynamic. The structure of the media of communication and the pattern of channels of dissemination of research findings and advice are obviously of major significance in information flow and hence in the dynamics of land use.

Age

Age can be an important variable in decision-making about land use. As has already been suggested, it can be significant in relation to the perception of the environment and the adoption of innovations. It seems also to be significant in relation to values and objectives. Ilbery (1983) reports that younger (under 45 years old) hop farmers in the West Midlands place more emphasis on meeting a challenge, making maximum income and expanding their business, while their older counterparts place more importance on the value of independence. Older farmers are apparently less inclined to accept indebtedness (Harrison 1972), and hence may tend to avoid decisions that would involve borrowed capital. In the north of Scotland, a clear contrast has been reported between the age structures of farmers applying to the regional development authority for assistance and the overall farming age structure in the region (Bryden and Houston 1976). Nearly 70 per cent of the farmers assisted by loans and grants were under 45 years of age, while only 24 per cent of all farmers in the region were under that age.

Older farmers seem to place less emphasis on economic considerations than their younger counterparts. This may be partly because some younger farmers feel that they have to pay close attention to economic objectives because of high land values, whereas older farmers have usually acquired land at much lower prices in the past. Another related reason is that younger farmers may have higher aspirations and higher levels of economic satisfaction. Older farmers may already have reached satisfactory levels of income, and thereafter have turned increasingly to other objectives such as leisure time or personal preference in cropping or livestock rearing. Perhaps the principle of decreasing marginal utility applies: given a sequence of equal increments in profit, the increments of marginal utility become smaller and smaller. The prospect of an extra £1,000 is probably less appealing to a farmer already earning £15,000 than to one who earns £5,000.

Age may also exert an influence on land-use decisions in other ways. In a survey of tobacco farmers in southern Ontario, Fotheringham and Reeds (1979) asked their sample to name their choice of substitute crops if demand for tobacco were to decline. Age was the most important variable in explaining farmers' choices. Older farmers tended to choose wheat, as a crop with almost assured yield and market. The youngest farmers chose strawberries, which were a riskier crop with an uncertain yield, but held the promise of high prices. The younger farmers in this case behaved more like gamblers, while their older counterparts placed more emphasis on security and stability of income.

Although the average age of farmers in England fell slightly between the 1931 and 1961 censuses (Harrison 1975), it is gradually increasing in many parts of the world. In the United States, for example, it increased from 48.7 to 51.7 between 1945 and 1974 (Coffman 1979). This increase reflects the changing structure of the population as a whole, but it is probably also the result of the increasing difficulty faced by new entrants into farming (and other land uses) at a time of high land prices. Change is slow, because many farmers spend 50 years or more in the occupation. But if significant changes do occur through time, then there may be some implications for prevailing objectives and their associated land-use decisions. Furthermore, differences in average ages may be detected between different areas. For example, farmers in the north of Scotland are on average older than their counterparts in England and Wales. In Ireland, farmers tend to retain their farms to an advanced age, and hence their sons are often middle-aged before they finally take over (Sheehy 1982). In these circumstances, the sons may be able to influence their fathers to a greater or lesser degree before they take over, but full control and decision-making by young farmers is uncommon, and regional and even national patterns of land use may be characterised by 'elderly' types of decision-making.

Education

Education is another socio-personal factor that can exert an influence in decision-making about land use. Better educated individuals are more likely to seek out information and to adopt innovations, and they may also have higher levels of aspiration. Their decision environments and their objectives may therefore contrast with those of less well-educated decision makers. Frawley *et al.* (1975), working in Ireland, found that 'successful' farmers (defined in terms of income) had higher levels of education and more progressive attitudes towards credit and risk than other farmers. In a study of rates of adjustment by American farmers to changes in the optimal quantities of nitrogen fertiliser in corn production, Huffman (1974) concluded that better educated farmers could grasp changes more quickly and adjust to them faster and more accurately than other farmers.

Intelligence and ability are less easily measured than level of educational attainment and are not synonymous with it, but they do have their own significance in decision-making about land use. Managerial ability was defined by Patrick and Eisgruber (1968), for example, as a key variable in explaining the successful growth of farm firms in the American South. At a more general level, Muggen (1969) in his review concluded that a positive relationship between performance and education had been established in most of the literature on the subject. It is obvious that the ability to assemble and process information about alternative forms of land use varies from individual to individual.

Personality and other socio-personal factors

Personality influences decision-making in a number of ways. It may directly influence objectives and aspirations: it may influence attitudes towards risk, and it is of significance in perception of environment and adoption of innovations. A significant relationship between strength of motivation and performance in farm management has been reported by Muggen (1969). The accuracy of subjective expectation of drought, floods or other environmental hazards varies with personality traits, as Saarinen (1966) has shown for the Great Plains wheat growers, and the acceptability or degree of aversion to risk, is also related to personality as well as to other factors. Various strategies to minimise risk may be devised or adopted by the risk-averse farmer. For example, he may seek to achieve the highest minimum return in the event of a poor growing season or a poor harvest, rather than seeking to achieve the maximum return that might be expected under more normal conditions. Such strategies may involve personality factors at two levels – the subjective estimate of the probability of a hazard, and the readiness or reluctance to accept the prospect of crop failure.

It has often been assumed that farmers who are averse to risk-taking are unlikely to be early adopters of new ideas or practices, and that they prefer to allow their neighbours to try out new ideas first. Recently, however, it has been suggested that the reverse may be the case, and that risk-averse farmers may be early adopters if the innovation is likely to assist in reducing the risks facing a particular crop or livestock enterprise (Mason and Halter 1980). Attitudes to risk are probably also related to the wealth of the individual. In a sample-based study of Californian farmers, for example, Pope and Prescott (1980) found that the wealthier farmers tended to have more specialised, less diversified operations, presumably because they found the risk arising from specialisation more acceptable than less wealthy individuals. Hobby farmers have also been found to be more specialised (Gasson 1966), perhaps for a similar reason: they have other income to fall back on. The degree of risk in farming has generally declined in the last few decades as a result of advances in farming technology (for example, in the use of pesticides) as well as because of government intervention in price support or other forms of price policy (Chapter 3). But while risks may have decreased overall, variability of risk from crop to crop remains, and risk aversion may remain a significant element in decision-making.

One important socio-personal attribute of a land user is the extent to which he possesses urban or cosmopolitan traits, as opposed to those of a rural or local nature. These traits may have been acquired during upbringing and education, and they probably also depend on the lifestyle of the individual and especially on his mobility. An individual's position on a continuum between rural–urban or localite–cosmopolite poles appears to be significant. The more cosmopolitan the personality and sociological traits of the individual, the greater tends to be his readiness to accept new agricultural practices (Jones 1963). Conversely, a position closer to the rural or localite pole is more likely to be associated with more conservative forms of decision-making.

Cultural factors

If personal and social factors are significant influences on decision behaviour at the individual level, cultural factors may also be important at the group level. At the very broad scale, it is well known that certain culture groups have aversions to certain animals or crops. For example, pig farming is not usually regarded as a possible land use by a Moslem. These cultural influences may also operate in less pronounced ways. Scobie (1964) asserts that the psychology and habits of coastal Argentinians in the mid-nineteenth century were powerful deterrents to grain farming. Sustained labour and residence were quite foreign to the value systems of the gauchos with their nomadic habits, and pastoralism persisted as the dominant use of the

57

pampas until the late nineteenth century. Conversely, in North America the woodsmen settlers coming from the east to the extensive grasslands of the American West never conceived or considered a range-based economy, and when ranching was introduced, it came from Texas and Spanish America rather than from Anglo-America (Kollmorgen 1969). Broad cultural contrasts are sometimes manifested along a political boundary. Different grazing histories and management practices on either side of the US – Mexico frontier are reflected in landscape contrasts, with taller grass and greater vegetation cover on the American side (Bahre and Bradbury 1978).

It has also been suggested that different national or ethnic groups have different characteristics in relation to land use. In Queensland, Buchanan (1976) found tobacco growing to be strongly concentrated among Greek and other south European immigrants. In south Brazil, a zone of mid-nineteenth century Italian settlement remains a major area of viticulture (Dickenson 1982). In North America, much has been written about the distinctiveness and sometimes superiority of certain ethnic groups. Kollmorgen (1941, 1943) has referred to the cultural 'islands' formed by various groups of immigrant farmers. Within these 'islands', there were often different forms of organisation and structure of farming, different combinations of land enterprises, and even different amounts of soil erosion compared with neighbouring areas. Cozzens (1943) claimed that there was less soil erosion on German farms in the Ozarks than on the farms of other groups, while many writers have drawn attention to the eminence of certain national groups in certain types of farming. For example, Trewartha (1925) observed the involvement of Swiss in cheese production in Wisconsin, and the association between Norwegians and tobacco growing in the same state has been documented by Raitz and Mather (1971). Baltensperger (1983) has shown how Russian-German farmers settling on the Great Plains in the late nineteenth century brought with them experience from the sub-humid environment of their homeland. Their farming systems contrasted with those of settlers from the humid Mid-West, and although they adopted some elements of the Mid-West system, they also retained important and distinctive features from their homeland. In particular, they practised a highly diversified cropping system developed as a safeguard against drought in their previous sub-humid environment.

Distinctiveness may fade through time. Californian cotton growers migrated into the Namoi Valley in New South Wales after a new dam was built, permitting controlled irrigation. The immigrants prospered, using their new environment to the full. At first, the locals continued their traditional land uses, and indeed were resentful of the newcomers. Gradually and slowly, however, they began to adapt and to make new appraisals of their surroundings, and eventually they themselves ventured into cotton growing (Pigram 1972).

Claims of ethnic or national superiority in agriculture have been questioned by writers such as Lemon (1966), who found no evidence of German superiority over other national groups in his study of eighteenth-century Pennsylvania. Lemon did conclude, however, that certain religious groups such as Quakers were consistently among the best farmers as defined by various criteria. Perhaps it is to be expected that religious groups, with their own systems of values, will pursue distinctive forms of farming. The goals and practices of groups such as Mennonites, Hutterites and Old Order Amish have attracted special attention because of their distinctiveness (e.g. Warkentin 1959). Using farm size as a measure of financial success, McQuillan (1978) found that Mennonites emerged as the most successful group in his study area in central Kansas.

These religious groups may be extreme examples, but less pronounced cases of cultural distinctiveness can be found in many areas, especially if they are relatively remote or isolated. For example, Hart (1977a) has referred to Appalachia as an 'island' of non-material values in a materialistic nation. Some of the contrasts in types of farming pursued by whites and minority groups (mainly blacks) in the American South are illustrated in Table 2.6.

Table 2.6 Types of farms, white and minority small farm operators in the South, 1969

	White	Minority
Cash-grain	9.4	8.6
Tobacco	15.1	19.6
Cotton	5.2	18.0
Poultry, dairy, livestock	50.2	28.0
General	7.6	7.6
Other	12.5	19.2

Source: Lewis (1976).

Clear contrasts exist in relation to involvement in cotton growing and in livestock farming: in general terms, such contrasts between culture groups may arise either directly through preference, or more indirectly through economic factors and the history of the culture groups.

Within the culture group there may be strong pressures to conform with group norms. The individual may be inhibited from purely personal decision-making by real or perceived group pressures. In nineteenth-century North America, for example, an individual who departed from the well-established rotations of the conventional system of farming was regarded as neither moral nor intelligent (Hart 1972). More recently, it has been suggested that one of the barriers to the adoption of no-tillage systems of cultivation using herbicides instead of ploughing is the rather untidy appearance of the treated field (Gersmehl 1978). This contrasts with the neat and tidy appearance of the conventionally ploughed field, where the farmer could display his technical skill in ploughing and hence achieve real or imagined status in the eyes of his neighbours. This reminds us of the intrinsic and expressive values held by some land users, and that utility may be perceived in the means and practice of land use as well as in its ends.

CHOICE OF USE AND MANAGEMENT

In conclusion, it becomes apparent that three layers or levels are involved in decisions about the use of resources in general and land in particular. To be selected, a type of use or management must be perceived as physically possible in the physical environment of the decision maker. His choice of use or management must be acceptable within his cultural milieu, and he must perceive utility in it. Firey (1960) sums up these requirements as possible, adoptable and gainful. The final decision about land use or management must successfully negotiate this three-layer sieve. Each layer of the sieve consists not of hard, objective phenomena but rather the individual's subjective perception of his physical and cultural environment as they interact with his own goals and personality. Each individual will select from his own practical range of choice of land uses or forms of management. This practical range will differ from the theoretical range of options open to him (White 1961). In one sense, the theoretical range of choice may be enormous, as it is limited only by human ingenuity. But even if the theoretical range of choice is defined as including all the types of use that have been practised on similar land in any part of the world, the practical range of choice is normally much narrower. The individual is unaware of some of the theoretical possibilities, and he rejects others as being unwise in his circumstances. Both theoretical and practical ranges of choice are normally wider in areas of good land where environmental constraints are weaker than in poor land where they are more severe. The general relationship is illustrated in Fig. 2.4.

Each individual has his own personal characteristic curve of practical range of choice, which diverges from the theoretical curve by a greater or lesser degree according to his personal and social characteristics. From the practical range the final decision is made on the basis of the land user's objectives. If land use is the outcome of

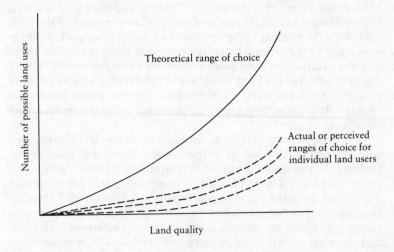

Fig. 2.4 Land quality, range of possible uses and range of choice.

individual choice on the part of the person controlling the land, then a complicated and perhaps random pattern of land use might be expected to develop. Yet it is well known that clear patterns of land use have developed in many places. For example, the Cotton Belt of the American South was a well defined land-use region during the first half of the twentieth century. The clarity of some of these regions probably encouraged early workers in the field of land use to seek explanations in direct terms of environment and economics. If land use is the product of human decision, why should so many land users in an area make the same choice? Once initiated, it is easy to see how a certain crop or other form of land use may be perpetuated. Group pressures may perhaps encourage conformity: marketing arrangements will have been worked out for the crop in question, and inputs and know-how will be readily available. Similar factors may help to explain how regional specialisation develops. In an important study of hop-growing in Kent in the nineteenth century, Harvey (1963) concludes that three basic processes governed the location of the hop acreage. Agglomeration of production meant economies of scale in and around the established locations, for example in marketing and in the supply of specialised inputs such as hop poles. 'Cumulative change' encouraged land owners to switch to hops: since hop land could bear higher rents than land used for other purposes, land owners could by raising rents encourage farmers to switch to hops. On the other hand, 'diminishing returns' tended to impose a ceiling on the proportion of land that could be devoted to hops at the farm level. Because of heavy requirements of manure, hop-growing was usually confined to less than one-third of the farm area, with the manure being produced by animals supported on the remainder of the farm. The costs of imported manure would mean that the returns resulting from expansion of hop-growing beyond this proportion of the farm would rapidly diminish. With an effective ceiling at the farm level, an increase in demand would result in a spatial extension of hop-growing, governed by agglomeration and cumulative change.

Thus good reasons may be adduced for both the development of a land-use region and for its perpetuation. There still remains the problem of the initial stage of the evolution of the region. This process is perhaps more difficult to understand; in a paper entitled 'How does an agricultural region originate?', Spencer and Horvath emphasise psychological factors; the ways in which farm populations accept new ideas; the manner in which farmers influence each other and the ways in which institutions and media such as newspapers influence practices. The controller of each piece of land may have to make a decision about how to use and manage it, but this decision is not taken in a vacuum. The individual will have in common with his neighbours various cultural and historical background factors, and may have the same types of objectives and levels of aspiration. It is not surprising, therefore, that he may make similar decisions about land use. Also, because of a tendency to make habitual decisions and to conform to the group of which he is a member, it is not surprising that a land use may persist long after the conditions under which it was first selected have ceased to operate. Inertia is probably as common in choice of land use as it is in other realms of human activity.

RESEARCH ON DECISION-MAKING IN LAND USE

It is clear that the making of decisions about land use and land management is an extremely complex process, and investigation is fraught with difficulty. This difficulty exists at several levels. In the first instance, few researchers have the necessary breadth of skills in agriculture, economics, sociology and psychology: the problem requires multi-disciplinary rather than inter-disciplinary attention. Most work on the subject has been based on a single discipline, so that only partial pictures emerge. Even the synthesis of these partial pictures is a difficult task requiring familiarity with the various disciplines involved. Furthermore, most of the work that has been undertaken on decision-making in land use has been concentrated in the agricultural sector. If comparatively little is known about agricultural decision-making, far less is known about decision-making in other sectors, and extrapolation of findings from agriculture to other sectors may be dangerous.

A second level of difficulty is the role of past decisions. Few decisions about land use are worked out on a clean slate. The past has left a legacy of existing land use and perhaps equipment and buildings as well as experience. The relationship of this legacy to contemporary conditions, and perhaps especially to economic conditions, is a key variable in decision-making. There may well be a tendency to perpetuate the familiar ways from the past, until or unless these ways are clearly out of tune with contemporary conditions. Even then, when it is recognised that change is required, the nature of the change will probably be influenced by the legacy from the past.

Thirdly, it is apparent that many variables such as age, level of education and form of tenure are inter-related. The relationship may be a two-way one, for example between type of land use and type of land unit. Therefore the role of individual variables cannot easily be isolated or measured.

Fourthly, problems surround the execution of research. Farmers and other land users can be questioned about their land-use decisions, and answers may be given in good faith. Yet there is always the problem of *post-hoc* rationalisation: the individual may work out a rational basis for a decision after it was taken. Whether the decision was actually reached in that way is another matter. Rutherford (1970) suggests that many decisions are based primarily on hunches rather than on more rigorous procedures, and certainly hunches may serve to define the possibilities for more systematic consideration even if they do not actually determine the outcome.

Finally, various attempts have been made by workers such as Ilbery (1977) to devise quantitative techniques to measure the relative importance of various factors in decision-making. Promising though some of these techniques may be, their results should be interpreted with caution. Even if individuals are capable of verbalising the factors of importance in their decision-making, problems still exist in quantifying these factors. These problems become especially acute at the aggregate level.

For various reasons, therefore, decision-making is a difficult field to investigate. The fact remains, however, that the use of land reflects human decisions, and an understanding of land-use patterns requires an understanding of these decisions. Serious methodological problems confront the investigator in this field. His task is complicated by the inter-relatedness of many of the factors that appear to be significant in decision behaviour. Much of the work that has been undertaken thus far is empirical in nature, and there is a need for more theoretical work to be carried out if major advances are to be achieved.

FURTHER READING

Bradley, M. D. (1973) Decision-making for environmental resources management.

Found, W. C. (1971) *A theoretical approach to rural land-use patterns.* Chapter 7 contains a concise and readable introduction to behavioural concepts in relation to land-use decisions. Innovation and perception are considered in Chapters 8 and 9 respectively.

Ilbery, B. W. (1978) Agricultural decision-making: a behavioural perspective.

Jones, G. E. (1963) The diffusion of agricultural innovations.

Lund, P. J. and Slater, J. M. (1979) Agricultural land: its ownership, price and rent – a guide to sources of statistical information.

Mitchell, B. (1979) *Geography and resource analysis.* Chapters 11 and 12 are concerned respectively with institutions and with policy-making in relation to resource management.

Muggen, G. (1969) Human factors and farm management: a review of the literature, *World Agricultural Economics and Rural Sociology Abstracts*, 11(2), 1–11. A concise and wide-ranging review with a lengthy bibliography.

Land use and government

The governments of most (if not all) countries exert direct or indirect influence on land use. This almost universal influence reflects something of the ambivalent attitudes held by man towards land. While land may be bought and sold like any other commodity, it is often perceived to have special qualities or attributes which require or justify government intervention. Although land may be a commodity, it also has certain characteristics of common-property resources such as water or the atmosphere. The extent to which land is regarded as private or common property obviously varies, depending on the political outlook of the government in question. However, there are usually at least some restraints on private-property rights in land even where right-wing governments hold sway. These restraints reflect the basic attachment that man feels towards land, and the fact that he is dependent on land for his sustenance and living space.

One of the fundamental reasons for government intervention in land use is that individual and societal utility do not always coincide. The type of land use or land management that is optimal for the individual or company is not necessarily optimal for the community or for society in general. It may be in the interests of the individual, for example, to sell his farm land at a high price for housing, but it may be in the interests of the community to retain the land in agricultural use so that food supply can be safeguarded. Similarly, it may be in the interests of the individual to produce agricultural crops from a piece of land, while society might prefer to use the land for recreation. The relation between individual and societal utility and objectives is therefore fundamental to the whole question of government influence on land use. The nature of this influence varies from country to country, but in many countries at least three broad types of influence are felt.

At the first and most basic level, the type of land policy pursued is a pervasive influence on the structure of land ownership and on the extent of private-property rights in land. A second level of government influence consists of support policies directed towards certain types of land use. Many western governments intervene in agriculture and forestry to safeguard home supplies, to stabilise production and to ensure the well-being of farmers and other land users. Thirdly, government may take direct action in using land at its own hand. In this case, government is the owner, controller and user of land, and pursues objectives that private land users are unwilling or unable to pursue.

LAND POLICY

Historical legacies

The nature of land policies pursued in the past often leaves a legacy which exerts a persistent if indirect influence on land use at the present day. The influence is exerted through the size and shape of the basic units in the structure of land ownership. There is no better example than the United States of America, where the land policy adopted during the nineteenth century determined a farm structure that has substantially survived in many parts of the country to the present. The land policy epitomised in the role and status of the family farm sprang from the yeoman ideal so closely associated with Thomas Jefferson. On the philosophical side, this ideal grew from the French Physiocrats; on the religious side it grew from the identification of the settlers in the New World with Israel gaining the Promised Land, where they 'dwelt safely, every man under his vine and under his fig tree' (I Kings 4:25) (Paterson 1967). The ideal was a reaction against the overcrowding and oppression of Europe whence the settlers had come, and democracy was its correlate. Similar ideas of a 'sturdy yeomanry' were present in Australia from about 1870 onwards, and were applied to soldier-settlement schemes after both World Wars (Williams 1970).

The yeoman or family farm was given legislative substance in the United States in the Homestead Act of 1862 at a time when the frontiers of settlement still lay in the humid and sub-humid parts of the country. A standard farm size of 160 acres (a quarter of one square mile section, or 65 ha) became established as the norm, in relation to established farming practice in eastern North America. Such a farm could be worked by family labour, and the large capitalist farms and estates from which many of the European settlers had sought to escape would not be replicated in the New World.

The concept of the family farm therefore determined the nature of the land units that were made available to settlers, and this concept became enshrined if not fossilised in the 160-acre farm. However suitable such a farm may have been for family subsistence and family labour in eastern North America, it was hopelessly inadequate in parts of the more arid American West. Yet it was tenaciously retained as the basic land unit, and suggestions that much larger units were required in the west were stubbornly rejected until the early decades of the twentieth century. By then, many homesteaders in the drier areas had given up the unequal struggle to survive on a 160-acre farm.

In pursuing policies of establishing and maintaining family farms, the US government was expressing a sense of values: the family farm was a Good Thing that had an intrinsic value almost irrespective of its economic efficiency. The independent family farmer was the bastion and the building block of democracy. With his family, he was responsible for running the farm; if he worked hard, he would 'make good'. These values have outlived the period and the circumstances in which they evolved. The yeoman farmer ideal dates essentially to a period of subsistence, and under later commercial conditions the 160-acre farm could be quite inappropriate especially as machine power became available to replace human labour. But within the family-farm ideal was the belief that the farming family should receive a fair price for their products. In return for hard work, they should enjoy a good standard of living, and not be burdened by poverty or destitution. As farming became more commercial and as its output grew faster than demand, it became clear that market forces alone could not be guaranteed to ensure a decent standard of living for the family farmer, however hard he worked. And so policies of government support were introduced in order to reconcile the contradictions in the family-farm ideal which began to emerge as mechanised, commercial agriculture developed. Not only did the idea of the family farm exert a crucial influence on the structure of land holding, it also was one of the factors leading inexorably to government support measures.

Gilson (1973) has shown how the family-farm ideal has influenced many Canadian agricultural policies since the passing of the Canadian Homestead Act of 1872, and its influence has lingered on to the present day in the form of legislation in many states in the United States which imposes restrictions on land ownership by corporations and aliens (see p.72): these forms of ownership are still regarded as less worthy than that of the family farmer. The ideal of

67

the family farmer also lingered on in policies of frontier settlement in Alaska in the twentieth century. The failure to attract pioneer family farmers there was a reflection of the survival of the ideal in policy long after it had faded from the minds of individual Americans (Shortridge 1976). Perhaps this is an example of the point made by Williams (1976) to the effect that in rural matters, the administration often seems to be a couple of decades out of touch with the actions and feelings of farming communities, because of the tendency of government to behave conservatively and to adhere to old concepts and ideals.

This point was made in relation to Australia, and that country offers another example of how land policy adopted in the past has influenced land use at the present. The states of Queensland and New South Wales had different policies towards land settlement, and pursued these policies with different degrees of vigour. The result is that the state line is now a boundary separating areas with contrasting characteristics of land use (Rose 1955).

Southern Africa also offers interesting examples of the effects of land policies. Natal was perceived as excellent grazing land by the Cape Trekkers entering from the interior, but was seen as potentially good arable land by the British arriving directly by sea (Christopher 1971). These different perceptions persisted for decades, and strongly influenced land-settlement policies. The Cape-Dutch tradition gave rise to large farms, low population densities and a low intensity of land use, while British attempts at close settlement and small, intensively worked arable farms were pushed in some instances too far into the more arid areas of grassland, and subsequently failed.

Elsewhere in Southern Africa, other elements of land policy conditioned the basic units of land allocation in other ways. During the early eighteenth century, the Dutch East India Company began to regulate land occupancy through the demarcation of areas to be occupied by each grazier. In the absence of land surveyors, a grazier was permitted to stake out a circular farm by riding at walking pace for half an hour from a chosen point (Christopher 1982). The area thus enclosed was approximately 2,500 ha, and this area, translated into square form, became one of the standard farm sizes in the Cape.

The terms under which land was occupied during colonial periods also influenced land-use regimes. Some land-disposal policies had the objective of increasing local agricultural production. The terms of leases offered to some farmers in Natal, for example, enforced sugar cultivation in order to maintain supplies to sugar mills built as settlement progressed, and ranching companies in Rhodesia had to undertake to graze a certain number of livestock per unit area (Christopher 1983). In some of the early colonies in New Zealand as well as in Australia and South Africa, attempts were made to encourage close settlement and intensive land use by charging high prices for land. These policies were difficult to maintain in other than small and localised areas because of the sheer extent of land around the initial colonies. Large tracts of grazing land surrounded the colonies, and the ready availability of such land, in contrast to the scarce resources of labour and capital, encouraged very extensive use. If land were made available cheaply, then it was sometimes regarded as being of little inherent value and was treated accordingly. This may have been one of the reasons for the exploitative use of land in many frontier zones, and for the resulting problems of land deterioration. These problems were especially acute where tenure was insecure and the occupier had little incentive to conserve or improve his land. Fixed-term grazing leases on state land in Australia have been blamed by writers such as Pick (1942) for severe degradation of land: the lessee had every incentive to use the grazing land to the maximum but no incentive to look after it carefully. This problem was recognised as early as 1814 by the British colonial administration in Southern Africa, and perpetual leases were introduced in the hope of encouraging the grazier to adopt a sedentary existence and to improve his land and livestock (Christopher 1982).

Although policies of close settlement and intensive land use met with limited success in the initial colonies, they were pursued once more towards the end of the nineteenth century in New Zealand, for example, against the background of the new development of refrigerated shipping, which made possible more intensive pastoral farming geared to European markets. Legislation was introduced to allow advances to be made to settlers, and the occupancy of farms could be obtained on favourable terms (e.g. MacLachlan 1966). Farm size became smaller in many parts of the country, and farming became more intensive. In the Canterbury Plains of South Island, there was a switch from extensive wheat growing to more intensive mixed-farming systems, with an emphasis on fat lamb for the British market. This switch is a good example of the complexity of influences on land-use decisions: it resulted not from one single factor, but rather from the combination of an advance in technology, making possible the production of meat for the European market, a growing population and labour force, and government policies of closer settlement. Individually, these factors might have had little effect on land use: in combination they were a powerful influence for change.

Government land policy is of significance in land use in long-settled countries as well as those opened up during the nineteenth century. Many governments have sought to re-organise or reform the structure of land ownership or occupancy, and Tuma (1965) quotes numerous examples of land reform ranging from classical to modern times. In Japan, sweeping land reform after the Second World War eliminated absentee ownership and rent payments in kind, and restricted land holdings to not more than 3 ha (for self-cultivation) and 1 ha (for renting out) in Old Japan, with corresponding ceilings of 12 and 4 ha in Hokkaido (Kornhauser 1982). In many parts of Europe, governments have intervened to sub-divide large private estates into smaller units. Social pressures usually underlay these policies of land division, and indeed Tuma concludes that the policies were usually intended to pacify rather than to change the social order or to solve fundamental rural problems. Some national policies, however, produced change on a very considerable scale. In Denmark, for example, around 27,000 small-holdings were created following legislation in 1899 and 1919 (e.g. Skrubbeltrang 1953), and in Ireland over 80 per cent of the agricultural area passed from large land owners to small farmers in the late nineteenth and early twentieth centuries (Colbert and O'Brien 1975). The precise nature of the effect of such changes

Table 3.1 Land settlement in Scotland

(a) Comparison of properties before and after land settlement (1920)

	6 arable farms		6 pastoral farms	
	Before	After	Before	After
No. of families	52	90	29	243
Area under crop (ha)	450	645	89	496
Area under hay and grass (ha)	854	594	2,710	2,300
Horses	71	160	43	368
Dairy cattle	63	334	132	562
Other cattle	668	303	440	897
Sheep	1,667	593	5,583	6,051
Pigs	39	290	—	—

(b) Comparison of settlement scheme with undivided neighbouring farm of same size, lowland Ross-shire, 1927.

	Scheme	Farm
Grain crops (ha)	160	110
Other crops (inc. grass) (ha)	240	290
Ewes	107	400
Cattle	85	100
Horses	16	10
Labour	18*	9†

*   14 holders plus 4 hired men
†   9 hired men
Source: Mather (1978b).

in land occupancy on land use is difficult to determine, because it is not possible to know with complete confidence what changes in land use would have occurred if land reform or redistribution had not occurred. Nevertheless, one common feature is an increase in labour input in the sub-divided unit. The corresponding increase in output may not be forthcoming immediately, but may be delayed until after recovery from the general disruption of re-organisation. Examples of 'before and after' and 'side-by-side' characteristics of land re-organisation in the north of Scotland are illustrated in Table 3.1.

While government influence is manifested clearly in policies of land allocation and distribution, a more subtle and indirect influence on land occupancy and hence ultimately on land use may be exerted through the laws of land inheritance. In parts of mainland Europe, for example, the civil codes provided for equal sub-division estates between heirs (e.g. Brun 1978), and this legal tradition resulted in acute fragmentation of many land units. While fragmentation could lead to increasing intensity of land use, if continued to extreme levels it became very inefficient, as tiny plots became enclosed within almost endless field boundaries. Some mainland Europeans took these traditions overseas with them, and divided inheritance was especially prominent among the Dutch-speaking peoples of Southern Africa, for example. Sometimes it resulted in multiple-ownership farms, where the controlled breeding of animals (essential for the production of good-quality wool and beef) became impossible. Christopher (1976) quotes an example of a farm in Cape Colony in the early twentieth century where one individual's share was 1/48141, and in another example in Transvaal where physical sub-division had occurred, a farm of 60 ha had a total of 19 km of boundaries. In such cases, fencing became prohibitively expensive, and many holdings became too small for the grazing of livestock to be continued.

In Chapter 2, the cultural factor in the making of decisions about land use was briefly discussed. One of the ways in which the cultural factor is mediated is through government policy towards land allocation and through the laws of land inheritance. In these ways, broad cultural influences can take concrete form, and leave an almost indelible imprint on the rural landscape. One of the clearest illustrations of the strength and significance of this cultural imprint is the contrast in the pattern of land units in French and Anglo-America. Under the seigneurial system of the French areas, blocks of land were granted to seigneurs, who then divided their blocks into strip farms (Harris 1966). The 'long lots' of rectangular strips of land laid out in Quebec and parts of Louisiana contrast fundamentally with the square quarter sections of the Anglo-American Mid-West. (The origin of the rectangular survey that lay behind these square quarter sections, its implementation in the upper Mississippi country and some of its implications for land use and management are discussed by Johnson 1976). Different peoples have developed different traditions of land occupancy, and their legal systems have perpetuated these traditions long after the circumstances in which they emerged have ceased to operate.

Controls on land ownership and occupancy

The influence of government is contemporary as well as historical. Many western countries maintain controls, with varying degrees of stringency, on the ownership and occupancy of land. In some instances, these controls are legacies of old policies that were perhaps more relevant in the past than at present, but in other cases they are maintained because of a firm belief that certain types of occupancy are related to efficient land use and that other types are undesirable. In the United States, both federal and state regulations apply to land ownership by aliens and corporations (Harris 1980; Morrison and Krause 1975). Federal regulations have fairly minor effects, but seven states prohibit alien ownership within their borders and several others impose various forms of restrictions (Fig. 3.1).

Several states also prohibit the ownership by corporations of farmland or even of any land (e.g. Reimund 1979). Most of these states are in the Mid-West, where family farming has had both a dominant and favoured position for more than a century. Restrictions on corporate ownership are clearly intended to protect family farming from competition by farming corporations or agribusinesses. It is noticeable that corporations are permitted in some states to engage in forestry but not in farming, which is strictly defined in legal terms. Although the restrictions are intended more for social reasons than for direct purposes of land use, they may have an indirect influence on land use, since corporations with access to capital and with limited liability are perhaps likely to make choices and decisions that differ from those of family farmers. For example, commercial objectives may be stronger and more dominant, and risky enterprises may be more acceptable.

Restrictions also exist in Canada. Controls on the sale of land to aliens were imposed in Prince Edward Island as early as 1859 (Brown 1975; see also Misek and Lapping 1984). During the 1970s, no fewer than seven provinces enacted legislation directed wholly or partly against absentee or foreign ownership of farmland (Troughton 1981). For example, the Saskatchewan Farm Ownership Act of 1974 is aimed at ensuring that agricultural resources are controlled by resident, full-time farmers. Non-residents may be prohibited from owning more than a quarter section (65 ha) (Bray *et al.* 1979).

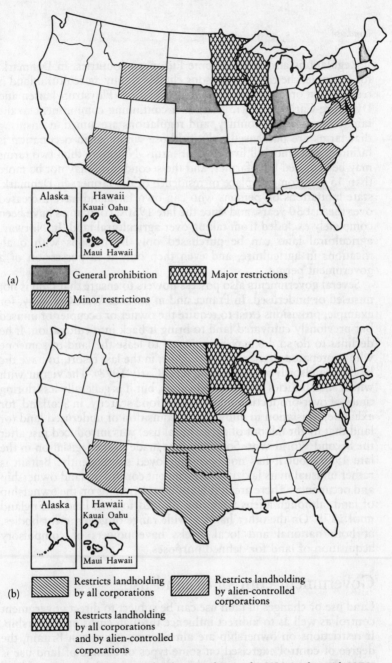

Fig. 3.1 State restrictions on land ownership in the USA in the mid-1970s.
(a) State restrictions on alien ownership of land
(b) States with restrictions on corporate landholding
Source: Morrison and Krause (1975) (USDA).

Regulations also exist in some European countries. In Denmark, for example, the range of persons eligible to buy agricultural land is restricted in order to control land speculation (Fløystrup-Jensen and Dyreborg-Carlsen 1981). There is a continuing commitment to the family farm in that country, and regulations are aimed at ensuring that farms are purchased only by those whose main occupation is farming, and who will live on their farms. Not more than two farms may be acquired by a farmer, and the second farm may not be more than 15 km from the place of residence of the farmer. In Denmark, state limitations on persons who can own farmland have increased over the last 30 years, and since the late 1950s, companies have been completely excluded from taking over agricultural land. In Norway, agricultural land can be purchased only by persons with qual-ifications in agriculture, and even then only if in possession of a government permit.

Several governments also possess powers to ensure that land is not misused or underused. In France and in parts of West Germany, for example, provisions exist to require the owner or occupier of unused but previously cultivated land to bring it back into cultivation. If he declines to do so, he may be required to lease the land to someone who is prepared to use it more fully or, in the last resort, to have the land compulsorily acquired from him (Carty 1978). The vigour with which such policies are enforced varies, but it is generally less during times of over-production than times of food scarcity. In Scotland, for example, legislation to allow state acquisition of underused land (or land that might fall out of agricultural use) was introduced just after the Second World War. Some use was made of the legislation in the late 1940s, but it has not been employed subsequently. Britain is rather unusual in its laxity of government control on land ownership and occupancy. There are at present no restrictions on the ownership of land, although aliens were not allowed to own land in England until 1878. On the other hand, a wide range of government bodies, at both national and local levels, have powers of compulsory acquisition of land for defined purposes.

Government control of land use

Land use or changes in land use can be subject to direct government control as well as to indirect influence through curbs on ownership. If restrictions on ownership are almost non-existent in Britain, the degree of control exercised on some types of change of land use is strict. The source of this control is a recognition that a type of land use that is optimal for the individual is not necessarily optimal for the community or for society in general. The foundation of direct control of land use in Britain is the Town and Country Planning Act of 1947, which introduced the idea of 'development control', 'development' being defined as the making of material change in the use of land or the carrying out of building, engineering, mining or other operations on the land. Local government, usually operating within broad guidelines from central government, exercises development control by granting or refusing planning permission for proposed changes in the use of land. In practice, many types of change require no planning permission. In detail, these types may be modified from time to time, but broadly speaking developments in agriculture and forestry require no planning permission, while changes of use from agriculture to urban, industrial or some forms of recreational use do require planning consent. In other words, some types of land-use change can proceed almost regardless of the planning system and direct government control, while others are tightly constrained. Government intervention in controlling land use in this way can have a major effect on land values, as these are influenced by prospects for change and development as well as by current use (e.g. Goodall 1970).

One of the main effects of the planning system in Britain has been to control the transfer of agricultural land to residential or other urban uses (Ch. 5), and it is noticeable that the rate of transfer of agricultural land in this way has been lower since the introduction of the planning system than it was during the 1930s. In contrast, the rate of urbanisation of farmland in North America, where planning controls of this type are generally weaker, has been maintained at high levels during the post-war period.

In North America, urban zoning ordinances were introduced in New York City in 1916, and by that time Los Angeles had already had for seven years a regulatory system that divided the city into residential- and industrial-use districts. Under the New York ordinance, the city was divided into residential-, commercial- and unrestricted-use districts. By 1926, zoning had spread to over 420 American cities, representing more than half the urban population (Nelson 1977; Platt 1976). In that year, it was questioned as to whether zoning was constitutional: it was subsequently held to be so by the US Supreme Court. The system works through the delegation of state power to municipalities, who may exercise it although they are not required to do so. Zoning ordinances may prohibit certain land uses from certain areas, and may also control the types and intensities of land use. For example, the development of low-cost, high-density housing may be prohibited, but high-cost, low-density housing permitted on the grounds that it will contribute more to local taxes and be less of a burden on the budgets of education and other services. Zoning power is usually exercised only within towns and cities, and in many rural areas there are virtually no controls.

Indeed the local fiscal arrangements whereby taxes are assessed on the value of a piece of land may encourage urbanisation and the spread of urban sprawl. The value of land as a potential site for commercial or residential development is usually much higher than its agricultural value. If the owner is assessed for tax on the basis of this higher value, then this is a positive inducement for him to discontinue farming in favour of the new urban use. Although zoning is employed mainly in urban areas, there are some examples of its use in non-urban settings. Part of the Los Angeles milk-supply area has survived the threat of urbanisation because land has been zoned exclusively for agriculture (Fielding 1964).

Land-use control is generally weaker in North America than in Britain, and in the mid-1970s only about 14,000 of the 38,000 units of local government in the United States regulated land use in some way (Healy 1976). In general terms, controls are stricter in densely populated countries than in those with more favourable man:land ratios, but an important trend during the twentieth century, and especially during the last 30 years, has been for controls to be strengthened and extended almost world-wide. In the United States, public efforts to control land use have extended from concern with separating conflicting urban land uses to means of directing economic and population growth, preserving or improving environmental quality, and preserving open space, prime agricultural land and critical natural areas (Ervin and Fitch 1979). The extent of strengthening varies from country to country, but in many parts of the world it has been one of the most significant trends in land use in recent decades.

SUPPORT POLICIES AND LAND USE

The second major form of government influence is exerted through economic rather than legal or tenurial measures. Problems in agriculture in many western countries in the twentieth century have stimulated government intervention by various means such as price-support policies, subsidies and production grants, as well as by the funding of research and development programmes and the provision of advisory services by which information may be disseminated.

Government aid has also been given to forestry, although usually in different ways and on a smaller scale. One of the great ironies in rural land use is the juxtaposition of the intrinsic value of independence, cherished by so many rural land users (Ch. 2), and the extent of government intervention in the economics of rural land use. In few other realms of activity is this intervention so extensive or so significant.

Why do governments intervene?

The goals of agricultural policy are usually multiple and complex rather than single and simple. They are sometimes in conflict with each other, and they are often intertwined almost inextricably. Nevertheless, they do vary through time, and they also vary more especially from country to country. Different countries have different emphases on the goals of their policies, but two main elements are usually present. The first of these is the seeking of a useful contribution from agriculture to the national economy, while the second is the wish to treat the agricultural sector equitably in comparison with other parts of the economy (Self and Storing 1962). A broad division may be made into utility goals and equity goals, but this distinction is not always sharp or clear.

Figure 3.2 sets out the sub-divisions within utility and equity goals. This distinction is useful as an analytical tool, but it would be misleading to suggest that government policies are always as clearly defined or differentiated as the diagram may imply. In many if not most policies, there is a blurring between economic and social goals, and a measure which may have begun as a means of encouraging production, for example, may be perpetuated for social reasons. Conversely, measures stimulated by social objectives such as a wish to maintain or protect the family farm sometimes have an effect on the role of agriculture in the national economy. One major goal, pursued especially in small, densely populated countries, is to ensure an acceptable degree of self-sufficiency for purposes of national security. This has been a major objective in British agricultural policy, and also in countries such as Japan, Austria and Switzerland (see OECD reviews of agricultural policy for discussion of national policies).

Underlying government intervention in agriculture in the western world is the fundamental fact that demand for food in developed countries increases only slowly. There may be some growth in demand as population increases, but population growth has been very slow in recent decades. There may also be changes in the nature of demand, as staple diets based on basic foodstuffs become more varied as a taste develops for more exotic materials and the ability to procure them increases. However, in general terms, the proportion of real *per capita* income spent on food decreases as incomes increase. In contrast to timber and many manufactured goods, demand for food increases only slowly during economic growth. This in itself means that agriculture becomes a declining industry in a growing economy. If the farmer responds to static demand by increasing production, then he may encounter problems of over-production and falling market prices. Attempts to improve his efficiency by using

77

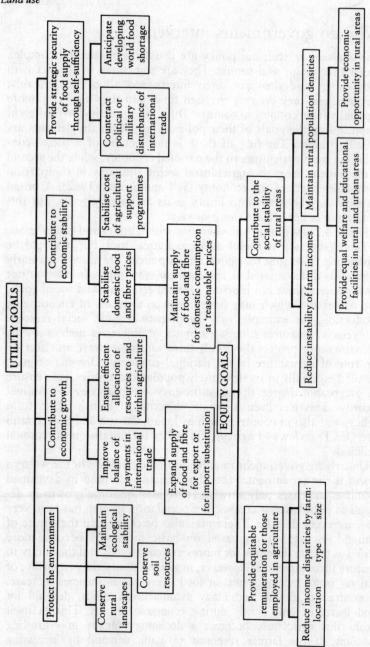

Fig. 3.2 Goals in agricultural policy.
Source: Bowler (1979).

better crop varieties and better techniques of production have the same effect. The progressive or innovative farmer seeks out new technology or new practices which increase revenue or decrease the cost of production. As others emulate him, overall output is increased, and prices are depressed. If this cycle is repeated, a 'treadmill' is set in motion (Cochrane 1958). Relatively static demand for food in a growing economy would in itself pose a problem for the farmer, but the problem is made more acute because inputs such as fertilisers and machinery have to be purchased from other parts of the economy, where prices are rising faster than in the food sector. The farmer is thus caught between static prices for his products, and rising costs of production. If left exposed to these forces, he would find almost no escape from the trap of falling income. Even the radical response of seeking to leave farming altogether is no easy solution. As has been suggested in Chapter 2, farmers value their way of life, and may have neither inclination to abandon the land nor aptitude for urban or industrial employment. Furthermore, the option of reducing the farm population so that those remaining could each have a larger share of agricultural 'cake', and hence maintain comparability of incomes with other sectors of the population, comes into conflict with other goals such as the maintenance of rural population densities (Fig. 3.2). It is obvious then that the problems are deep-seated and incapable of easy solution. The variety and range of measures introduced by various governments over the last few decades serve simply to indicate and illustrate this complexity. The means and mechanics of government intervention vary from place to place, as does the precise nature of the initial objectives of intervention. The range of measures is so extensive as to be almost bewildering, and instead of attempting to consider them systematically, it is preferable to consider them within the setting of individual national agricultural policies.

Britain

British agricultural policy is a feature of the twentieth century and especially of the period since the Second World War. During the second half of the nineteenth century, a policy of *laissez-faire* prevailed, and agriculture was left exposed to the forces of demand and supply on the international market. From around 1870 some sectors of British agriculture suffered a decline as the New World entered the international market. Imports of wheat from the Prairies undercut home production, and much land in eastern England passed out of cropping. Similarly, sheep farming on the hill grazings of Scotland could not readily compete with sheep farming in Australia and New Zealand, and large areas of land passed out of agricultural use. Most

European countries were affected by cheap imports from the New World, and several, such as France, Germany and Italy, embarked on policies of protecting home agriculture by tariff barriers (Tracy 1982). In Britain, policies of free trade prevailed, and while manufacturing industry benefited and the urban-industrial population enjoyed the benefits of cheap imported food, agriculture remained unprotected. Denmark and the Netherlands also avoided protectionist policies, but instead began to change their agriculture away from the vulnerable basis of cereal growing, which was now undercut by overseas producers, and towards pigs, milk and horticultural products which were much less affected by imports. In Britain many cereal-growing areas were badly hit, with land passing out of arable crops and into grass.

This era was brought to a sudden halt during the First World War, when the disadvantages of relying on imported food became all too apparent. In the preceding years, Germany had protected its farmers from competition from imports, and so was in a better position than Britain to feed itself. Government intervention became inevitable in Britain: minimum prices for cereals were introduced, and a variety of other measures designed to increase home food production were adopted. These measures were withdrawn during the post-war financial crisis, but in the economically depressed 1930s, state intervention became firmly established. Intervention occurred on three fronts – import controls, marketing controls and price subsidies, by which government contributed the difference between the market price of wheat and an agreed standard price. These measures were on a relatively small scale, but were nevertheless a clear indicator of the prevailing trend. The state was now involved in agriculture, as well as in a number of other sectors of the economy.

During the Second World War, the need for greater self-sufficiency in food supplies led to dramatic changes in British agriculture. At the outbreak of war, Germany was self-sufficient in basic foodstuffs such as grain, potatoes and sugar beet. During the 1930s, policies of support to agriculture had been pursued in Nazi Germany. These policies were motivated by both ideological and practical considerations. The wish to protect the peasantry as a bulwark against liberalism and socialism was paralleled by a wish to maximise domestic food prices. Guaranteed prices were offered for a full range of agricultural products, and by 1933 German grain farmers were effectively cut off from the vagaries of the world market (Farquharson 1976). In contrast, Britain was only about one-third self-sufficient in total food supplies, and a great drive to increase home food production began. Plough-up campaigns led to a great increase in the arable area, and land which had lain under grass for half a century or more was converted to the production of wheat and barley. The government became the sole buyer of agricultural produce, at pre-determined prices set high enough to encourage individual farmers to increase production. In addition, capital grants for drainage and other improvements were made available. In short, government intervention had now arrived on a grand scale.

During the war years, the government gave a commitment that it would not allow agriculture to decline in the future as it had in the past, and the Agriculture Act passed in 1947 became the foundation of post-war agricultural policy. Few pieces of legislation have had such a significance for rural land use. Several objectives were defined in the Act, one of the fundamental ones being the achievement of a stable agricultural industry, 'capable of producing such part of the nation's food ... as it is desirable to produce in the United Kingdom'. This food was to be produced at minimum prices consistent with the proper remuneration and living conditions for those engaged in the industry. Goals of utility and equity were combined; strategic considerations of self-sufficiency of food supply were emphasised. Agriculture was no longer at the mercy of demand and supply within an open market.

The means by which these objectives were sought were primarily through guaranteed prices. Prices for the main agricultural (but not horticultural) commodities were set annually, and if the market price fell below the guaranteed price, then the shortfall was made good by a 'deficiency' payment from government. This arrangement had the advantage that consumers could still enjoy the benefits of cheap food, as imports were not excluded by tariff barriers as was the case in many other European countries. Furthermore, by adjusting guaranteed prices, selective increases in certain products could be obtained, although in the first few years after the war, increases were sought across the board. Gradually, as supplies increased both on the home and international markets, some relaxation was introduced. By the mid-1950s, the government was no longer the monopoly buyer of farm produce, and guaranteed prices for some commodities were now offered only for fixed 'standard' quantities rather than for unlimited amounts. The degree of government intervention declined as the stringencies of the war-time period faded, but there was no suggestion of withdrawal. The overall costs of government support stabilised, but the system of deficiency payments was retained, along with a range of production grants and capital grants for the improvement of land and farms.

In the mid-1960s, the import-saving role of agriculture was emphasised by the Labour Government, and programmes of selective expansion, notably in beef, were proposed. Existing measures and modes of intervention were retained, but changes in the relative emphases of objectives could be perceived. Policies of a social nature were reflected in the Agriculture Act of 1967, where the economic problems of small farmers were recognised and new measures were introduced to encourage farm amalgamation. Special provision was also made for hill farmers. At this time agriculture as a whole was being encouraged to release labour for manufacturing industry, and machine power was rapidly replacing man power. The continuing cost-price squeeze, resulting from a faster increase in costs than in prices, encouraged a continuing search for economies of scale, and growing specialisation at the level of the farm and of the region.

The structure and mechanisms of British agricultural policy remained substantially intact from 1947 until accession to the European Economic Community in 1972. Several other European countries had comparable agricultural policies in the post-war years, but with varying forms and degrees of intervention. In Germany, for example, the overall intensity of agricultural land use was higher than in Britain, although population and land area were similar. The difference in intensity was attributable to a greater degree of intervention, in the form of restrictions on imports, in Germany (Grotewold and Sublett 1967). Both British and German policies are now subsumed within the broader Common Agricultural Policy of the EEC.

The Common Agricultural Policy (CAP)

The agricultural policy formulated and operated by the EEC is not dissimilar to that pursued in Britain after 1947, but it has different emphases and it employs different means. Objectives within the CAP include stability of the market and security of supplies of food at reasonable prices, as well as a fair standard of living for the farm population. These objectives include some conflicts and contradictions, notably between the prices of food to the consumer and the level of income of the producer. In the EEC area, problems of small farmers and inadequate size of holdings are more serious than in Britain, and they have been given greater emphasis than in earlier British policy.

The main difference between the CAP and previous British policy is in the mode of government intervention. Whereas deficiency payments played key roles in the British system, they play smaller parts in the CAP. Price support is achieved through the medium of intervention buying. An 'intervention' price for the major commodities is set annually. The intervention agencies will purchase the commodity at that price (as long as it meets prescribed standards of quality) irrespective of the level of demand in the open market. Intervention buying therefore serves as an effective floor to the market. Furthermore, home producers are protected from overseas competition by import levies which ensure that cheap supplies do not flood in. On the other hand, commodities acquired by the intervention agencies are often exported at subsidised prices to other countries.

Several major consequences follow from the use of this method of price support. One is that the consumer does not enjoy the advantages of cheap food which might be offered by the international market or by the system of deficiency payments. (Poorer consumers benefit from the deficiency-payment system through relatively cheap food, and contribute relatively little to the financing of the system since they pay less income tax than richer consumers.) Another consequence is that government through the intervention agencies has to meet the full cost of 'intervention' buying, and not just the difference between market price and support price. But perhaps the most fundamental problem stems from the conflict inherent within the policy. If support prices are set high enough to enable small producers to enjoy a 'reasonable' level of income, then over-production is likely to be encouraged and large-scale efficient farmers may reap very high incomes. Surpluses accumulate and the costs of support measures increase.

Structural policies are also incorporated within the CAP. In order to reduce the number of small, uneconomic farms, two main measures were adopted. Assistance was (and is) give to farmers to take up alternative occupations or to retire, and the remaining small farmers are offered help to modernise and develop their farms. Grant aid is made available so that farms can be improved or developed, usually over a period of years, so that they can offer full-time employment with income similar to that in non-agricultural employment in the area. By reducing the number of small farmers and helping those who remain to expand their farm business, it is hoped to make the land users more commercial in outlook and thus to respond better to market trends. In this way it is hoped that the twin problems of over-production and inadequate living standards can be alleviated.

Both British agricultural policy and the CAP which has superseded it recognised that regional dimensions exist in farm problems, especially in areas of hills and mountains. Farmers in these areas are at a disadvantage compared with their counterparts in more fertile lowlands. Yields are usually lower, and the range of choice of land use is usually narrower. Measures such as headage payments for livestock and cropping grants for the production of winter fodder have been offered in these areas, largely for social reasons concerned with the well-being of the farming population, but also, in the case of early post-war Britain, in order to bring marginal agricultural land into fuller production at a time of food scarcity. These measures play important roles in maintaining agriculture in many of these areas and in averting a flow of land out of agriculture and into other uses. At the same time, however, some of them have encouraged the substitution of capital for labour, and their effect in helping to maintain employment (and hence population) has therefore been limited.

North America

North American agricultural policies have given greater emphasis to farm prices and incomes, and strategic considerations of self-sufficiency have been given much less prominence than in countries such as Britain. Perhaps this different emphasis is only to be expected in light of the different population:land ratios and the almost effortless ability of the United States and Canada to feed themselves. In both of these countries, government intervention began in the 1920s with measures to strengthen farmer co-operation in the marketing of farm products (Brandow 1973). The main phase of intervention was during the troubled years of the 1930s, when the combination of collapsing prices during the Depression and environmental stress in the form of drought affected large parts of Canada and the USA, and gave rise to the conditions of farm poverty and destitution so vividly portrayed by John Steinbeck in *The Grapes of Wrath*. In Canada the Prairie Farm Rehabilitation Act was passed in the mid-1930s at a time when two-thirds of the farm population were destitute. Within a few years, the drifting of soil had been controlled, in part by seeding and fencing abandoned land and converting it to permanent pasture, and in part through an aggressive programme of extension of better cropping practices (Plaunt 1973).

Although soil erosion and rural poverty have been more prominent reasons for government intervention in North America, some of the measures adopted resemble those employed in Britain and the EEC: for example, price supports, marketing controls and export subsidies. One of the main differences is in the more extensive use of acreage quotas or allotments. These are not unknown in Britain; for example, potato growers in Britain operate under a system of quotas allocated by the Potato Marketing Board in order that control be maintained over the area devoted to potato growing, and hence some control imposed on the production of potatoes. This helps to avoid problems of over-production in some years leading to drastic falls in price and hence to greatly decreased production in the following year, with consequent rises in price and the emergence of a cycle of over- and under-production. A quota system was also introduced in dairy farming in Britain in 1984, in an attempt to deal with the growing surpluses of dairy products in the EEC. Under this system, dairy farms are allocated a fixed level of production. Such a system may have important long-term implications. Dairying may be perpetuated in its existing areas. Farm prices may be affected by the existence and size of a quota, and if a tenant farmer decides to give up dairying then the capital value of the farm could be reduced and the landlord thereby adversely affected.

In the United States, crop quotas or allotments were introduced for several major crops during the 1930s, and many of them have survived in some form ever since. In the leading wheat-producing states, for example, acreage allotments and marketing quotas appear to have been more important than prices in the allocation of acreage between wheat and other crops in at least some post-war years (Morzuch *et al.* 1980).

Crop acreage allotments are means by which government may impose limits on the acreage of land under certain uses, and in-directly on the spatial pattern of land use. In the case of cotton, for example, acreage allotments brought about a reduction in the area used for cotton growing when they were first introduced, and new uses such as the growing of soybeans and the feeding of cattle on grass and forage crops were found for land previously under cotton. The growing of soybeans expanded after government price support was offered in 1941, against a background of fears that imports might be threatened (Fornari 1979). Cotton allotments were determined on the basis of historical acreage (OECD 1974), and the system helped to slow down the shift of cotton growing from the traditional south-eastern states to irrigated land in the west and south-west. It helped to 'hold' the crop in the area in which it was established at the time when the system was introduced.

Crop allotments alone, however, failed to solve the problem of over-production, and by the 1950s more radical measures were introduced. Farmers were now offered payments to take land out of production. In the mid-1950s, a programme to reduce the acreage of crops such as wheat, cotton and peanuts was introduced, and direct payments to farmers were offered if they diverted away from these crops. At the same time, a longer-term diversion programme, directed towards a reduction in the total cropland area, was also introduced (Lidman and Bawden 1974; Garst and Miller 1975). By the late 1960s, an area similar to that of the whole of Britain had been 'idled' in this way: total cropland withheld in 1972 amounted to around 25 million ha (OECD 1974), of which more than 90 per cent related to wheat and feed-grain programmes. As with many other types of government intervention, the impact of these measures varied spatially, and the area most affected was on the more marginal zones of the Great Plains and parts of the south. During the years between 1956 and 1960, for example, farmers were given the opportunity to 'rent' cropland to the US government, in order to reduce crop surpluses and to conserve land resources through land retirement. The level of payment was, relative to the profitability of crop production, more attractive on poor land than good land, and so land placed in the Conservation Reserve tended to be concentrated in areas marginal for cropping. A tendency for preferential participation by elderly landowners was also evident in some areas (Hewes 1967). Varying spatial effects of national policies have also been reported from many other areas. For example, Dragonvich (1980) has described the varying regional impact of government subsidies and reconstruction schemes directed at the declining dairying industry in Australia. A regional dimension was not intended in the policy, but one emerged, with the greatest effects being evident in the parts of the country where there were clear alternatives to which dairy farmers could turn.

Government programmes to diversify land use or to set aside land from production have sometimes been motivated by environmental reasons rather than over-production and low prices. During the 1930s, programmes were introduced to encourage the growing of grass and forage crops in an effort to reduce rates of soil erosion in parts of the American South, and especially in the Tennessee Valley. Elsewhere (for example, in New Zealand), the idling or 'retiring' of mountain land susceptible to soil erosion has resulted in the destocking of sheep in these areas (Howard 1979). In other words, similar measures such as incentives offered to farmers *not* to use land may be motivated by different objectives. Generally speaking, however, over-production has been the most widespread and persistent problem, and the problem of reconciling adequate price-support levels and acceptable levels of production has never been satisfactorily resolved. A novel response was introduced in the United States in 1983. Following a federal outlay of around $12 billion on the support of farm commodity prices and income in 1982, a Payment-in-Kind (PIK) program was launched in 1983. Under this program, farmers were encouraged to take land out of production in exchange for payment, partly in cash and partly in commodities from government stores built up over previous years. The response from farmers greatly exceeded the expectations of the US Department of Agriculture, and around one-third of the nation's wheat land and two-fifths of its rice and cotton land were fallowed (e.g. Goodenough 1984).

The significance of price support

Government intervention in the market for farm produce is of primary significance because it means that land use is determined not solely by the free play of market forces but at least partly by government decision. The significance extends beyond the crops and commodities directly affected, because competitive ability and balance of comparative advantage depend at least partly on levels of support. Numerous examples of the effects of government intervention, manifested in trends and changes of land use, can be quoted. At the broad scale, the expansion of cereal growing in Britain during the 1970s is at least in part a result of attractive 'intervention' prices offered under the Common Agricultural Policy. In contrast, livestock farming did less well during the same period, partly because it depended to some extent on expensive bought-in feed. A spectacular example of the effects of price support is offered by the case of oil-seed rape (see Bowers and Cheshire 1983; Lane 1983). The production of this crop in Britain prior to the 1970s was not an attractive proposition because British growers could not compete with those in areas more favoured environmentally. But during the 1970s, EEC price support was offered at increasingly attractive levels, in order to increase home production and to reduce dependence on imported oil seeds. The result was that the area of oil-seed rape grown in Britain increased by about 20-fold between 1972 and 1980. If price support were removed, the probability is that the crop acreage would dwindle very rapidly.

Examples of the effects of price support are by no means confined to Britain. The case of soybeans in the American South has already been mentioned. In Ireland, Walsh (1975/76) has concluded that the main trends in the five major farm crops between 1950 and 1971 resulted from government decisions. These examples are perhaps not surprising: in theory, government, if it decides to intervene, can dictate how land is used by adjusting the relative levels of price support for the various crops that can be produced. In practice, however, the extent to which government can determine land use in this way is limited. At one level, farmers are often more powerful voices in government than their relative numbers in the country's population would suggest. Strong pressures may be exerted on government both to maintain overall levels of price support and to avoid undue or over-rapid lessening of support for individual commodities. Secondly, adjustments in levels of price support within individual commodities may be of less importance in determining the area devoted to that crop than would appear at first sight. In New Zealand, for example, there are extensive government price controls, and wheat growing is often thought to be largely a response to the level of state incentives. However, the idea that the wheat acreage is directly related to price-support levels was found not to be substantiated (Fielding 1965). Instead, it was found to be inversely related to lamb prices. In other words, government cannot necessarily manipulate the acreage of, say, wheat just by manipulating the wheat price: the level of price available for lamb was a stronger influence. When it rose, the area devoted to wheat fell, and *vice versa*. Perhaps if the entire spectrum of land uses was subject to price support, then adjustments in support levels could have a stronger influence. When some enterprises are related to export markets or to other outlets where price supports are not maintained, then the significance for land use of adjustments in price-support levels is lower.

Other forms of intervention may be as significant as support levels. For example, Just (1973) concluded that the acreage for feed grain in the San Joaquin valley of California would have fallen by about 30 per cent if cotton acreage allotments had been dropped and all other factors remained constant. Policy programmes for various crops interact with each other, and the effects of adjusting levels of price support for one crop will depend on the programmes pursued in relation to other crops. On the other hand, identical policies may have different effects. For example, Sahi and Craddock (1975) showed that if the acreages of wheat and rape seed were each to be increased by 25 per cent on Canadian prairie farms, the price of the former would have to be raised by 40 per cent and of the latter by 20 per cent.

Although full control of land use is not established through policies of price support, their effects are both pervasive and fundamental. It has been suggested that each increase of 1 per cent in support prices in Britain results in increases of 10 per cent in land prices (Traill 1982). In this way, public expenditure in supporting agricultural prices leads to increases in private land values. The transfer of land between agriculture and other land uses such as forestry is affected, and conflict between agriculture and conservation is heightened when land of interest for purposes of nature conservation is improved for agriculture with the assistance of capital grants. Within agriculture, capital intensity increases, but the labour force decreases as it is replaced by machinery. Nor are these effects confined to the present. The effects of government protection in an earlier period are illustrated by the fact that many British cereal producers adopted mixed farming or moved out of cereals altogether and took up pastoral farming after the repeal of the corn laws in the 1840s and the removal of protection (by import duties) against cheap imports (Vamplew 1980).

Many modern agricultural policies are concerned with the efficiency of production as well as with its economic and social aspects. Large research and development programmes have been mounted in many countries, and agricultural extension services have been provided whereby knowledge of technological advances can be quickly transmitted to land users. Many of these advances tend to reduce the risks of crop failure, for example, by making possible the use of pesticides. Economic risks are also reduced by the provision of price support. One of the main roles of government has therefore been in reducing the degree of risk faced by farmers and other land users. One of the main effects of government price-supported policies is in reducing the amplitude of fluctuations in production, prices and incomes. In their review of American price-support policies, Nelson and Cochrane (1976) concluded that their effect was to keep farm prices and incomes higher than they would otherwise have been in the period from 1953 to 1965, but by so doing incentives were provided to achieve output sufficient to keep farm prices lower than they would otherwise have been from 1968 to 1972. Without such programmes, they concluded, there would now be more and smaller farms, less mechanisation and greater labour inputs.

Intervention in the economics of types of land use other than agriculture is usually motivated by other reasons. In forestry, for example, the problem is not one of stagnant demand for timber as the economy develops and standards of living rise, but rather the long interval that elapses between initial costs of establishing woodlands and eventual revenue when the timber is harvested. The time-lag of several decades deters many land occupiers from becoming involved in timber-growing, and to overcome its effects many national governments have introduced financial inducements to timber growers. These inducements may take the form of fiscal advantages, low-interest or interest-free loans, or direct grants for planting and management. In France and Italy, low-interest loans are offered. In Britain, the form of inducement preferred by government is favourable forms of tax assessment together with planting grants. Planting grants were paid under Dedication Schemes between 1947 and 1981, when a simplified Forestry Grant Scheme was introduced. Under this latter scheme, grant is paid at rates of £230 ha for conifers and £450 for hardwoods (these rates apply to areas of 10 ha and over, with higher rates being offered for smaller areas). In very approximate terms, these grants are likely to cover around one-quarter and one-half respectively of planting costs. Grants are a relatively simple and direct instrument of the national policy of expanding the forest area in Britain, but their significance in this respect is probably less than the incentives offered in tax concessions. Taxation arrangements in forestry in Britain are complicated, and special treatment is afforded in several taxes. Of these, one of the most important is income tax. An occupier may elect to be assessed either under Schedule B, where tax liability is at a flat rate based on the assumed value of the land, regardless of revenues or costs, or under Schedule D. Under this latter Schedule, losses in forestry can be offset against other taxable income. The establishing of forest plantations can therefore be a very attractive proposition for some individuals, especially if they pay tax at high rates, and the real cost, after tax-saving has been taken into account, can be reduced to a fraction of the actual cost.

Another form of tax of primary importance in forestry in Britain is capital transfer tax (CTT). This tax replaced estate duty as a form of capital taxation in 1974, and the rate of afforestation on private land slowed down dramatically thereafter: annual new planting rates decreased from almost 19,000 ha in 1973–74 to just over 6,000 ha in 1977–78. Estate duty regulations were extremely favourable in relation to capital in the form of forest land, while CTT offered few attractions. Modifications have subsequently been made to CTT regulations, and special treatment has once more been afforded to forestry. The changing climate of capital taxation is not the only factor affecting planting rates, but it is an important one, and by 1981–82 new planting in the private sector had increased again to over 12,000 ha/annum.

Important implications arise from this special treatment of forestry. One is that this means of encouraging an expansion of the forest area is difficult to quantify in terms of cost, since its real cost is in the form of taxes not collected rather than expenditure actually incurred. Another is that investment in forestry is much more attractive to the rich and to those burdened by large tax liabilities than to others. This, in turn, means that a differential exists in terms of land holdings. The occupier of a small farm, for example, would find fiscal inducements to afforestation unattractive, whereas another individual might find the idea of investing in forest land very attractive. A number of specialist companies have sprung up over the last two decades and offer services whereby individuals without expertise in forestry can become forest owners, and can thus enjoy the benefits of tax advantages.

GOVERNMENT AS LAND OWNER

While government can influence land use in a variety of indirect ways, it is also a major land owner and land user in its own right. In the Soviet Union, all land belongs to the state: land is viewed as a natural resource and not a product of human labour, and hence it cannot be owned privately (Syrodoyev 1975). It can, however, be allocated by the state to collectives or to individuals for specific purposes such as agriculture or housing, and this purposive allocation ensures (at least in theory) that the land is used in conformity with state plans.

The degree of state ownership and control in the Soviet Union is unusual, but substantial areas of land are also owned by the state in most western countries. In the United States, about one-third of the entire land area is owned by federal agencies, in addition to areas owned by individual states. In Britain, around 9 per cent of the land area is owned by central government agencies (Table 3.2), and local authorities and nationalised industries together own a similar extent (Massey and Catalano 1978). Almost one-fifth of the land area is therefore in the hands of government bodies of one form or another.

Table 3.2   Public land ownership

	Percentage of total area
United States*	
Federal	33.6
State	5.1
County and municipal	0.9
Total	39.6
Federal land	
Department of Interior	68.2
Department of Agriculture	24.7
Department of Defense	3.9
Other	3.2
Canada†	
Private	10.7
Federal	40.3
Provincial and territorial	49.0
United Kingdom‡	
Holdings of freehold farm and forest land by public bodies	
The Crown	0.8
Central Government Departments	5.2
Local authorities	1.7
Statutory agencies and nationalised industries	1.1
Total	8.8

Sources:
* Adapted from US Dept of Commerce Bureau of Census (1978) *Statistical Abstract of the United States*. Washington: Government Printer.
† Adapted from *Canada Yearbook*, 1972. Ottawa, Information Canada.
‡ Adapted from Harrison, Tranter and Gibbs (1977).

In many western countries, government, through its various agencies, is by far the largest land owner, and government ownership is especially prominent in the mountain lands of the New World

(Pearce 1979). Government's role in determining land use is therefore a major one, and the processes of decision-making involved in the use of government-owned land are as important in many areas as those of private landowners. As in the private sector, a variety of forms of ownership and occupancy are involved. In much of the western United States, for example, large areas of federal land are rented or leased to private individuals for grazing, and ownership by the nation does not necessarily mean that the nation can easily control the use or management of the land in question (e.g. Wallach 1981; Hagenstein, 1972). The remainder of this section, however, deals mainly with situations of government ownership combined with direct control.

The reasons for government involvement in land ownership and land use are numerous and varied. State ownership and control are not peculiar to the twentieth century, but extend back for millenia in some parts of the world. In China, for example, public ownership of land and the equitable distribution of arable land to peasant families is believed to date back to the last millenium BC (Leeming 1977). In Japan, 'official' pastures were set up by the state to supply horses for military purposes (Kobayashi 1975). In medieval England, a number of Royal Forests were designated where the king and his noblemen could enjoy hunting, and later they became sources of timber for naval shipbuilding. More recently, huge areas of land in colonial territories such as Australia and New Zealand were declared Crown land during the nineteenth century, and much of the western part of the United States was in the hands of the federal government. In the New World, land in this form of public ownership was gradually transferred to private occupancy under the prevailing land policies, but large areas have been retained under direct national control.

These examples illustrate some of the main reasons for state involvement in land ownership and land use: strategic supplies of timber or other materials; conservation and recreation, which do not always fit comfortably within private ownership and control of land; and reasons of equity or social justice. Since different reasons exist for government involvement, even within a single country, it is not surprising that different government agencies are involved. Perhaps a classic example is in the United States, where numerous federal organisations own and manage land. Much of the land under federal control is nominally in the hands of the Department of the Interior (Table 3.2), but three different agencies – the Bureau of Land Management, the National Parks Service and the Fish and Wildlife Service – are in effect the managers of the land under the umbrella of the Department, and these agencies have very different objectives. The other major federal agency involved is the Forest Service, for which the US Department of Agriculture has responsibility. Below the federal level, the states and local government bodies or agencies are also involved in land ownership or management. It is usually quite wrong, therefore, to imagine that government ownership is necessarily uniform or monolithic: it may display almost as much diversity as the private sector.

The diversity of government ownership is well illustrated by the case of New Zealand, where the government in one form or another farms around 5 per cent of the country's occupied area. Four different departments of state are directly involved in farming (Stover 1969). The greatest involvement is by the Department of Lands and Survey, which functions as a pioneer farmer, in improving land and acting as farmer for a few years until the farm is handed over to an individual occupier. The Department of Maori Affairs plays a similar role in relation to Maori lands with their own distinctive legal, social and environmental context, while the Departments of Agriculture and Justice also function as state farmers on a small scale. In other realms of land use, other state agencies such as the forestry service and the national parks authority are also significant land owners and land users.

The example of New Zealand illustrates some general points about government ownership of land in the western world. Ownership is often geared to a specific purpose such as land development or the production of timber. Land is usually acquired (or retained) for a specific purpose, and objectives may be defined narrowly in relation to that purpose. In practice, therefore, the agency or institution controlling the land may consider a narrower range of choice of land uses than would a private individual in a similar setting. There may be a diversity in the use of government land, as a result of the wide range of agencies involved, but each agency has its own remit which is often fairly narrowly defined. This fact is of significance for the broader field of national land-use planning (Ch. 8) as well as for the use of land in government ownership.

Diversity of government objectives extends also to broad land-use policies as well as to land under the direct control of government. In the case of Britain, for example, an agricultural policy of encouraging land improvement may conflict on some areas of land with a conservation policy of preserving wetlands. On other areas of land, grant-aid may be available both for afforestation and for agricultural improvements, and in general there is little integration or harmonisation of policies. A lack of coordination of policies has also been noted in Canada by McCormack (1975). He suggests that attempts to co-ordinate policies have been made only in recent years. In the case of Britain, these attempts have been half-hearted and ineffective. Most countries have policies towards individual land-use sectors: few countries have integrated, national land-use policies.

The great diversity of objectives among agencies actually owning or controlling government land reflects the diversity and complexity of government objectives for land in general, and bodes ill for the successful development of integrated national land-use policies that can be applied throughout a country.

While each government land-owning agency usually has its own objectives, there has been an increasing tendency in many countries in recent years to pursue several objectives within a single institutional framework. In the United States, the Multiple Use-Sustained Yield Act of 1960 and the National Forest Management Act of 1976 provided legislative bases for land in the hands of the US Forest Service to be managed not just for timber production, but also for grazing, conservation, and recreation. Following the 1960 Act, no single use was now to have priority, and economic return was not in all cases to be paramount (Steen 1976). In Britain, the objectives of forestry policy under which the Forestry Commission operates were broadened during the 1960s and 1970s to give more emphasis to conservation and recreation. Furthermore, general sections within the Countryside Acts of 1967 and 1968 required *all* government agencies and officials to 'have regard for the conservation of the environment'. But while the public through the legislature may seek to define multiple goals for land management, the relative importance of these goals is not always clearly defined, and they may be difficult to translate into an order of priority for action on the ground. In practice, officials of agencies play important roles in interpreting and implementing broad policies, and in effect are, in many instances, the decision makers in the use of publicly owned land.

These roles tend to persist despite an increasing tendency for pressure groups to seek to influence decisions about the use and management of public land, and for mechanisms of public participation in decision-making to be established. One of the many examples of the latter was the setting up by the Victoria state government in 1970 of the Land Conservation Council to advise the Minister of Lands and Conservation on the 'best' future use of the state's public lands. Ostensibly, mechanisms for a high level of public participation were built into the decision-making procedures of the Council (Mercer 1979). In Canada, extensive public participation has been involved in the drawing up of plans for national parks such as Riding Mountain in Manitoba (Hoole 1978). In this case, participation was positively encouraged, and alternative plans were presented for evaluation.

In many other cases, pressure groups have strongly represented the viewpoints of sections of the public, and have been successful in achieving changes in plans and practices of public agencies. In the early 1970s, for example, new forest practice acts were introduced in California, Oregon and Washington (Duerr *et al.* 1979), as a result of pressure from environmental groups. In New Zealand, environmental pressure groups have been effective in influencing state forest service attitudes to logging in indigenous forests (Wright 1980), while in Western Australia similar groups have achieved the setting aside of forest parks in state forests being harvested for the woodchip industry (Conacher 1977). In England, bodies such as the Council for the Protection of Rural England have exerted influences on various planning issues in the green belts (e.g. Munton 1983a) and national parks (MacEwen and MacEwen 1981).

GOVERNMENT, DECISION-MAKING AND LAND USE

Decision-making at the institutional level is perhaps even more complex than at the level of the individual. For the institutional decision maker, rationality may have a meaning quite different from that of his counterpart at the individual level. He may be concerned with political goals rather than economic ones (see, for example, Alston and Freeman 1975), but he can rarely ignore all considerations of economics. Optimal land use and optimal forms of land management may therefore represent a compromise between political and economic criteria, and may result in an outcome that offers room for adjustment and manoeuvre in the future rather than a commitment to a policy that is irrevocable, or from which it is difficult to change course.

Differences between public and private lands also extend to planning. Public agencies have the ability to draw up and to implement land-use plans on their lands: public bodies can draw up plans for the use of private lands but may have great difficulty in implementing them. Plans for the use of public lands may serve as formalised policy statements, and they may be drawn up in a formal, institutional structure that provides a mechanism for handling various demands, including in some instances public participation (see Ch. 8).

The complexity of public decision-making about resource management has been reviewed by Moore (1975) in terms of the five clusters of variables – situation, participants, organisation, process and outcome – first identified in a broader setting by Robinson and Snyder (1965). *Situation* includes the context and setting, the precise nature of the issue about which a decision is required, including the time-scale in which it has emerged and the prevailing values within which it must be resolved. *Participants* are the individuals (politicians, officials and members of interest groups) involved in the decision, with all their personal and sociological attributes, perceptions and attitudes. *Organisation* is the framework within which the participants operate, and may relate to the interaction of the politicians, officials and interest groups. *Process* has a meaning similar to that discussed in Chapter 2, namely the means by which decisions are taken, while *outcome* includes both the output of the process in terms of the decisions taken and the effect of that outcome, which in turn sets the scene for the next cycle of decision-making.

While this five-cluster framework may be helpful in analysing public decision-making, at the same time it illustrates the bewildering complexity which the researcher faces in this field. The number of variables in each cluster is large: the number of combinations is enormous. Most of the variables that are relevant at the individual level of decision-making are also relevant in decision-making by government agencies, and in addition at this level there is the complication of structure and organisation.

Governments and their agencies may determine the use of land in their possession; they may control the use of land in a more general way by imposing legal constraints on the range of choice open to the private decision maker; and they may support or encourage certain forms of land use by intervention in the market or by financial inducements. Determination, control or encouragement may be set at different scales ranging from the level of national government to that of the local municipality.

Some examples of the ways in which central government can influence land use in Britain are reviewed by Carroll (1979): controls and other influences have grown and expanded substantially in recent decades, and especially since the Second World War. This trend is not confined to Britain, but is paralleled in most other western countries. Such is the clarity and significance of the trend in the United States, for example, that Bosselman and Callies (1972) have felt able to talk of a 'quiet revolution in land-use controls'. Indeed Callies (1980), in looking back over the decade, has concluded that the incursion of federal influences and controls has been on a far greater scale than even that envisaged in 1970.

This revolution in the degree of public influence on the use and management of land reflects a changing view and attitude. Public interest in land is now more widely recognised and accepted than some decades ago, and a new balance between private property rights in land and public interests is being established (e.g. Bock 1974; Andrews 1979). This swing reflects a shift from the view that land is merely a commodity or form of private property to one in which it is seen more clearly also to be a natural resource in which the public have a general interest, which the private owner can no longer ignore completely.

FURTHER READING

Bowers, J. K. and Cheshire, P. (1983) *Agriculture, the countryside and land use.*

Bowler, I. R. (1979) *Government and agriculture : a spatial perspective.*

Carroll, M. (1979) Rural land use control in Great Britain, *Natural Resources Journal*, 19, 145–60.

Josling, T. E. (1974) Agricultural policies in developed countries : an overview, *Journal of Agricultural Economics*, 25, 229–63.

Moore, P. W. (1975) Public decision-making and resource management : a review. *University of Toronto Department of Geography Discussion Paper, Series No. 17.*

Platt, R. H. (1976) *Land use control : interface of law and geography.*

Tracy, M. (1982) *Agriculture in Western Europe : challenge and response, 1880–1980.*

Structures and trends in land use

Choice of land use is made by the individual land user, operating within broad environmental limitations and government influences. It is not surprising, therefore, that contrasts should exist in the structures of land use in different countries, even within the western world. Striking differences occur in climate and other aspects of the physical environment, in population density and land area and in complexion of governments. These factors all have a bearing on the structure or composition of land use within national boundaries. Yet a few similarities can be seen between various countries, and when current trends in land use are examined, the similarities become clearer. There is a tendency for some land-use trends, such as the loss of farm land to urbanisation, to be viewed within individual countries as purely internal issues, but a clearer perspective on these problems is obtained if a broader view is taken at the international level. The purpose of this chapter is therefore to review land-use trends and structures in the latter part of the twentieth century, with a view to establishing the extent of similarity between countries and, as a corollary, the extent to which structures and trends are peculiar to individual countries.

PROBLEMS OF DEFINITION AND DATA

Before land-use structures or trends can be considered, a cautionary note must be sounded about the basic data sources. All worthy scientific publications contain reviews of sources and methods. Such reviews are usually of less than absorbing interest, but in few fields is an evaluation of sources more essential than in land use. Land uses are notoriously difficult to classify and measure, even within small areas. Several problems are encountered when international comparisons are attempted. A fundamental problem lies in definitions of land-use categories, and in particular much confusion has arisen between land use and land cover. Land cover relates to the physical nature or form of the land surface, and can be identified visually by traditional ground-based survey or by remote-sensing techniques. Categories such as heathland or rangeland can be readily identified by these means and indeed feature on many land-use maps. The idea of land cover applies not only in rural areas, but also in urban areas where the type or form of building can be readily identified. In many cases in both rural and urban areas, the type of land use can be easily deduced from the nature of the land cover; a field of wheat, for example, indicates agricultural (cropping) use, while a particular type of building indicates residential use. But there is not always such a direct and obvious relationship between land cover and land use. Heathland or rangeland may be used for the grazing of livestock at low intensities, or for recreation or wildlife conservation, but these uses may not be readily apparent either on visual examination in the field or by remote-sensing. Similarly, a particular type of building does not necessarily always indicate a particular type of use.

The mapping of land use on the basis of formal, visual expression in the landscape may thus involve dissimilar classes or categories, which may not be mutually exclusive. In practice, many maps purporting to show land use actually show mixtures of land use and land cover.

Numerous other problems are encountered in designing systems of classification for land-use surveys (see, for example, Rhind and Hudson 1980). Constant tension exists between incorporating large number of classes so that maximum detail can be stored, and restricting the classification to a few classes for manageability and ease of interpretation. Such tension is common to classifications in many fields, but special problems exist in relation to land use. Scale and emphasis are obvious examples. The classes to be employed at a scale of, say, 1:100,000 will be different from those at a scale of 1:5,000, especially in urban or horticultural areas. Similarly, a classification designed for a country as a whole is likely to give most emphasis to agriculture and forestry, perhaps having only one class for all urban land. On the other hand, a classification designed for a largely urban area will probably contain numerous categories for the various land uses encountered in an urban area. In other words, there can be no 'ideal', all-purpose classification; instead, different classifications will be appropriate for different purposes. Another basic problem is the fact that some areas of land may simultaneously be used for two or more purposes. The problem of multiple use is tackled in different ways in different classifications.

Land use

Land-use surveys

The lack of uniformity or comparability of classifications is one reason why the comparison of land-use structures over time or between areas is very difficult. Another is the sheer difficulty of carrying out land-use surveys. Traditional surveys involving field mapping are costly, time-consuming and difficult to organise. Only a few national surveys have been completed by these means. The best known examples are the First and Second Land Utilisation Surveys of Britain, conducted during the 1930s and 1960s respectively. Traditional land-use surveys such as these, based on detailed local fieldwork, are very labour-intensive and hence costly. The use of volunteers is obviously welcome as a means of reducing costs, but at the expense of speed and rigour of organisation.

The two land utilisation surveys of Britain are unique and invaluable records. But while they do permit some measurement of land-use changes between the survey dates, they are beset by unfortunate features which prevent a full analysis. For example, rotational grass was included with arable land in the first survey, with permanent grass being defined as a separate category. In the second

Table 4.1 Classification of land use (first order of hierarchy)

First Land Utilisation Survey (FLUS)
1. Forest and woodland
2. Meadow land and permanent grass
3. Arable or tilled land, fallow, rotation grass and market gardens
4. Heathland, woodland, commons and rough hill pasture
5. Gardens and allotments
6. Orchards
7. Nurseries
8. Land agriculturally unproductive
9. Ponds, lakes, reservoirs

Second Land Utilisation Survey (SLUS)
1. Settlement (residential and commercial)
2. Industry
3. Transport
4. Derelict land
5. Open spaces
6. Grassland
7. Arable
8. Market gardening
9. Orchards
10. Woodlands
11. Heath and rough land
12. Water and marsh
13. Unvegetated land

World Land Use Survey (WLUS)
1. Settlements and associated non-agricultural lands
2. Horticulture
3. Tree and other perennial crops
4. Cropland
5. Improved permanent pasture
6. Unimproved grazing land
7. Woodlands
8. Swamps and marshes
9. Unproductive land

United States Geological Survey (USGS)
1. Urban or built-up land
2. Agricultural land
3. Rangeland
4. Forest land
5. Water areas
6. Wetland
7. Barren land
8. Tundra
9. Perennial snow or ice

National Land Use Classification (NLUC)
1. Agriculture and fisheries
2. Community and health services
3. Defence
4. Education
5. Recreation and leisure
6. Manufacturing
7. Mineral extraction
8. Offices
9. Residences
10. Retail distribution and servicing
11. Storage
12. Transport tracks and places
13. Utility service
14. Wholesale distribution
15. Unused land, water and buildings

Sources: FLUS – Stamp (1948); SLUS – Coleman and Maggs (1962); WLUS
– Kostrowicki (1970); USGS – Anderson *et al.* (1976); NLUC –
Study Team (1975).

survey, however, rotational grass was not included with arable land,
but was mapped in a grassland category (Coleman *et al.* 1974).

After the completion of the First Land Utilisation Survey in
Britain, an attempt was made to launch a World Land Use Survey
(WLUS) under the aegis of the International Geographical Union and
L.D. Stamp who had been the organiser of the British survey. The
suggested classification for the WLUS is illustrated in Table 4.1 along

the classifications for the British surveys. Although a few countries were mapped (see Board 1968), the monumental task was, perhaps not surprisingly, never completed.

In recent years air photographs and remote sensing have made the task of land-use survey easier, and much progress has been achieved. Fundamental problems about the distinction between land use and land cover remain, since these techniques are based on the formal expression of land use rather than on the actual activity itself. This problem is reflected in the title of the classification drawn up in the United States for the eventual mapping of the country at a scale of 1:100,000 or 1:250,000 (see Table 4.1), commencing in 1974 (Anderson 1977; Anderson *et al.* 1976). The use of satellite imagery makes the compilation of land-use maps for whole countries or even groups of countries a much more realistic proposition than when field survey was the only available technique. As yet, limitations exist in the use of these techniques, and some types of land-use can be identified more accurately and reliably than others (e.g. see Gordon 1980, for an assessment of the accuracy of mapping of land uses in Ohio by LANDSAT). Despite these limitations, the use of satellite imagery and similar techniques seems set to revolutionise land-use survey. Nevertheless, the basic problem remains that the classification must be geared to the type of information that can be yielded by remote-sensing techniques rather than that which is most relevant for planning and other practical purposes.

Recognition of the generally unsatisfactory state of information on land use in Britain is reflected by significant developments during the 1970s. The Department of the Environment undertook a survey of urban areas in England and Wales, employing a simple classification geared to air photography (Smith *et al.* 1977). Also a suggested National Land Use Classification was devised by a joint team from local and central government in response to the growing need for better information on land-use information for planning purposes. Like many classifications, it is hierarchical, with 15 orders, 78 groups, 150 sub-groups and over 600 classes. The primary classification, at the level of the order, is shown in Table 4.1. Its methodology has been criticised by Dickinson and Shaw (1978), but it has been welcomed as an attempt to collect land-use data systematically. The intention was that the classification be used by local authorities in making annual returns to central government from 1974 onwards, so that compatible data would be available for the whole country. This in itself was a recognition of the unsatisfactory state of information on the composition and trends of land use in the country.

Other sources

These examples from America and England show that significant advances in land-use survey have been achieved over the last decade. Other than survey, the main source of information on land use is the censuses conducted by agricultural ministries and other government departments. These censuses are usually based on the individual farm or other land unit, with the results being aggregated to various spatial levels such as the county, region or country. In the absence of regular comprehensive land-use surveys, agricultural censuses have usually been the main source of information. The quality and reliability of its results have generally improved over time, but sometimes the improvements themselves, such as redefinitions of categories to avoid ambiguity, can lead to a difficulty of comparability over a period of years. Also the quality of information may be uneven across the categories. In the agricultural censuses conducted in Britain, for example, areas quoted for cropland are usually much more accurate than those for rough grazings, for which the farmer may only know the approximate extent and which in any case are often not sharply defined on their higher margins.

Greater problems confront the measurement of urban, industrial and recreational areas, which are often less amenable to measurement by census. There has been a frequent tendency to estimate some of these land uses merely as residuals remaining on the subtraction of agricultural and woodland areas from the total land surface. Clearly this is inadequate, especially in relation to the controversial issue of urban expansion. Fortunately, some of the advances of recent years in land-use survey have led to improved quality of data in this respect.

Although agricultural censuses yield valuable information on land use, their purpose is usually to cast light on trends in production rather than on land use *per se*. Furthermore, they are conducted by agencies such as agricultural ministries for their own purposes, rather than by organisations with overall responsibility for land use. In the United States, for example, no government agency assembles comprehensive land-use statistics (Raup 1982). Understandably, therefore, data are oriented to individual sectors, and there will not necessarily be compatibility or comparability between sectors.

From what has been said about surveys and censuses as sources of information about land use, it will be clear that available pictures of land use in individual countries are imperfect and incomplete, although some information is usually available in national statistical yearbooks. At the level of international comparison, the problems are even greater, because of different definitions, procedures and timings. The most accessible and convenient source of international statistics of land use is the FAO *Production Yearbook,* published annually. It employs a broad classification of land uses: arable land and land under permanent crops; permanent meadows and pastures; forests and woodland; and other land. The last class includes urban areas, parks, unused land and various other land-use types not otherwise defined. Definitions of the other classes are given in the publications, but the fact that the yearbook is a compilation of national statistics should not be over-looked. The collection of statistics at the national level may have proceeded on the basis of national definitions rather than expressly on the FAO classification. The yearbook is careful to give warning about this problem of definitions, and the abundance of asterisks and other qualifiers on the tables serves as a reminder that caution is required in interpretation.

THE STRUCTURE OF LAND USE

The structure or composition of land use varies greatly from country to country, and the search for generalisations or norms at the global level is rather fruitless. Too many significant variables exist for extensive similarities to emerge between countries in different settings, and some of these variables, such as the nature of the environment, population density, history and government policy are very influential. Some examples of the structures of land use, using FAO classes, are illustrated in Table 4.2.

Table 4.2 Land use *c.* 1970

	Arable and permanent cropland	Permanent pasture	Forest and woodland	Other land
	(Percentages of the total land area)			
World	10.8	23.9	32.2	33.1
USA	20.9	26.7	32.0	20.4
USSR	10.5	16.8	41.3	31.4
UK	29.9	48.8	7.8	13.5
EEC	36.2	28.0	21.6	14.2
Australia	5.4	59.4	18.1	17.1
Brazil	6.4	17.0	70.2	6.4
India	55.4	4.4	21.8	18.3
Japan	14.7	0.8	67.5	16.9
Nigeria	32.8	21.7	19.3	26.2

Sources: FAO Production Yearbook, 1980; Best (1979).

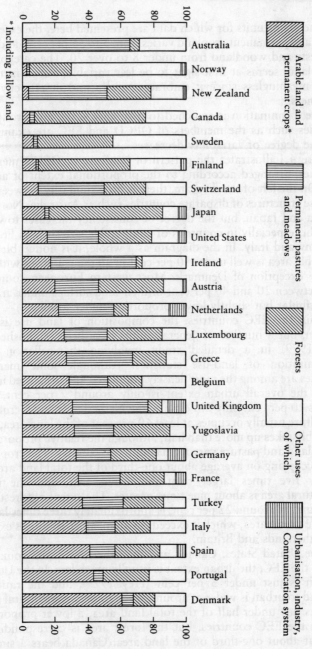

Fig. 4.1 Land use in OECD countries (percentage of total area 1970).
Source: OECD (1976).

In the major units for which data are presented here, the extent of arable and permanent cropland varies from 5 to 55 per cent, and that of forests and woodland from under 8 to over 70. The category of 'other land' seems at first sight to be less variable, but in fact it is rather meaningless since it embraces tundra and desert, city and wilderness.

If the examination is switched to a smaller scale, and groups of countries such as the members of OECD and EEC are examined, then the degree of variability decreases.

Figure 4.1 illustrates the pattern of land use in OECD member countries, arranged according to the proportional extent of arable land. On the left of the diagram, there is little similarity between the land-use structures of disparate countries such as Australia, Norway, Canada and Japan, but the degree of consistency increases towards the right, especially in countries of comparable size such as France, Germany and Italy. In the diagram as a whole, it is noticeable that the arable area is well under 50 per cent in all the countries with the solitary exception of Denmark. Most western European countries have between 20 and 40 per cent of their land surface under arable, and a similar but slightly lower proportion under forest.

Within the EEC countries, the composition of land use is not uniform, but a number of general points have been established by Best (1979) in a detailed study involving the collation and harmonisation of land-use statistics. Although some member countries are among the most densely populated and urbanised in the world, the overall urban extent is only around 7 per cent, and exceeds 10 per cent only in Belgium, the Netherlands and Germany. Agriculture usually occupies at least 60 per cent of the land area, and invariably takes up more than half, although the relative proportions of cropland and pasture vary from country to country. The cropland area, occupying on average about one-third of the total land area, is roughly five times larger than the urban area, and the total agricultural area is about nine times greater. The extent of forest and woodland, at around 22 per cent, is approximately three times larger than the urban area, which it exceeds in all member countries except the Netherlands and Britain.

In the United States, Canada and the other developed countries outside the EEC, the urban extent is usually much less. In the United States it is just under 3 per cent (Frey 1979), and the ratio of cropland to urban is wider at around seven to one. Agricultural land occupies just under half of the total land area, a lower proportion than in the EEC countries, but the forest area is correspondingly larger at about one-third of the land area. Canada bears a similar relationship to the United States as the latter does to the EEC countries. It has a much smaller urban area, a smaller agricultural area and a larger forest area. Urban and cropland areas are also very small in Australia, but forest growth is precluded over much of the country because of climatic limitations, and well over half of the land surface is under permanent pasture, mostly on natural or semi-natural grassland. Japan has an unusual structure of land use with over two-thirds of the mountainous country under forest and a negligible area of permanent pasture.

Variability in structure of land use extends also to the relative extent of national parks and similar areas. Statistical problems abound here, because land within such parks may also be forest land and recorded as such, illustrating the basic difficulty of confusion between land use and land cover. The definition of parks is also variable: in England and Wales, for example, national parks occupy about 9 per cent of the land area, but these parks are mostly also used for agriculture and forestry and are not national parks in the internationally accepted sense. Designated parks with more natural environments, however, also occupy about 9 per cent of the land area of New Zealand, 3.6 per cent of that in the United States, and about 3 per cent in Australia (OECD 1976). In most other countries, their relative extent is smaller, amounting to only 0.39 per cent and 0.16 per cent respectively in Belgium and Finland, for example. There is some evidence of an inverse relationship, albeit a weak one, between population density and the relative extent of land set aside as 'natural' parks and similar areas. In sparsely populated countries, a larger extent of land is usually designated as parks than in more densely populated lands.

At the global level, a weak relationship can also be discerned between population density and proportional extent of cropland and forest. In general terms, the extent of cropland increases with population density, while that of forest decreases. This relationship is complicated by variables such as the nature of the economy (and whether agriculture, for example, is geared to the home or export market) and degree of government intervention, as well as by basic environmental factors. Numerous exceptions to the general pattern spring to mind, including Japan, 'city' states such as Hong Kong and Singapore, and countries in arid or semi-arid areas.

The structure and pattern of land use also show enormous variations within individual countries. Many of these variations are based fundamentally on environmental contrasts between mountain and lowland or humid and arid areas. It follows, therefore, that even if individual countries have similar overall land-use structures, the actual patterns of land use within them may vary, and different problems and trends will be experienced within the different regions.

TRENDS IN LAND USE

The problem of adequate statistics is even greater in relation to trends in land use than it is in relation to static structures. The detailed monitoring of trends at the international level is in fact almost impossible: surveys or censuses are not held annually in each country, and the accuracy and reliability of data vary over time. A particular problem is the changes in definitions of classes or categories that occur from time to time. Annual figures presented in sources such as the FAO *Production Yearbook* must be viewed with caution, but even so a number of general trends are apparent, and a greater degree of consistency exists in land-use trends than in the case of land-use structures. The broad-brush classification employed in the

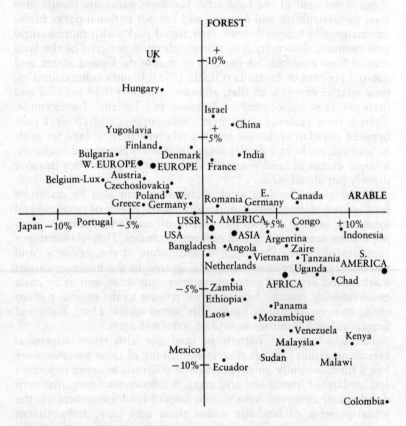

Fig. 4.2 Percentage change in forest and arable areas 1970–79.
Source: FAO Production Yearbooks.

FAO Yearbook precludes analysis of trends in urban and other small-scale land uses, but a basic grouping of countries can be made on the basis of trends in arable and forest areas. Figure 4.2 shows such a grouping relating to the 1970s.

Most countries lie on one of two quadrants of the graph, displaying either an increase in forest and decrease in arable land, or conversely a growth in arable and decrease in forest. European countries have undergone an expansion of forest and a reduction of arable during the last decade, while many developing countries in Africa, Asia and Latin America have combined a growth in arable land with a sizeable loss of forest. Relatively few countries lie on the other two quadrants of Fig. 4.2; those which do tend to be very large, or to have unusual land-use structures.

One of the major global land-use trends in recent years is the expansion of the arable area. During the 1970s, this area expanded in all continents except Europe, and in South America as a whole as well as in several individual countries, the amount of expansion exceeded 10 per cent during the decade. This expansion is the continuation of a long-established trend which has been outlined by Grigg (1974) and Robertson (1956). Over the century from 1870, the arable area has approximately doubled, firstly with the opening up of the New World and more recently with expansion in the developing continents.

Over the period from 1870 to 1910, the arable area increased by about half, as compared with an increase of just over a quarter during the decades from 1930 to 1970. Few developed countries have experienced a growth in arable area in recent years. Those which have, such as Canada and Australia, are unusual in the developed world in that they have expanding populations and still-expanding frontiers of cultivation and settlement and they are major exporting countries. Overall, the arable area in the developed world decreased by 0.5 per cent during the 1970s, and increased by around 5 per cent in the developing world during the same period.

Globally, the arable area extends to only around 11 per cent of the land area, but in Europe the proportion is much higher at approximately 30 per cent. It is interesting to speculate that a relationship exists between, on the one hand, the continental and national extents of arable land, and, on the other, the trends depicted in Fig. 4.2. It is noticeable, for example, that Europe, which is the continent with the highest arable extent, has seen a downturn in the arable area, while the other continents have experienced an expansion. Whether these trends will result in a convergence of land-use structure towards some common pattern remains to be seen.

Population pressure is, of course, a major driving force underlying the expansion of the arable area in the developing countries. Yet the rate of expansion of arable land is far slower than that of population. During the 1970s, for example, the global population grew by around 20 per cent, as compared with an increase of only 2 per cent in the arable area. Growth in food production has come from improvements in yield rather than increases in cropland. (The reverse may have been the case in the United States, where it has been suggested that three-quarters of the growth in output in the 1970s is accounted for by bringing additional land into cultivation (NALS 1981).) A corollary to these trends is the shrinking arable area per person. During the 1970s, this area fell from 0.36 ha to 0.31 ha world wide, and it is likely to fall by half in the developing countries during the second half of this century (Barney 1980). Conflicting estimates have been made of the maximum area that can ultimately be brought into arable use, but it seems likely that the rate of expansion over the next two decades will be slower than that of the last 30 years, because most of the potential arable land lies in remote areas which are difficult and costly to bring into use. Furthermore, growing problems of soil erosion, waterlogging and desertification are leading to losses of productive cropland. These are not easily quantifiable in terms of areas, but nevertheless they are of great significance for land production.

Expansion of arable land in the developing world is largely at the expense of the area of forests and woodland. This reduction has itself been the subject of great environmental concern, as it may give rise to undesirable environmental consequences such as accelerated soil erosion. In a sense, this phase of rapid deforestation in many developing countries corresponds to similar phases in medieval Europe and in the New World during the nineteenth century. To-day, in most European countries the trend has been reversed, and the forest area is once again increasing. Land has been and is being released from agriculture, which suffers more often from problems of overproduction than of inability to feed the population. The growth of demand for forest products as standards of living improve has led many developed countries to transfer 'surplus' agricultural land into forest. The mode of transfer is usually indirect rather than direct; arable land is not usually afforested directly, but the more marginal areas may pass into permanent pasture. In turn, the more marginal areas of pasture may be planted with trees. There is some evidence that rates of afforestation are highest in those countries with the smallest extents of forests. In the UK, for example, an increase of around 10 per cent in the forest area was achieved during the 1970s, and Ireland, which in 1970 had under 4 per cent of its land surface under forests, experienced an increase of nearly 40 per cent in the woodland area during the decade. Percentage increases must be interpreted cautiously in the light of small absolute areas, but these trends in forest area may lend support to the idea of some convergence of land-use structures. Just as some convergence is evident in arable extents, so it may also be present in forest areas, with the most-wooded countries registering a contraction and the least-wooded ones an increase.

One of the fastest growing types of land use in many parts of the world is national parks and related areas. Statistical information is especially deficient in this respect because of problems of definitions and the multiplicity of designations that may be made for purposes of recreation and conservation. In absolute terms, the area devoted to parks is usually very small, amounting to around 2 per cent of the world land area (Eidsvik 1980), and small absolute additions may represent large proportional increases. Nevertheless, the trends in some countries are striking. The average annual rate of expansion of 'natural' parks in the United States during the 1960s was nearly 3 per cent per annum, and that in New Zealand was over 2 per cent (OECD 1976). Average annual rates may give a slightly misleading impression of the pattern of growth, which is usually discontinuous, as new designations are made sporadically, rather than steadily. Decennial or longer term periods may therefore be more appropriate for considering trends. Nevertheless, the same general pattern emerges at this time-scale, and increases of 20 and 70 per cent in Spain and Turkey respectively were registered during the 1970s (OECD 1976). There is little doubt that the trends involving parkland are more dynamic than those in other sectors of land use.

Outside Britain, most of the land in designated parks is unused or little used for agriculture, and bears few signs of human modification. On the other hand, much of the land used for urban purposes was previously cropland. Demand for land for building and other urban purposes is usually keenest around the existing towns and cities, which historically have grown up on the more fertile lowlands suitable for arable farming. The loss of agricultural land for urban purposes has given rise to much controversy and concern in Europe and North America, especially during the last two decades. Indeed it has often been seen as the most important issue in land use. The view is usually taken that the transfer of arable land to urban use is irreversible, and hence that it is undesirable in the light of long-term trends in population and food supply. On the other hand, it has been argued that urbanisation does not necessarily mean an end to food production. In England in the 1950s, for example, Best and Ward (1956) found that the value of vegetables produced in garden plots was similar on an acre-by-acre comparison to that of food produced on farmland.

Concern about the loss of farmland to urban and related land uses has been reflected in the adoption of government policies to protect farmland in many countries. In Canada, for example, the provinces of British Columbia and Quebec in the 1970s introduced legislation to preserve farmland (e.g. Pearson 1975; Pierce 1981). The rapid expansion of urban areas lies at the root of concern about the loss of food-producing land. In Italy, for example, the urban area grew by 31 per cent between 1961 and 1971, while comparable figures for the UK and France were around 11 per cent (Best 1979). Annual losses of farm land of between 0.1 and 0.8 per cent have been registered in most OECD countries (OECD 1979), but higher figures have been recorded in several countries. In Canada, for example, the urban area grew by 18 per cent during the 1960s (Hansen 1981). Even when the relative rate of transfer is low, the absolute areas involved may be considerable; for example over 1 million ha are transferred annually from agriculture to urban uses in the United States (OECD 1979), and concern is heightened by the fact that much of the land built over has an above-average productivity. It has been suggested that land urbanised in Britain during the 1950s was 70 per cent more productive than the average for all farmland (Edwards and Wibberley 1971), and Vining *et al.* (1977) concluded from Soil Conservation Service data that prime farmland was three times more likely to be built over than non-prime land in the United States during the period from 1967 to 1975. Plaut (1980) estimates that 44.5 per cent of the reserve of prime agricultural land (see Ch. 8, p.220 for discussion on definition of prime land) could be urbanised by the end of the century, the reserve being the area of land not currently being farmed but which could be brought into agricultural production if required. Furthermore, the rate of growth of urban areas has been approximately twice the rate of increase in population, and a stabilising population does not necessarily mean that the urban area will stabilise.

In Britain, much controversy has been engendered over both the rate of land loss and its significance. The crucial period of formulating agricultural and planning policies was during and immediately after the Second World War, when a food shortage was being experienced. At this time, the need to safeguard the means of food production was readily accepted, and policies to protect agricultural land were adopted. New urban areas were built at high densities in order to save farmland, and indeed the rate of land loss in England and Wales during the 1950s and 1960s was around 15,000 ha/annum compared with 25,000 ha during the 1930s when there was little or no planning control (Best 1978, 1981). This decrease in the rate of land loss, despite a rapid increase in rates of house-building, has been interpreted as an indicator of the success of post-war planning and control of land use. Best, who has based his work extending over many years on statistics derived from the agricultural census, is convinced that this is so and that there is no serious problem of availability of agricultural land in Britain. Indeed he is dismissive of what he regards as the 'myths' of disproportionate amounts and rates of agricultural land loss, and argues that land-use planning in Britain, which has as one of its objectives the safeguarding of agricultural land, is based on what he regards as the 'myths' of threats to the agricultural potential (Best 1978, 1981). He argues that there is no reason why urban expansion, with spacious layouts and attractive settings, should not continue.

On the other hand, Coleman (e.g. 1976, 1978), basing her views on the comparison of the First and Second Land Utilisation Surveys, adopts the contrary position. In her opinion, the rate of land loss has been far greater than the agricultural census indicates. This rate is alarming, she claims, because of the loss of food-producing potential. In her view, post-war planning has failed to safeguard agricultural land. This remarkable controversy, which is summarised in Rogers (1978), serves to illustrate the different conclusions that may be reached when different sources and methodologies are employed, and is eloquent testimony to the imperfections of basic land-use data in Britain. In the United States, there has been a similar controversy, culminating in the setting up of the National Agricultural Lands Study, whose Final Report (NALS 1981) was published in 1981. During the 1970s, the rate of land loss to urban uses appeared from surveys carried out by the Soil Conservation Service to be accelerating at an alarming rate, increasing from around 0.5 million ha annually in the period from 1958 to 1967 to over 1 million ha during the period from 1967 to 1977. Doubt has been cast on the accuracy and reliability of these figures because of changes in survey procedures over the years (Fischel 1982), and this doubt undermines the conclusions of NALS, where it is argued that strong government policies should be introduced to preserve agricultural land.

As in the case of many other land-use issues, NALS was plagued by data problems (Raup 1982), and in the period leading to the setting up of the study, Hart (1976) drew attention to the wide variations in estimates for the transfer of agricultural land to urban uses. These ranged from 350,000 to 5 million acres (140,000 to 2 million ha) per annum. Since there is so much uncertainty over the true rate of loss of agricultural land, it is not surprising that there is disagreement over the extent to which policies of land preservation are necessary. This question is reviewed by Jackson (1981), and the relationship between the NALS study and policies of agricultural land preservation is considered by Rose (1984).

Disagreement over the extent of land loss perhaps overshadows the basic issue of how generous provision should be made for urban areas and for other land uses such as recreation and forestry, and how far agricultural land should be safeguarded for future use. Over the last few decades, changes in yields and productivities have a far greater influence on food production than changes in the agricultural area. These changes have stemmed from plant breeding and from the intensive use of fertilisers and other inputs. If these improvements can be expected to continue indefinitely in the future, then liberal policies towards the outflow of land from agriculture are fully justified. If, on the other hand, the last three or four decades have been an exceptional period for technological improvements, then there is more justification for policies which seek to safeguard the agricultural area. Which of these outlooks is more likely to materialise is a matter for judgement, but what is clear is that the policies of recent decades in Britain have rested on shaky foundations of inadequate data.

While the dominant trend in developed countries (at least in Europe) has been for land to be transferred from agriculture to forestry and urban uses, the detailed dynamics of land flows are usually extremely complex. Even if the agricultural area remains constant in terms of area, this may merely be the outcome of the loss or abandonment of land in one part of the country, and the bringing in of new land elsewhere. This process is well developed in North America, where the abandonment of farmland in areas such as the Maritime Provinces and the Appalachians has been offset by the bringing into arable use of new land in areas such as Western Canada and Arizona (e.g. Hart 1968; Dorling and Barichello 1975). In other words, the apparent trends operating at the national level are sometimes merely the resultants of conflicting trends operating at the regional scale. Similarly, regional trends simply express the net direction of changes resulting from numerous individual decisions at the level of the basic land unit.

While the directions of dominant trends in land use are usually reasonably clearly defined (despite arguments over their strengths), the detailed dynamics of land flows are generally very poorly understood. These dynamics may be very complex, involving the decisions of hundreds of thousands of individual land users. The pattern for the Netherlands is shown in Fig. 4.3.

The Netherlands is an unusual case, both because additions are being made to the land area through the reclamation of polderlands, and because national land-use statistics are sufficiently detailed to allow such a diagram to be constructed. Although the forest area of the Netherlands is reported to have contracted during the 1970s (see Fig. 4.2), the country during the 1960s was seemingly typical of Western Europe, with a net loss of agricultural land and an increase in the urban and woodland areas. These trends remain typical of

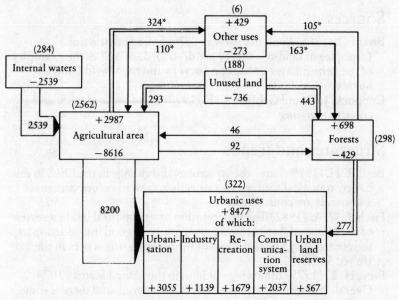

( ) Total area of the category in question, in thousand ha, in 1970.
* These flows are accounted for partly by changes in the statistical classification and improvement in surveying.

Fig. 4.3 Flows between the various uses in the Netherlands – average
annual values 1961–1970.
Source: OECD (1976)

Europe, but in relation to agriculture and forestry they are the
opposite of those in the developing world. Unfortunately, there is
little prospect of comparable flow diagrams being constructed at
the global level, or for many countries other than the Netherlands
in the foreseeable future, such are the inadequacies of information.
The lack of detailed, accurate information is frustrating from the
viewpoint of academic curiosity. It is much more serious in relation
to policies about how land should be used over the next few
decades. Policies all too often are based on inadequate factual
information. In the words of Hart (1976), myths abound where
facts are few, and in the land of the blind, the one-eyed man is king.

FURTHER READING

Sources

Board C. (1968) Land use surveys : principles and practice.
  Principles of land-use survey are described, as well as the examples
  of the British Land Utilisation Surveys and the World Land Use
  Survey.
Coppock, J. T. and Gebbett, L. F. (1978) *Land use and town and
  country planning*.

Structures and trends

Best, R. H. (1979) Land-use structures and change in the EEC. In this
  paper, statistical sources are critically reviewed before structures
  and trends are considered.
Fischel, W. A. (1982) The urbanisation of agricultural land : a review
  of the National Agricultural Lands Study. A good introduction to
  the controversy about the loss of farmland to urban uses in the
  United States.
Frey, H. T. (1979) Major uses of land in the United States : 1974.
  Overall and sectoral composition is considered, and there is some
  analysis of land use by land ownership.
OECD (1976) Land use policies and agriculture. This is a useful
  account of structures and trends in land use in member countries,
  considered in relation to potential problems in rural communities
  and to policies adopted.
Rogers, A. W. (ed.) (1978) *Urban growth, farmland losses and
  planning*. This is the most compact account of the Best-Coleman
  debate, containing papers by each of the protagonists together
  with an introduction and summing up.

5

Urban and peri-urban land use

The city and its environs offer an excellent case-study of land-use issues and conflicts. Land-use patterns are usually more complex and dynamic than in the deeper countryside. Demands for the use of land as space and as ecosystem come into contact with each other, and the conflicting concepts of land as private property and as a common-property resource come into contact with each other as social (planning) controls are imposed on the extent to which economics are allowed to dominate land-use competition. Most of the classical models of land use have been derived in relation to the city and the rural area around it, and it is here that the degree of public control of land use is strongest, at least in the western world. Urban and peri-urban areas therefore can illustrate many of the basic principles of land use, and many of these principles can be more easily demon-strated here than anywhere else. In this chapter, three main themes will be considered in relation to the city and its surroundings: theories and patterns of land values and their significance for land use; dynamics of land use in the zone of contact between town and country; and public responses, expressed in the form of green belts and other measures, to the pressures underlying these dynamics.

LAND VALUES

As indicated in Chapter 1, land values vary both with fertility (and with other physical or environmental factors) and with location. Fertile tracts of land usually produce greater levels of output for given levels of input than infertile tracts, and are therefore more valuable and command higher prices. Land values will usually therefore vary with soil types and climatic conditions, especially when agriculture and forestry are the main land uses. But for some types of land use, location is far more important than physical land type. Some locations are highly prized because of their high degree of accessibility to large numbers of potential shoppers, or because of their convenience for travel to work, or for ready access to markets. Competition for the use of these locations is intense, and they command high prices. Prices, in turn, are an important factor in the use to which a piece of land is put. Very expensive land, for example, is more likely to be used for retailing than for ranching. Enormous differences in land values can exist over distances of a few kilometres or even a few hundred metres, especially within and around cities. As a result, land uses may be sorted or separated according to their ability to pay for land, although economics is, of course, not the only factor that determines the use to which land is put, and economic forces are usually circumscribed by a variety of social, legal and political factors. Nevertheless, these economic forces remain strong, and they cannot be ignored in any analysis of land use, especially around cities.

The ideas of Johann Heinrich von Thünen underlie and pervade theories of land values and land use. Von Thünen was the owner of an estate near the town of Rostock on the Baltic coast of what is now East Germany. In 1826, he published a work entitled *Der Isolierte Staat in Beziehung auf Landwirtschaft* (The Isolated State in relation to Agriculture), in which he tried to work out the most profitable pattern of land use on an area of uniform land surrounding a single market for land produce (see Hall 1966, for an English translation). The main variable factor in his analysis was transport costs, which were, of course, related to distance and the nature of the commodity (and especially its ratio of value to bulk). He made various assumptions which simplified his analysis: for example, he assumed that the cost of transport was proportional to distance and that costs of production, other than transport, were constant. For a given crop, net returns or economic rent (see Ch. 1) would decrease with increasing transport costs and hence with increasing distance from the city. However, the gradient of decreasing rent would vary from crop to crop. The produce of some crops would be more sensitive to transport costs than other crops. Bulky, low-value commodities would be more sensitive than higher value commodities such as wheat. If demand existed for several land products (within an 'isolated state', with no foreign imports), then the most profitable land use for a given location could be identified by constructing the graphs of economic rent of the various alternative land uses, as indicated in Fig. 5.1.

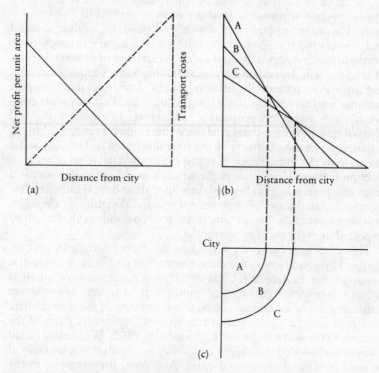

Fig. 5.1 Von Thünen analysis and pattern.
(a) Graph of profit per unit area for single land use
(b) Graph of profit per unit area for three land uses
(c) Resulting pattern of rural land use around one quadrant of city.

If land-use decisions were determined by economics alone, and if the assumptions on which the analysis was based were valid in reality, then the pattern of land uses around a city market would be in the shape of concentric zones or rings. In *The Isolated State*, horticulture and dairying dominated the innermost ring immediately around the city, followed successively by timber-growing, intensive arable farming, less intensive arable with long ley, three-field arable, and finally ranching. There is a clear gradation of intensity within the arable zones, it being sensible to use the innermost arable zone most intensively, and there is an ordering of the rings in accordance with the sensitivity of their products to transport costs. Perhaps the position of timber-growing in an inner ring seems surprising, but an early nineteenth-century city used large quantities of timber (a commodity bulky in relation to its value) for both fuel and construction.

119

The mode of analysis devised by von Thünen is far more important than the actual sequence of land-use rings prescribed in *The Isolated State*. The ordering of the rings obviously depends on levels of demand and on relative transport costs, both of which vary through time. Furthermore, the regularity and even the existence of concentric rings of land use will depend on the initial assumptions. Variations in land fertility are one potentially distorting factor. Another is that transport facilities tend to develop along specific lines, and that transport costs are not necessarily proportionate to distance. In addition, the real costs of transport have decreased since von Thünen's time, resulting in a flattening of the gradients of the type illustrated in Fig. 5.1, and a decrease in the importance of transport costs relative to other production factors. Most cities in the western world are to-day supplied from areas extending far beyond their immediate hinterlands, and few exist in 'isolated states'. For numerous reasons, therefore, few modern cities are surrounded by the concentric zones of land use that might be expected from the von Thünen model.

This does not, however, invalidate the form of analysis first attempted by von Thünen, nor does it mean that no traces of concentric zonation may be detected. Clear elements of zonation were apparent around nineteenth-century London, with dairying and market gardening in the innermost zones, cereal growing in the intermediate locations and the equivalent of ranching in the remoter parts of the country to the north and west (e.g. Chisholm 1962). Within this broad pattern focusing on the capital city, other local patterns were centred around provincial towns and cities. Aberdeen, for example, in the nineteenth century was partly surrounded by market gardens and nurseries (Fig. 5.6a, p. 142).

Much of the concentric pattern has now disappeared at both the national and local scales, but some traces remain, especially in the form of horticulture. Concentric patterns have been reported from around cities such as Montevideo (Griffin 1973) and Addis Ababa (Horvarth 1969), where supplies of food and other land products still come largely from the local hinterland. At the broader scale, elements of concentric zonation reminiscent of von Thünen were detected by Jonasson (1925), who mapped the decreasing intensity of agriculture in Europe (as indicated by the levels of yield of eight crops) with increasing distance away from a core area encompassing Belgium, the Ruhr and part of lowland England, where the dense populations offered a market that could be likened to the central city of the isolated state. More recently, Belding (1981) has found a statistically significant relationship between net return per farm (corrected for size) and per unit area, on the one hand, and accessibility to aggregate demand, centred on Benelux and decreasing radially outwards, on the other.

Peet (1969, 1972) has extended the scale still further, seeing north-west Europe as the focal market of a global producing system made possible by the great reductions in real transport costs with the development of the railways and cheap ocean shipping during the nineteenth century. The average distance of transport of agricultural products increased markedly during the century, but the average distance of transport for each commodity remained in similar rank order. This suggested that at least some elements of zonation in land production remained, even if the zones were becoming wider and had been displaced outwards. As transport costs fell relative to other costs of production, the control exercised on land use by distance and location weakened, and the role of environment factors such as land quality became relatively stronger.

Traces of concentric zonation of rural land use are still visible around some cities even in the western world. Nurseries and market gardens constitute one element; dairy farming may constitute another, but even if all these traces had disappeared, the significance of von Thünen and his mode of analysis would survive. In recent decades, his work has been the foundation on which others have built, and indeed have extended his analysis from the country into the heart of the town. One of the names most closely associated with this extension is Alonso (1960, 1964), although Alonso himself built on the work of other American land economists of earlier decades. Notable among these were Hurd (1903), Haig (1926) and Ratcliff (1949).

The premise underlying the work of Alonso and his predecessors is that central, and therefore accessible, sites are attractive to most if not all land users. Accessibility is obviously a prerequisite for re-tailing if the potential shopping market is to be tapped effectively. Other commercial land users may seek central sites for the same reason, and accessible sites may also be sought by manufacturers so that they can assemble their raw materials and distribute their products easily and cheaply. House purchasers may seek central sites so that travelling costs to work, shopping and entertainment are minimised. Farmers will want a location near to the city if their produce is directed at the city market. A wide range of land users may therefore value accessible sites near the town centre, which historically has been the focal point of the local road and rail network, and which therefore has been the point of maximum accessibility.

Some land users, however, may value centrality more than others. For example, the importance of a central site is much greater to a shopkeeper than to a farmer. Each type of land user will therefore place different evaluations on centrality and on how important it is to his enterprise. Each user may be prepared to pay more for a central, accessible piece of land than for a remote, peripheral one,

121

but the price differential and hence the price gradient away from the most accessible site will depend on the type of land use and on the extent to which it depends on easy accessibility. Alonso summed up these ideas by saying that each type of land user can be assumed to have a characteristic bid-rent curve. These curves will reflect the prices that the user is prepared to pay for sites at various distances from the centre: some types of land user may place a higher premium on centrality and accessibility than others.

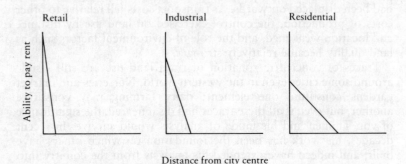

Fig. 5.2 Bid-rent curves: ability to pay rent against distance for three urban land uses. By superimposing the curves, the comparative advantage of each use in each location can be established (as in Fig. 5.1) and a theoretical pattern of urban land use determined.

If these bid-rent curves (Fig. 5.2) are superimposed, it can be seen that the types of land use with the steeper curves will outbid those with flatter curves in the central zone, and that the reverse will be the case in the periphery. In other words, a pattern of concentric zonation of land use, akin to the von Thünen model of agricultural patterns, will be found *within* the city. This pattern will only exist, of course, if economics is the primary factor in decision-making, and if assumptions about the uniformity of land and the proportionality of transport costs to distance are valid.

Inherent in this model is the idea that land becomes cheaper with increasing distance from the centre; and so within the residential belt, for example, it becomes possible for a potential residential land user to buy (or rent) a smaller site in the inner part of the ring, or a larger more spacious one for the same price further out towards the periphery. If he chooses the more spacious option, he must 'trade off' the benefits of the larger site against the higher costs of travelling to the city centre. The same principle can be applied to other zones such as retailing. All types of shop may seek sites of maximum accessibility, but furniture stores, for example, may need larger sites for storage than, say, shoe shops, and may therefore be forced to 'trade off' the benefits of a site of maximum accessibility against the disadvantages of very high land prices.

A further implication of the model is that bid-rent gradients are proportional to transport costs. If these costs fall over time, as they have done during the present century, then the influence of location and accessibility on land values and land use will decrease.

MODELS OF URBAN LAND USE

In theory, a direct relationship should exist between land value and location, between land use and land value, and hence between land use and location. To what extent does this relationship exist in reality, and to what extent do cities and their environs conform to the patterns of concentric zonation that might be expected from analyses such as those of von Thünen and Alonso?

In 1925, long before Alonso's work was published, Burgess suggested a concentric zonation model of urban structure (Fig. 5.3a).

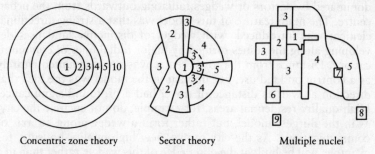

| Concentric zone theory | Sector theory | Multiple nuclei |

THREE GENERALISATIONS OF THE INTERNAL STRUCTURE OF CITIES

DISTRICT:

1. Central business district
2. Wholesale light manufacturing
3. Low-class residential
4. Medium-class residential
5. High-class residential
6. Heavy manufacturing
7. Outlying business district
8. Residential suburb
9. Industrial suburb
10. Commuters' zone

Fig. 5.3 Models of urban land use.
Source: Bourne, L. S. (1971) *Internal structure of the city.* Oxford: Oxford U.P., p. 71.

This model, or simplified, idealised representation of reality, was based on Chicago, and was intended to describe the structures of contemporary, rapidly growing industrial cities in North America. Burgess did not claim that the model was relevant in other settings, but it has sometimes been assumed subsequently that he intended that the model be more widely applicable. The model has attracted enormous attention because of its apparent elegance and simplicity, and it is thoroughly reviewed and criticised in all standard texts on urban geography.

Some themes of criticism have been widely rehearsed. One is that gradual belts of transition are more common than sharply defined zonal boundaries. Related to this criticism is the view that land uses are heterogeneous rather than homogeneous, and that single-use zones cannot validly be identified or defined. In other words, many critics have taken the view that the model is an over-simplified version of reality. The basic lack of conformity between the Burgess model and actual patterns is its most obvious weakness, and this lack of conformity has led to alternative models of urban structure being suggested.

In 1939, Hoyt put forward his sectoral model of urban structure, based on an analysis of the patterns of rent in residential areas in 25 American cities (Fig. 5.3b). This analysis revealed that the pattern of rent (or land value) was neither random nor annular, but rather was dominated by sectors or wedges radiating outwards from the urban centre. The main feature of this model was that a strong directional element was introduced, with wedges of distinctive land uses developing along the spines formed by major radial lines of communications. Distance from the town centre was not discounted entirely as a control on land use, but implicit in the model was the idea that direction as well as distance of travel had a profound significance. High-quality residential areas, for example, do not encircle the city, as in the Burgess model, but rather form a wedge along an axis of communications. As the city grows, new high-quality housing, for example, will be built at the outer edge of this wedge, rather than in a narrow ring around the city. Industrial land use may also extend radially outwards along a river, canal or railway to form another wedge, separated as far as possible from the high-quality residential zone.

Hoyt's model was based on the more objective analysis of real residential rent patterns. It is perhaps not surprising, therefore, that the Hoyt model is usually regarded as a more accurate and faithful representation of the land-use structure of western cities than the Burgess model.

A third model has been suggested by Harris and Ullman (1945), which was less simple and elegant than those of Burgess and Hoyt, but perhaps closer to reality. The multiple nuclei model (Fig. 5.3c) recognises that many cities do not grow outwards only from a single centre, but rather absorb other, previously separate nuclei in the course of their growth. As the city grows, specialised land use develops on separate tracts of land, which are square, rectangular or irregular in shape, and not in the rings and wedges of Burgess and Hoyt. This model is purely descriptive, and has no deductive basis. Its structure, however, perhaps reflects the reality of rectilinear land units typical of much of the United States better than the models of Burgess or Hoyt. It is much less specific than the other models, and perhaps implicit in it is the view that a simple generalisation of urban land-use patterns is not possible. However, if definite and regular patterns of land use can be expected from land economics, as discussed in the previous section, why are more distinct patterns of land use not apparent in the real world?

Land economics and models of land use

Part truth or whole truth?

A variety of answers can be suggested in response to the question of why more distinct patterns of land use are not apparent. At one level, each model may be valid as a partial but incomplete representation of reality. Vance (1971), for example, observes that the 'natural' physical tendency for accretion to occur in rings makes the concentric-zone theory logical and the corresponding model accurate in part. The notion of 'filtering down' of housing from the richer to the poorer, allied to the association of social status and location of residence, lends credibility to patterns of the Hoyt type, and the growth of cities to engulf previously separate towns and villages is a historical fact that accords with the multiple-nuclei model. Vance concludes that the existence of this set of theories of *partial* truth indicates that urban patterns can be understood only in terms of a *series* of explanations, which in combination approach completeness, and not in terms of a single-factor explanation. He proceeds to relate different elements in the urban structure to what he calls different land-assignment systems, distinguishing the medieval, capitalist and post-capitalist views of land. During the capitalist period, for example, when the American urban models were being propounded, land was viewed as property valued primarily for its economic return. Vance contrasted this view of land with both the medieval notion of land as a site for urban activity rather than as property, and with the post-capitalist view of land in which there is social as well as economic value.

Land values : theory and reality

A second level of answer to the question may be sought within the realm of ideas about patterns of land values within the setting of twentieth century American cities, which have been the seed-bed both of urban models and of theories of land economics. To what extent do the theoretical patterns of land values expected from bid-rent theory exist in reality? Relatively few comprehensive studies of patterns of land values have been carried out, perhaps because of data problems and the paucity of reliable and comprehensive sources, but one major study by Yeates (1965) in Chicago is instructive. Yeates attempted to reconstruct the pattern of land values decennially between 1910 and 1960. He found that land values decreased with distance from the city centre for each time period. Interestingly, however, he found that there was a steady decline in the strength of the association: a clearer gradient of land value was evident in 1910 than in 1960. Indeed by 1960 he found that in some sectors, land values actually increased towards the periphery, leaving a trough of lower values in the intermediate zone. He concluded that the rise of subsidiary business centres had weakened the influence of the main centre as the primary focus of high land values. Furthermore, the influence of recreational and physical amenities on land values appeared to have increased over the decades. A zone of high-value land extended along the shore of Lake Michigan, probably as a result of a combination of amenity reasons and proximity to the communications axis of Lake Shore Drive. In short, elements of a radially decreasing pattern of land values could be discerned, but the pattern had become more complex down through the twentieth century, and it was clear that it was influenced by other factors as well as by distance from the centre. More recently, Chicione (1981) has concluded that proximity to the urban core in the Chicago area is still reflected in farmland prices in the rural fringe, despite the extensive suburbanisation and decentralisation that have occurred in recent decades. Within the fringe, the influence of soil productivity on farmland values is over-shadowed by locational factors. These, however, are not the only influence on land values, and in particular, the uses of neighbouring areas of land may also be a significant factor.

Broadly similar conclusions emerge from studies of other American cities. Brigham (1965) found that the pattern of variation in residential land values in Los Angeles revealed a positive correlation with accessibility to employment opportunities in the central business district, but that this relationship was sometimes overshadowed by low amenity levels near the main concentrations of employment, and by the effect of secondary employment centres. In a study of Milwaukee, Downing (1973) found a significant correlation of land value with distance from the commercial centre, but a large proportion of the variation in land values remained unexplained by this variable alone. He concluded that other factors such as air quality and proximity to competing or complementary land uses may be important.

Outside North America, further support for the idea of decreasing land values with increasing distance is not lacking. Distance was found to be a significant variable in relation to the unit price of land purchased for municipal housing around Edinburgh (Richardson 1974): an average gradient of £1,089 ha/km was found, for the period between 1952 and 1967. Again, variables other than distance were found to be significant in relation to variations in land values. For example, price gradients were steeper in some directions than in others, and the type of seller (e.g. whether a farmer or institutional owner) was a complicating factor.

The influence of distance from the Central Business District (CBD) on the value of land in the periphery of Auckland has been analysed for a number of years between 1955 and 1970 by Moran (1978), who found not only a significant relationship but also one which strengthened over this period, in contrast with the conclusion of Yeates in Chicago.

In short, there is clear evidence that distance from the city centre is a significant factor in determining land values, and hence in influencing land use, but it is by no means the only influence. Perhaps on a homogeneous, isotropic plain without the complication of river, lake, hill or valley, and in an isolated city, the spatial pattern of land values might conform more closely to one of concentric zonation. In the real world, such plains and such cities are rare.

Land units and land ownership

Another reason for real patterns of land use to deviate from theoretical patterns of concentric zones is the effect of the pattern of units of land ownership and the behaviour of land owners. If land units were small, regular in size and shape, and in the hands of owners or controllers who behaved consistently and identically, then the influence of the pattern of land holding might be minimal. In the real world, of course, these conditions rarely occur. For reasons of land history, perhaps they might be approached more closely in some parts of the Mid-West of the United States than in most other areas. In the case of Chicago, Fellman (1957) has shown that the initial sub-division of land units prior to building contains elements of each of the three main urban models: on secondary or re-subdivision, concentric zones and sectors are clearer than multiple nuclei, but at the level of individual lot sales, nuclei are a clearer pattern element than circles or sectors. In other words, different (partial) patterns are discernible at different stages in the physical process of urban development.

127

In the Old World, the impress of the pre-existing pattern of land holdings may be stronger than in cases such as Chicago. Numerous examples have been reported on how the morphology of cities in England has been affected by patterns of land ownership. In the case of Birmingham, for example, rapid growth on the north side during the eighteenth and nineteenth centuries contrasted with much slower growth on the south and east. This uneven pattern has been attributed to the pattern of land holdings, since the owners of four landed estates on the south were unwilling to release land for building (Wise 1948). In the case of Sheffield, the influence of the Fitzwilliam estate on the pattern of growth in the 1920s and 1930s has been reported by Rowley (1975), who concluded that social and political factors were more important than the motive of maximum profit in the Fitzwilliam thinking. Indeed, Rowley rejects urban theories based on concepts of rent maximisation and the market mechanism as being incomplete and incorrect before the late nineteenth century, when an effective land market developed. If economic motives are not present, or if they are over-shadowed by other factors, then bid-rent theories cannot explain urban land-use patterns.

At the more detailed level, the layout of streets and buildings in the urban plans of cities such as Leeds and Bradford have been shown to be related to the framework of land ownership at the time of development (Ward 1962; Mortimore 1969). Street layouts and building patterns are typically discontinuous and fragmented, because development proceeded in a piecemeal and uncoordinated fashion on small land holdings as they became available during the nineteenth century. The larger land holdings and estates remained in the hands of their traditional owners, who resisted urbanising pressures more strongly than their smaller brethren who were more strongly motivated by economic considerations. At first, these larger estates formed gaps in the urban fabric. Some eventually became urban parks, and when others eventually succumbed to building pressures, their scale offered possibilities of more regular and compact layouts than had been possible when development had to operate within the framework of small land units. Some of the larger estate owners imposed restrictive stipulations or covenants on releasing land for urban development, constraining the type or form of development in a way that cannot be explained solely in terms of land economics.

The type of decision taken by the estate owner and the influence on urban morphology could vary through time. For example, in the 1840s the Ramsden Estate strictly controlled the form of building in the growing town of Huddersfield, but by the latter part of the century it was unable to attract builders on its terms and so the degree of influence and control lessened (Springett 1982). The role of the pattern of land holdings continued down into more recent times with the development of the large peripheral municipal housing areas which are characteristic of most British towns and cities. In the case of Bradford, for example, large estates were sought for this purpose in preference to smaller units, because of the convenience they offered at the various stages of negotiations leading to acquisition, planning and construction. Indeed, Mortimore (1969) felt able to conclude that in the growth of Bradford during its formative period from 1850 to 1950, 'the existing property units became an invisible skeleton for the growing body of the town'.

If the detailed pattern of the city is at least partly a reflection of the pattern of land ownership at the time of its growth, the urban land-use pattern is the product of numerous separate decisions on land use and land development. This obvious point has often been overlooked in work on urban structure. Bourne (1976) has made a notable attempt to relate the broad evolution of urban structure and the behaviour of developers, but such efforts to bring together the broad pattern and the individual decision have been few in number. Bourne also points out that different types of developer are responsible for different types of development: private developers for suburbs; public authorities and planners for roads and utilities; and corporations for industrial facilities. The implication is that with different types of developers and land owners, different goals and different decision behaviour are to be expected.

The pattern of land use in cities is usually more complex than simple models would suggest, and some parts of many cities consist of mixtures of land uses rather than single land-use types. Broad zones of transition may exist, rather than sharp zonal boundaries. One possible reason may lie in the basic concept of bid-rent relationships, which might at first sight be expected to give rise to clear and simple concentric land-use zones. Whitehand (1972), however, points out that bid-rent relationships are not constant. House-building, in particular, is characterised by booms and slumps. During booms, housing may have a steeper bid-rent gradient than institutional uses such as schools or hospitals or parks, which may then become established in locations beyond the housing zone. During housing slumps, however, the housing gradient may be flatter, and institutional land use may then compete more success-fully for land which in boom times would have been in the housing zone. In other words, the relative locations of housing and in-stitutional uses may alternate, and Whitehand suggests that parts of the fringe zones of cities such as Glasgow may reflect these alternations and cyclical patterns of development.

One area of the city which displays particular complexity is the transition zone around the city centre. This is a more or less continuous belt separating the retail-orientated heart of a city from the surrounding area given over mainly to non-commercial land uses. Within this zone, different processes may be active in different sectors. In one, commercial uses may be expanding, as offices take over previously residential properties. In another, commercial uses may be contracting, as the core of the CBD shifts slightly (see, for example, Griffin and Preston 1966) or even contracts. Historically, the city centre has always been the focus of retail activity because of its easy accessibility, but in recent times it has become less accessible. Whereas it was the focal point of tramway and rail services, it may be relatively inaccessible for a car-using population. Some retail enterprises may thus seek locations on the urban periphery, where easy accessibility by road may be combined with large car parks laid out on relatively cheap land. Manufacturing industry may be attracted to peripheral locations that offer easy accessibility from motorways, in contrast to the now congested inner cities. Changing transport modes may therefore give rise to different interpretations of accessibility, and ultimately to changing bid-rent gradients.

Finally, yet another reason for the lack of conformity between real cities and models of urban structure is suggested by the growth of municipal housing areas. Although economic factors may play some part in the selection of such areas, the process is not determined solely by market forces. Public intervention, expressing social goals and values, constrains the free play of market forces, as indeed does (at least in theory) the whole structure of the town and country planning system in Britain. In the terms of Vance (1971), the mode of land assignment is now post-capitalist, and is based not solely on economic but also on social values.

Although the major urban models conform only partly with the land-use patterns of modern western cities, this does not mean that they are of no value or interest. The concentric zone model, for example, is useful in illustrating the pattern that would result if land-use decisions were determined by economics, and if rents were simply a function of distance. Deviations from the model indicate the extent to which other factors play parts in land-use decisions. The same conclusion can be reached for the peri-urban zone around the city as for the city itself.

PERI-URBAN LAND USE

If the assumptions employed in von Thünian analysis are correct, the city should be surrounded by concentric zones of different types of agriculture and woodland, arranged according to their products and their characteristics in relation to transport. In practice, few cities in the west are surrounded by well-developed rings of agriculture, although traces of such a zonation may be the surviving remnants of formerly better developed zones. The evident complexity of much rural land use around the modern city reflects the facts that the assumptions of von Thünian analysis are simplifications, and that factors other than distance and transport costs play important roles in land-use decisions.

One of the main characteristics of cities in the western world during the last century and a half is rapid growth. Any assumption that the city is a static entity is a gross over-simplification. Also, as cities expand, they not only displace agricultural land at the urban edge, but also cast a shadow ahead of them. Urban influences, in one form or another, are felt on rural land use long before bricks and mortar displace corn and grass. The strength of these influences will vary with rates and pressures of urbanisation, and with the ways in which they are constrained by planning systems or other public controls on land use. They may give rise to consistent features of land use, whose extent and degree of development vary according to the strength of the influences.

Urban and rural land values

Land used for residential development or other urban purposes is much more valuable than land used for agriculture, by a factor of 10 or more. For example, Schmid (1968) quotes examples from a wide range of American cities and states: the prices paid to farmers for land for urban or other non-farm purposes ranged from about four to over 100 times those paid for farm purposes. At around the same time, agricultural land values in the vicinity of Copenhagen ranged from 1.0 to 2.5 DKr/m^2, as compared with 13.0 to 33.0 DKr/m^2 for land for development (Darin-Drabkin 1977). With such differentials, urban uses will almost invariably displace agriculture (unless other controls are imposed). Furthermore, land where urbanisation is *expected* to occur is more valuable than land where agriculture is expected to continue. The mere anticipation of urban development on an area of land increases its value. If this expectation is strong and confident, urban developers or speculators may purchase the land from the farmer, and be content to leave the land unused until it is developed, reaping capital appreciation rather than steady income. If the expectation is rather more vague, the land may not change hands, but the farmer may be reluctant to invest capital and effort in maintaining levels of fertility, drainage, fences or other capital equipment, and in particular he may be reluctant to invest in land uses such as orchards which require a number of years to mature and

131

become productive. Agricultural land use may therefore be discontinued, modified, or dis-intensified ahead of actual urban encroachment. The innermost ring of rural land, therefore, may not be given over to highly intensive agriculture or to the production of poorly transportable commodities, but it may instead be characterised by a lower level of agricultural activity than that prevailing further from the advancing city.

The Sinclair model

These characteristics of rural land use around the expanding city were considered to be sufficiently consistent and widespread by Sinclair (1967) for him to suggest a revised pattern of concentric zonation of rural land uses (Fig. 5.4).

In contrast to the von Thünen model, the three inner zones are characterised by negative influences exerted by the city on agriculture, while the fourth zone, some distance beyond the city edge, is distinguished by dairying and similar types of farming, oriented towards the city market but displaced from it by a belt in which urban pressures are dissipated. Beyond this zone, the regional type of agriculture, which was feed-grain/livestock farming in the Mid-West setting of Sinclair's model, prevails. In the Sinclair model, agricultural land values are depressed in the fringe immediately around the city where urban pressures are greatest, although the development land value is highest here.

Bryant (1973) has subsequently refined this aspect by pointing out that different types of agriculture are affected differently by possible urban encroachment. Types of land use requiring initial investment which yields only long-term returns (such as orchard trees) are more likely to be adversely affected than shorter-term investments. Therefore, there may be several curves on the graph of agricultural land values against distance, and not just one.

The Sinclair model is not based on rigorous deduction as was the von Thünen one, although it has a clear logical basis. Regularity and circularity will require uniform physical conditions and uniform rates of urban expansion in all directions. Neither of these prerequisites is likely to exist in reality. Nevertheless, elements of the patterns suggested by Sinclair can be seen around many cities, and perhaps his model has a widespread though partial validity. Areas of derelict agricultural land, with tall, ungrazed grass and broken-down fences, are not unusual on the urban fringe. These areas have probably been acquired by builders or speculators seeking capital gain rather than annual income, and agriculture has simply been discontinued. Another common feature is grazing land of modest quality, in which some grazing use is maintained, perhaps seasonally or for

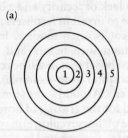

1 Urban farming
2 Vacant and grazing (temporary)
3 Field crops and grazing (transitory)
4 Dairying and field crop
5 Specialised feed-grain livestock

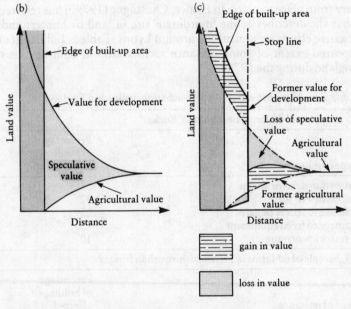

gain in value

loss in value

Fig. 5.4 The Sinclair model and land values around a city.
(a) Sinclair model
(b) Land values: urban and agricultural
(c) Land values: urban and agricultural with planning controls in urban expansion
Sources: (a) Sinclair (1967); (c) Modified after Boal (1970).

special purposes. Land where development is likely to occur fairly soon but is not imminent may be let on an annual or seasonal basis by the farmer-owner, or more probably by the builder or institutional owner. With a lack of security and a likelihood of develop-ment, there is a reluctance to invest in fertilisers and other inputs, and the quality of management is often modest. Institutions and other public bodies may maintain such tenure and use for many years, retaining the land against a belief that it will be required eventually for the expansion of the hospital (for example), and letting it out meantime on an annual basis. Around some segments of the city, there is a demand for such land for the grazing of horses and ponies, to the extent that traces of a zone of 'horseyculture' may be apparent.

Factors other than the pressures created by urban/rural differentials in land values may also contribute to the relatively low level of agriculture immediately around the city. The first of these is nuisance effects. The theft of crops, disturbance to animals, and dangers from litter and refuse may all discourage the farmer from continuing certain or all of his land enterprises. The nature of these nuisance effects may vary from place to place. In France, Chassagne (1979b) has referred to what she describes as the 'inordinate' use of land by hunters and its negative effects on agriculture around Lyons. Table 5.1 illustrates the reported extent of some nuisance factors around built-up areas in England during the 1970s.

Table 5.1   Nuisance effects on peri-urban agriculture in England

(a)   Sample of 100 farms near Slough, Bucks.*

Type of nuisance	Percentage of holdings affected
Crops damaged or stolen	35
Rubblish left	32
Damage to fences or gates	25
Damage to fixed equipment	15
Livestock worrying	10

(b)   Sample of 69 farms in Hertfordshire urban fringe†

Type of nuisance	Percentage of holdings affected
Trespass	88
Trespass resulting in damage	78
Rubbish dumping	71
Livestock farming problems (e.g. worrying)	29
Theft of crops or livestock	16

Sources: * Based on data in ADAS (1973); †   Hall (1976).

In a survey parallel to the one on which Table 5.1a is based, 84 per cent of a sample of 91 farms in the green belt around Newcastle upon

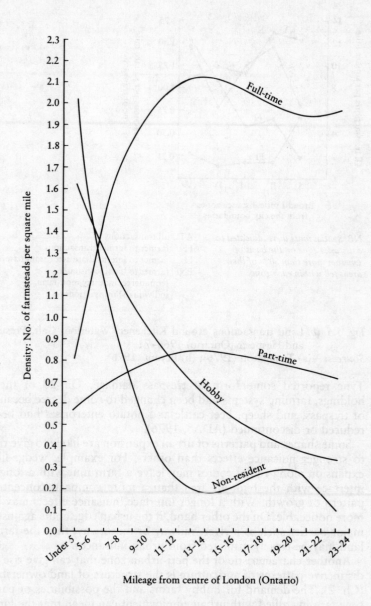

Fig. 5.5 (a) Comparative density occurrence of full-time, part-time, hobby
farmsteads and non-resident farm properties, London (Ontario)
area, 1975.

135

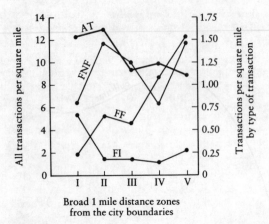

Broad 1 mile distance zones
from the city boundaries

NB *Spatial units were allocated to*   AT   all transactions
a distance zone on the basis of   FF   farmer to farmer transactions
whether more than 50% of their   FI   farmer to intermediate actor transactions
areas fell within each zone.   FNF   farmer to 'final' consumer
                                                   (commerce, industry, non-farm
                                                   individuals) transactions

Fig. 5.5 (b) Land transactions around Kitchener, Waterloo, Galt, Preston
            and Hespeler (Ontario) 1966–71.
Sources: (a) Troughton (1976); (b) Bryant (1976).

Tyne reported some form of trespass damage. On 20 of these
holdings, farming systems had been changed to some degree because
of trespass, and sheep, beef cattle and potato enterprises had been
reduced or discontinued (ADAS, 1976).

Some shapes and patterns of urban expansion are likely to give rise
to stronger nuisance effects than others. For example, wedge-like
expansion along radial routes may leave a farm unit with a longer
interface with the built-up area than a more compact, concentric
pattern of growth. With a longer interface, nuisance effects may be
more noticeable. On the other hand, if the urban edge abuts against a
major barrier such as a river, railway or motorway, then the farmland may be largely insulated from urban nuisances.

Another characteristic of the peri-urban zone that can give rise to
distinctive patterns of agriculture is the structure of land ownership
(Ch. 2). The demand for hobby farms and the possibilities of part-
time farming allied with urban employment can mean that the farm
structure is different from that in more rural areas. With a different
framework of land ownership and different user-motives, then the
prevailing land-use decisions may be different from those in the

deeper countryside. An interesting example from around London (Ontario) is presented by Troughton (1976) (Fig. 5.5a).

Hobby farmers predominate in the inner ring, and part-time farmers are also fairly numerous. The number of full-time farmers increases steeply with increasing distance from 8 to 16 km beyond the city. In other words, there is a distinct spatial pattern of decision makers in the rural fringe, and this pattern may have implications for land use and land management. For example, Munton (1983a) reports that a relationship exists between hobby farmers and run-down farmland in the London (England) green belt. (He also concludes that agricultural dereliction is associated with detached fields, and especially those next to new roads or housing, and with short-term lets.)

The degree of activity in the land market also tends to be greater around cities. Bryant (1976) presents data for some cities in Ontario that indicate that the overall density or frequency of land transactions decreases outwards (Fig. 5.5b), and that farmer-to-farmer transactions increase rapidly in that direction, in contrast to the pattern of farmer to non-farmer deals. Changes in land ownership, as well as in the character and use of the land, can begin more than 20 years before the rural countryside is actually converted to urban use, according to Brown *et al.* (1981) on the basis of their work around a number of North American cities. But the timing of the initial sale varies according to the financial position of the landowner. Generally, institutional landowners can hold out longer for a better price than small farmers. Absentee owners, elderly farmers and those who have held the land for only a short time are most likely to sell (Kaiser *et al.* 1968). Around Padua in Italy, Merlo (1979) found that non-agricultural landowners were the first to sell, and that when agricultural owners did eventually sell, they retained part of their land and remained in part-time farming. It may be speculated that hobby farmers, motivated by factors other than purely economic ones (for example, status or amenity – Munton 1974), may resist pressures to sell more strongly than some other types of owners.

Effects arising from the distinctive patterns of land ownership may combine with nuisance effects to strengthen the influence of expected agricultural encroachment in discouraging intensive agriculture around the urban edge. Numerous examples from different parts of the western world could be cited in support of Sinclair's concept. For example, Mattingly (1972) presents empirical evidence from a case study of Rockford (Illinois) which indicates that the labour input per unit area increases for some distance outwards from the urban edge. He also finds that part-time farms are twice as common in the inner zone, and that the relative roles of dairying and cash-grain farming change outwards from the city. Dairying becomes more prominent outwards: in the inner zone farmers seem to be reluctant to invest in the necessary fixed equipment amidst uncertainty about the long-term survival of their farms in the face of urban pressures. Grain farming requires less investment in fixed equipment, and is thus perhaps more suited to the inner zone (Berry 1979). Around Belfast, Boal (1970) found clear evidence of reduced intensity of inputs and greater use of conacre (see Ch. 2), as compared with the deeper countryside. In England, Thomson (1981) has characterised the typical urban-fringe farm, on the basis of parish summaries of the agricultural census, as being smaller and as having a higher proportion of permanent grass and a lower stocking rate than the average 'national' farm. In Germany, large areas of land have passed out of agricultural use and remain unused while weeds, bushes and scrub take over. This 'social fallow' is related to alternative employment opportunities taken up by the former farmers, and is not confined exclusively to the peri-urban zone, although it is very pronounced there. Between 1965 and 1970, for example, the area of social fallow around Hamburg and Bremen more than doubled (Kunnecke 1974). A decline in livestock farming around the Ruhr cities has been reported by Mrohs (1979), although the number of horses has increased as farmers have catered for nearby urban recreational demand by developing equestrian enterprises. One of the reasons for the decline in cattle and pigs, as described by Mrohs, is the need to feed and tend the animals regularly, which does not fit in well with part-time farming. Another reason is complaints from the nearby urban population about bad smells. This factor seems to be especially significant in Sweden (Brasch 1979). Under the Environment Protection Act, permits are required for buildings for large-scale pig, poultry and fur farming, and distance from neighbouring residential areas is considered as an important factor in the granting of permits.

These European examples illustrate *some* distinctive features of farming on the urban-rural fringe, rather than the full development of a Sinclair model. In North America, clearer elements of a Sinclair zonation may be apparent: for example, Clawson (1971) refers to the complete abandonment of farmland and to the resulting large areas of idle land in the great urban complex of north-eastern America. After analysing air-photographic evidence of land-use change in 53 rapid-growth counties in the United States between 1961 and 1970, Ziemetz *et al.* (1976) concluded that 33 per cent of the land developed for urban use had been idle immediately previously.

On the other hand, Heaton (1980) reports that the gradients of land values and value of farm products per unit area slope outwards from metropolitan centres in the United States. Working at the broad scale, he concludes that the more centrally located areas are more likely to be characterised by capital-intensive production and by highly intensive land use. This is in accordance with what might be expected from von Thünian analysis, and the apparent conflict and contradiction with the Sinclair model can be explained at least partly in terms of different scales. At the broad scale, land use in the vicinity of cities is usually more intensive than in the remoter rural areas, perhaps because historically cities have tended to grow up in fertile lowlands where intensive agricultural land use is rewarded, as well as because of the influence of the urban market. At the more local scale, however, expected urban encroachment casts a shadow around the rural fringe, and the belt of maximum intensity may be removed from the urban edge by a distance proportional to the rate and likelihood of urban growth. It would be an over-simplification, however, to suggest that the pattern of rural land use discernible around a city is solely a function of scale. Numerous cases of at least some aspects of von Thünian elements have been reported close to the urban edge. Around Christchurch and Auckland in New Zealand, for example, intensive market gardening and orchard farming have been reported respectively by Smith and Mears (1975) and Moran (1979). Urban encroachment and loss of land in the case of the former was met with a response of further intensification and specialisation. Furthermore, the negative effects of the urban shadow may be so controlled or counteracted that no elements of a Sinclair zonation are discernible, as Moran (1980) illustrates in his case study of the Auckland area.

Around Auckland, dairy farms supplying the urban market occupy much of the inner part of the fringe, with similar types of farm supplying processing factories in an intermediate band, and grazing and fattening farms further out still. The main town-dairying zone has been static for some decades, and Moran concludes that elements of a Sinclair pattern are absent or, at the most, very poorly developed. This he attributes partly to historical factors, and indeed he concludes that Sinclair under-estimates the historical legacy. The location of town dairying around Auckland has perhaps been stabilised, in the face of the expanding urban area, by a system of supply quotas. Production is controlled by the allocating of these quotas, with preference being given to farmers close to the urban area. There is therefore a tendency for the pattern in existence when the quota system was first introduced to be perpetuated. Another factor identified by Moran as contributing to the absence of Sinclair elements is the growth of direct-sales and 'pick-your-own' fruit and vegetable enterprises around the city. Proximity to the urban market is obviously a distinct advantage here, and in this case a peri-urban location has more advantages than disadvantages. Indeed, Blair (1980) on the basis of his work in Essex concludes that the disadvantages of farming in the fringe have been over-rated and the advantages under-rated. He found that 29 per cent of his large sample of farmers in the country derived an income from farm- gate sales, averaging 19 per cent of total farm income. On the other hand, although 70 per cent of his sample farmers complained of nuisances, 78 per cent of these took no action, and of the remainder only 15 per cent actually changed their farming systems or methods.

Planning and the peri-urban zone

Rural land use in the urban fringe can contain elements of both von Thünen and Sinclair patterns. Indeed the zone is one of great variability in intensity of land use. The historical legacy may be one important factor in the existence of von Thünen elements: the rate of growth and the nature of expected growth are likely to be the major determinants of Sinclair elements. If the relationship between agricultural and urban land uses is determined solely or primarily by economic forces, then agriculture will almost inevitably be displaced by urban uses, and a dense shadow may be cast on the rural area around the expanding city. However, market forces are now usually constrained, to a greater or lesser degree, by mechanisms that express social values of land. If the relationship between urban and agricultural uses is regulated by a planning system, then the urban shadow should be smaller and much less dense. Indeed, if the planning system exerted complete control on change of land use, then there should be no shadow at all. Boal (1970) has attempted to modify Sinclair's representation of the spatial pattern of agriculture and other land uses in the rural fringe for situations where 'stop lines' or boundaries to permitted urban development have been imposed by planners (Fig. 5.4b). If a credible stop line is defined, then speculative or development land value beyond it should be negligible, and the value of land would be related solely to its agricultural use. On the other hand, the speculative value of land between the urban edge and the stop line would increase, and its agricultural value would fall. In theory, an intense urban shadow (with its effects on rural land use) should exist within the stop line, but it would be contained within that line and not overlap onto the land beyond it.

The intervention of planning and land-use controls on the urban fringe is epitomised by the green belt. Many cities in Britain are now wholly or partly encircled by formally designated green belts. The first and largest of these – around London – has had government approval since the mid-1950s, but the concept itself has a longer history, dating back to the early years of this century and before. It is closely associated with the names of the pioneers of town and country planning, such as Ebenezer Howard, Raymond Unwin and Patrick Abercrombie. But even among these early proponents of green belts there were different interpretations of the concept, and differences remain to this day in interpretation of its role and objectives. Unwin, for example, envisaged a narrow strip of land, perhaps only 2 km wide, where land would be acquired by public authorities and made available for recreation for the citizens of London. In fact, during the late 1930s, some land was acquired in this way. Then during the Second World War, a plan was prepared by Abercrombie for the Greater London region. In this plan, the objectives for the green belt were broader. One was to restrict the growth of London; another was to maintain the character of existing but separate settlements by preventing their merging in an amorphous sprawl. Another again was to safeguard land for agriculture and recreation. This plan was incorporated into the rapidly evolving structure of town and country planning in the early post-war years (see Ch. 8), and in due course it became the basis of the approved London Green Belt from the mid-1950s onwards. Over the years the belt has been expanded, and it is now about 20–25 km in width and 4,300 sq. km in area.

Green belts are now an accepted and widespread planning designation, where particular policies apply towards changes of land use and their control. Ambivalence remains, however, in their objectives. In the case of the London Green Belt, Munton (1983a) distinguishes the aims of designation as seen by central government from those of local planning authorities. The former sees the green belt as a means of restraining urban growth at a strategic or sub-regional scale, while the latter place more emphasis on goals such as the protection of local landscape and provision of recreational facilities.

The primary means by which green-belt policies are implemented within the designated zone is through the development-control system, whereby the consent of the local planning authority must be obtained before certain changes in land use can be effected. Proposed residential and industrial developments, for example, require consent. Evidence from the London Green Belt indicates that all these land uses have tended to expand over the last few decades, and that complete control has not been achieved. There is little doubt, however, that the rate of expansion of these broadly urban uses has been retarded, and in any case green-belt designation did not necessarily mean that *all* development would be prohibited.

One consequence of the fact that some development has been permitted in the London Green Belt (as in others) is that at least some development value attaches to agricultural land within the designated zone. All speculative value does not disappear at the green- belt boundary, as Fig. 5.4 would suggest, and where there is some speculative value, and some expectation of urban development, then there may be a 'shadow' effect on agriculture. Munton (1983a) reports that 5.5 per cent of the agricultural land in the inner half of the London Green Belt is in a derelict or semi-derelict condition and that a further 30 per cent shows some management problems. Green- belt designation in itself has not shielded agricultural areas from all urban pressures, although it may have reduced the extent and severity of these pressures. Development-control powers on their own cannot, of course, ensure good land management, since they are essentially only a check or curb on certain types of land-use changes.

Recently, increasing attention has been paid to management agreements as means of achieving public goals in green belts and other peri-urban areas, as well as in the deeper countryside. Under these agreements, the land occupier may be compensated for foregoing certain proposed changes in land use, or for managing his land in such a way that landscape objectives are achieved. While this 'carrot' approach is a welcome addition to the 'stick' of development-control powers, it is probably more useful and practicable in small, selected areas than on an area-wide basis. Attempts may also be made to achieve recreational objectives by management agreements, while development-control powers are not usually helpful in this respect. The other major means of encouraging recreational use of land is by public acquisition, which, of course, also permits the use of management of land in accordance with other publicly defined objectives. Although significant areas of land are in public ownership in most green belts, the cost of acquiring entire green-belt zones (or other extensive parts of the rural fringe) would be enormous, not least because of the high development value of the land, and complete public ownership is not a practicable proposition in the foreseeable future.

Recreation

Recreational land use is a distinctive feature of many rural fringes. Several centuries ago, land adjacent to some Scottish towns such as Aberdeen and Ayr was set aside for public recreation, and this tradition has been maintained and extended in many cases in more recent years, so much so that Aberdeen is now almost encircled by recreational land (Fig. 5.6b).

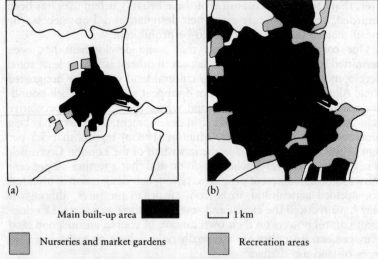

(a)   (b)

Main built-up area ■■■■   ⊢——⊣ 1 km

▨ Nurseries and market gardens   ▨ Recreation areas

Fig. 5.6 Aspects of rural land use around Aberdeen 1870 and 1980
     (a) Nurseries and market gardens 1871
     (b) Recreational land use *c.* 1980
Sources: (a) Keith and Gibb (1871) Plan of the city of Aberdeen; (b) Field survey.

Around the much larger city of London, as much as 9 per cent of the Green Belt is in informal recreational use, in addition to more formal areas such as golf courses and playing fields. Why should recreation often be a distinctive element in rural land use on the urban fringe?

As in many other aspects of land use in this zone, a simple, single answer cannot be given. In some cases, recreation may be the type of land use which is most profitable: the bid-rent curve for golf courses catering for an urban market may be steeper than that of agriculture, and so recreation can compete successfully in purely economic terms. Economic arguments may also be offered for providing facilities in the rural fringe for unpriced, passive forms of recreation such as walking and picnicking, it being argued that the optimal location is close to the centre of urban demand, and that summed transport costs (taken as a surrogate or indicator of the perceived value of unpriced recreation) may exceed potential returns per unit area from agriculture or other uses. In such cases, public acquisition or provision might be justified for purely economic reasons.

More frequently, recreational land (and especially sites for informal recreation) reflects a purely social evaluation. Green-belt and other urban control policies have sometimes contained a recreational component as well as ones directed at agriculture and urban pattern: recreational land uses may well be compatible with policies designed primarily to contain urban growth (e.g. Bowen 1974). It has sometimes been suggested that recreation has an important role to play in the fringe (e.g. Countryside Review Committee 1977) and that it should be actively promoted. The rural fringe is optimally located with respect to urban demand for recreation: recreation is a means of deriving social benefit from land which may be underused; the provision of recreational facilities in the fringe may intercept recreational demand which might otherwise affect other more sensitive parts of the countryside and coast; and recreational land use is an effective buffer separating town and country, and shielding agricultural land from the negative urban effects.

Recently, however, some of the assumptions on which the planning of recreation in the rural-urban fringe is based have been questioned by Harrison (1981, 1983). In a study of part of the London Green Belt, she found that little recreational use is made by inner-city residents, and that rural-fringe sites and facilities do not intercept demand for other countryside recreation. If her conclusions also apply to smaller cities than London, then perhaps the policies of providing rural-fringe country parks and other facilities ought to be reviewed. Nevertheless, she did find that considerable *local* use was made of the rural fringe for purposes of recreation, and this local demand may be considerable, irrespective of the city-wide demand.

143

CONCLUSIONS

The rural-urban fringe is a zone of transition between town and country. Urban influences are strong and diverse: they may take the form of demands for recreation or for agricultural products, or they may be expressed more negatively in the fear or reality of urban encroachment and in a general climate of uncertainty on the part of land occupiers, and they may be manifested in broken-down fences, derelict farmland and general landscape decay. The precise nature of urban pressures, as well as their intensity, varies from place to place, and their symptoms are variable rather than consistent. Elson (1979) concludes that there *is* a distinct urban fringe problem, but that its manifestations in land use are not evenly spread around cities. Perhaps it might be added that they are not evenly spread around fringes of individual cities, far less around all cities. Perhaps there has been a tendency to concentrate too much on metropolitan and other large cities and to ignore smaller urban centres, and to think solely or primarily in terms of single models such as those of von Thünen and Sinclair.

As long ago as 1942, Wehrwein observed that one of the characteristics of the rural-urban fringe was that most of its land uses were in a state of flux. Because of this state, he argued, they could be subject to planning control and direction. In theory, planning systems and other mechanisms for controlling land use ought to be effective in such a zone, and indeed Golledge (1960) concluded that zoning could gradually destroy the distinctiveness of Sydney's rural-urban fringe by removing many of the characteristics of its land uses. However, few would contend that complete control has been established even in British rural-urban fringes where planning controls are relatively stringent. Perhaps the basic problem is that planning controls can prevent certain changes in land use from taking place, but they cannot force land owners to use their land efficiently or in a way which maintains landscape quality. Zoning, as such, cannot ensure full and efficient land use. For this and other reasons, a number of experimental projects have been established in the rural fringes of English cities such as London and Manchester, under the aegis of the Countryside Commission (e.g. Hall 1976). The aims of these projects are concurrently to improve informal recreation facilities; to improve landscape (or at least to prevent further deterioration); and to maintain where possible the viability of farming in the face of urban pressures. Whether such projects can be effective in the long term in the face of such pressures, and whether they can provide for fuller and more efficient land use, remain to be seen. Sometimes it seems that land in the peri-urban fringe is valued by many (if land prices are an accurate indicator of values), used by relatively few and managed by none, so that dereliction and decay are all too familiar. But perhaps these characteristics are inevitable in the no man's land between town and country.

FURTHER READING

Barlowe, R. (1978) *Land resource economics.*
Ely, R. T. and Wehrwein G. S. (1964) *Land economics.*
Both of these are standard works on land economics and deal with the relationship between location, land value and land use.

Numerous general texts on urban geography are available. One of the most readable is:
Carter, H. (1972) *The study of urban geography.*

For a full and compact discussion of rural land use on the peri-urban fringe (with a strong North American flavour), see:
Bryant, C. R., Russwurm, L. H. and McLellan, A. G. (1982) *The city's countryside.*

A detailed account of the London Green Belt, and its history, land-use characteristics and planning issues is given in:
Munton, R. J. M. (1983) *London's Green Belt : containment in practice.*

Land use and environment

This chapter is concerned with the effects of land use on the natural environment. The next chapter discusses environmental conservation and questions concerning the control or management of these effects.

Environmental effects of land use date back for millenia. For example, pre-agricultural hunters left their own imprint on the landscape of parts of England such as Dartmoor and the North York Moors. By using fire as a means of managing vegetation, they had an influence on the condition and distribution of deer and other hunted animals (Simmons 1975). The use of fire in certain settings caused irreversible change, with peat moors replacing the original woodlands. But although environmental impacts are old-established, their magnitude and perceived significance are probably far greater to-day than at any time in the past. This stems from a combination of a rapidly growing population seeking food, clothing and shelter; expanding cropland and urban areas; new demands such as re-creation, and new abilities to clear, drain and level land by mechanical means. Impacts of land use are reported from almost every country on earth; removal of forests and other forms of natural vegetation have been reported in recent years from countries as diverse as Iceland, Ethiopia and Nepal (Bjarnason 1978, Kuru 1978 and Bjonness 1980a).

Although present-day forest removal is merely the continuation of a process initiated thousands of years ago, its rate is now probably far greater than at any time in the past. The story of forest removal in the Near East, China, Western Europe and North America is outlined by Eckholm (1976). He estimates that the original forest area had by the mid-twentieth century been reduced by at least one-third and perhaps by one-half. Around 15 per cent of the world's closed forest area in 1963 had been removed by 1973 (USCEQ 1979). In some countries, the rate of loss has been much greater. The Ivory Coast had by the 1970s lost 70 per cent of the forest with which it began the century (Eckholm 1982).

The clearing of the forest is one of the most significant forms of environmental impact. On the global scale, the effects of deforestation extend to changes in the reflectivity of the earth's surface and to possible changes in the carbon dioxide balance, and hence to climate. On a more local scale, a major change in land cover usually causes changes in hydrology and rates of soil erosion. These changes often extend beyond the locality directly affected, and may give rise to downstream flooding and siltation. These effects of forest clearance arising from the growth of population in some Third World countries attract much attention at present, but there were nineteenth-century counterparts in areas such as the French Alps where the growth of population and agriculture led to severe erosion in some localities (Combes 1982).

Forest is usually replaced by rangeland or cropland. In turn, urbanisation may swallow up cropland, and with each change of land use, a new set of environmental impacts is unleashed. In the same way in which a change in land use has environmental effects, changes in management and cultivation practices can have their own significance. Changing cropping practices in parts of Europe and North America over the last two or three decades, for example, have given rise to much concern about their environmental consequences.

The nature of impacts varies according to the type of land use and

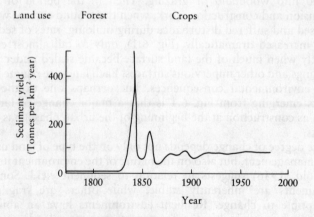

Fig. 6.1 Land use and sediment yield.
(a) Generalised history of erosion in the Frains Lake drainage basin (Michigan)

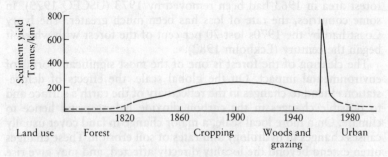

(b) Land use and sediment yield (mid-Atlantic region, USA)
Sources: (a) Davis (1976); (b) Wolman (1967).

land management. In general terms, man's use of land usually means a reduction in the diversity of plant and animal species and an increase in rates of soil erosion. Increased rates of erosion result from increased disturbance on the soil surface, and from the temporary (or in some cases semi-permanent) removal of vegetation. The magnitude of increase varies from area to area, depending on climate, soils and vegetation (Leopold 1956, Wolman 1967, and Davis 1976).

Figure 6.1 shows how different episodes in the land-use histories of parts of North America are associated with different rates of sediment yield. As cropping replaced the original forest cover from the early nineteenth century, sediment yield increased, only to fall again during the twentieth century when some of the cropland passed into woodland or grazing. Then in the period of urban expansion and construction work, when the ground surface was left exposed and suffered disturbance during building, rates of sediment yield increased dramatically (Fig. 6.1), only to fall almost equally quickly when much of the land surface became sealed under roads, buildings and other impervious surfaces. Each land-use regime has its own environmental consequences, but perhaps one of the main points emerging from Fig. 6.1 is that a major change of land use (such as construction at the beginning of the urban phase) has major effects.

The degree of change depends not only on the type of land use and land management, but also on the nature of the environment itself, as Leopold (1956) suggests in relation to sediment yield. Some environments are inherently stable, while others are fragile and susceptible to change. Resilient environments have an ability to revert to their original form after stress from a given land-use regime is discontinued (Hill 1975), while fragile environments have lesser abilities to do so. In general terms, mountain and arid environments are relatively fragile, and temperate humid lowlands are usually more resilient. In the former case, the steep slopes are readily eroded and stripped of their soil if the natural vegetation cover is breached, while the soils and vegetation of arid areas are vulnerable when stress from grazing or other land-use activities is superimposed on aridity. Humid lowlands, on the other hand, usually have greater powers of revegetation and recovery, but they are not immune from damage or change resulting from land use. Very few types of land use have a negligible effect on the environment, and when one type of use replaces another, the effects tend to be superimposed and cumulative. As certain types of natural environment and of land use are associated with severe forms of environmental damage, so also are certain types of land tenure within which land use is carried on. Few if any forms of land tenure preclude environmental effects, but some are associated with particularly severe forms. For example, leasehold tenure on state-owned grazing land in Australia was seen by Pick (1942) as a recipe for disaster: the leaseholder felt no personal responsibility for looking after the land well, and the state, or its officials, failed to insist on high standards of land management. It has also been argued that slavery under the plantation system contributed to the depletion of the soil in the American South (Genovese 1961). Reliance on a poor-quality labour force together with the whole structure of the plantation system meant that crop rotations could not easily be practised, and that soil depletion inevitably followed monoculture. On the other hand, certain groups, such as the Old Order Amish, have established reputations for good husbandry and for avoiding damage to the land which they cultivate.

AGRICULTURE

Agriculture is the biggest land use in terms of area, and at the global level it is the most significant land use in terms of environmental impact. Modern agricultural practices and techniques, backed by the application of machine power and the input of vast amounts of energy from fossil fuels, have transformed agricultural production, but at the cost of environmental consequences. These consequences are especially noticeable on cropland.

Cropland

Soil erosion and other soil effects

Soil erosion is probably the environmental effect which attracts the greatest attention. Soil erosion may be beneficial in certain circumstances, for example when it redistributes soil from unworkable slopes

149

to workable level ground, or when it removes the weathered, nutrient-depleted material from the soil surface in recent volcanic areas, thus exposing the more fertile, less weathered material below (Sanchez and Buol 1975). It is far more often detrimental, however, and it is undesirable from a number of viewpoints.

If soil is removed more quickly than it can form by weathering and related processes, then soil erosion means both a loss of nutrients required in plant growth, and a reduction in soil depth. On thin soils, especially, the loss of soil depth and hence a reduction in the thickness of the rooting zone can have serious adverse effects on plant growth. Soil erosion also leads to changes in river channels, and to sedimentation in rivers, lakes and reservoirs. These effects are described in a model suggested by Strahler (1958): when a drainage basin is devegetated, the channel network expands, resulting in increased erosion in much of the basin and sedimentation along the main channel.

One component of the cost of soil erosion is that arising from siltation in rivers and reservoirs. Estimates of as much as $500 million/annum have been made for dredging and other sedimentation costs (Pimentel and Pimentel 1980), and total costs may be as much as $1 billion/annum (Crosson and Brubaker 1982). The annual cost of soil erosion in the state of Iowa alone has been estimated at over $94 million (Heft 1977).

Rates of soil erosion are usually much higher on cropland than on grassland or forest because the soil surface is exposed for at least part of the year, during cultivation and the early stages of crop growth. Different crops have different characteristics in relation to soil erosion. Row crops are usually associated with higher rates of soil loss than other crops. In Ontario, erosion losses from crops grown in rotation with grasses or legumes were found to be about half of those resulting from continuous row cropping (van Vliet *et al.* 1976). Much depends on the nature of land management; on the type of cultivation, on whether the land is ploughed downslope or across slope, and on how much residue is left behind when the crop is harvested. Some examples of rates of soil loss under different crops and practices are given in Table 6.1.

The average annual rate of loss of topsoil from cropland may be as high as 30 tonnes/ha (Pimentel *et al.* 1976). These rates of soil loss are all far in excess of the rates of soil formation, for which estimates range from under one to under 4 tonnes/ha/year in the United States (Smith and Stamey 1965; Pimentel *et al.* 1976; Carter 1977). There is, therefore, a net soil loss of several tonnes per hectare per year over much of the area of cropland in America. In fact, a quantity of soil which takes 10 or more years to form may be lost in a single year of cropping. In other words, under these circumstances, soil is a wasting

Table 6.1 Annual soil loss from various crops in different regions

Crop	Location	Slope (%)	Soil Loss (tonnes/ha)	Year
Corn (continuous)	Missouri	3.68	49.5	1935
Corn (plough-disk-harrow)	Indiana		52.3	1967
Corn (contour)	Iowa	2–13	53.6	1974
Cotton	Georgia		51.1	1965
Wheat	Missouri	3.68	25.1	1935
Wheat pea rotation	Pacific NW		14.0	1961
Native grass	Kansas	5	0.8	1939
Forest	New Hampshire	20	0.3	1974

Source: Compiled from Pimentel (1976).

asset, and as the soil resource deteriorates, the usefulness of the land dwindles. It has been estimated that several million hectares of cropland have been completely ruined by soil erosion in the United States, and that one-third of the topsoil has been removed from the remaining cropland (Pimentel and Pimentel 1980). Productivity has been reduced over huge areas of land, and severe soil erosion has in places been a factor leading to the abandoning of cropland (e.g. Trimble 1983). Erosion at rates prevailing in the late 1970s is, it is estimated, likely to reduce potential corn and soy bean yields by 15–30 per cent over a 50-year period (Crosson and Brubaker 1982).

Some of the practical effects of soil loss may be masked by the use of artificial fertilisers to compensate for the nutrients lost in the soil. But while nutrients can be replaced in this way, there is no similar remedy for the loss of soil rooting depth. This loss is irretrievable, and permanent, at least on the human time scale.

In the humid parts of Europe and North America, the problem of soil erosion is usually less acute than in the continental interiors, because rainfall intensities are usually lower and less erosive. It is not absent, however, and changing farm practice in Britain during the 1960s and 1970s gave rise to some concern. Soil erosion on arable land was reported from a number of localities (Morgan 1980). In north Norfolk, for example, part of a 60-ha field suffered erosion estimated to result in a 3 per cent reduction in yield in spring barley and an 8 per cent reduction in winter wheat (Evans and Nortcliff 1978). It was concluded that enlargement of the field by the removal of field boundaries had been a contributory factor. Another factor was the low content of soil organic matter, which helps to maintain soil aggregates and so reduce soil erosion. Continuous arable cultivation results in a reduction in the organic matter content (e.g. Skidmore *et al.* 1975), and so may increase the susceptibility of soil to erosion. Most reports of soil erosion on arable land in Britain have implicated structural damage or downslope cultivation as initial causal factors (Trudgill and Briggs 1980).

While soil erosion has not yet been recognised as a major or widespread problem in England, continuous cropping combined with the use of heavy machinery during cultivation led to other problems of soil structure during the 1960s (especially in silty and clay soils), and soil degradation resulting from cultivation has since been reported from several other European countries (e.g. Boels *et al.* 1982).

Similarly, soil structure and fertility were found to be impaired by continuous potato growing in New Brunswick and Maine. Yields declined, partly as a result of the removal of stones which hampered the use of harvesting machinery. With the removal of stones, soil temperature and moisture were also reduced (Saini and Grant 1980). Cultivation-induced changes in agricultural soils have also been reported from Quebec (Martel and Mackenzie 1980). Organic matter was found to be 33 per cent lower on soils on dairy farms where a rotation of one year cereals and four years hay is practised than on virgin forest soils, and 60 per cent lower on farms with continuous corn cropping. With a change from the dairy-farm rotation to continuous cropping, structural stability and soil productivity both declined, even though nutrient levels were raised by fertilisers.

Some soils have stable structures and are little affected by cultivation, even when heavy tractors are used, but others such as fine sandy clays and silts are easily damaged, and the damage once initiated may be difficult to rectify (Greenland 1977). In other words, the effects of land-use practices vary according to the nature of the local soil conditions.

Fertilisers

Loss of soil or damage to the soil resource is usually readily perceived, since soil is basic to the whole agricultural system. Other consequences of cropping are often equally real, but may be more difficult to assess or identify since they do not affect agriculture directly. During the decades since the Second World War, the use of fertilisers and farm chemicals has grown enormously. In Britain, applications of potassium and phosphates more than doubled in the first two post-war decades, and then began to level off. Applications of nitrogen, on the other hand, continued to rise, and by the late 1970s had increased by more than ten-fold compared with immediate post-war levels. Nitrogen fertilisers are used on both temporary and permanent grassland as well as on cropland. Some fertiliser may find its way into watercourses or into groundwater, and there is evidence that nitrate levels in both rivers and groundwater have increased as a result of increased use of nitrogenous fertilisers. Fears have been expressed that health hazards may result from nitrates in drinking water, but the Royal Commission on Environmental Pollution (1979), in a study of fertilisers and other possible forms of agricultural pollution, concluded that anxiety was not justified by the information then available. However, even if no health hazard results, the effects of increased nutrient levels in water bodies may be both significant and undesirable in other ways. When nitrogen and phosphorus are added, water bodies undergo eutrophication or nutrient enrichment. Phytoplankton and other aquatic plants become more abundant, and when the increased mass of organic matter decomposes, the dissolved oxygen content of the water may be depleted. Under anaerobic conditions, foul odours are generated, fish populations are adversely affected, and the aesthetic quality and recreational value of water bodies are reduced. The Great Lakes (and especially Lake Erie) are the most celebrated example of eutrophication, but the process is by no means confined to very large bodies of water such as these. Small lakes in agricultural areas may well be seriously affected. In Loch Leven in eastern Scotland, for example, the build-up of nitrate levels during the 1960s correlated with the growth in the use of fertilisers in the catchment, and as much as 85 per cent of the nitrogen input was estimated to come from agricultural sources (Holden 1976). On the broader scale, an extensive survey of nearly 500 catchments (watersheds) in the eastern part of the United States during the early 1970s revealed a clear tendency for nutrient loadings in streams to be much higher in agricultural areas than in forested catchments (Omernik 1976). Mean nitrogen, concentrations were five times higher in the agricultural catchments, and phosphorus concentrations were almost 10 times higher.

Farm chemicals

In the post-war period, the growth in use of artificial fertilisers has been paralleled by a great increase in the use of chemicals to control pests and weeds. Collectively referred to as pesticides, these chemicals include herbicides, insecticides and fungicides. Almost the entire cereal area of the United Kingdom is now treated with pesticides, and 44 per cent of the cereal crop is treated more than three times during its growth (Royal Commission on Environmental Pollution 1979). In the United States, over 90 per cent of the acreage of corn, cotton and soy beans is treated, and about half of the wheat crop (Eichers *et al.* 1978). The use of pesticides plays a vital role in the control of weeds and pests, and together with the use of fertilisers, it has made possible a relaxing of the traditional systems of crop rotations previously required to maintain the fertility of the soil and to keep weeds and pests at bay. Pesticides play a vital role in modern intensive agriculture. Without their use, it has been estimated, the cereal crop would fall by 24 per cent during the first year, and by as much as 45 per cent in the third year (Royal Commission on Environmental Pollution 1979). If pesticides were not used in American agriculture, the value of crops lost could amount to as much as $8,700 million per annum (Pimentel *et al.* 1980).

Vital as pesticides may be in modern farming systems, they are the focus of much controversy and concern. Drift from aerial spraying may affect areas adjacent to the crops being treated, and there may be a tendency on the part of some farmers to make excessive applications in order to satisfy themselves that the pest (or potential pest) will be effectively controlled. Much of the criticism of pesticides and their agricultural use has been directed at the chlorinated hydrocarbons such as DDT. These insecticides are toxic to a wide range of insects, and so affect other insects as well as the target species. They are also extremely persistent, and tend to become concentrated in the higher parts of food chains. High concentrations built up in birds of prey in particular, and it was discovered that decreases in the populations of a number of predatory species of bird in Britain during the 1950s and 1960s were due to declining breeding performance through the thinning of eggshells as a result of pesticide residues (Ratcliffe 1967, 1970). The use of organochlorides in agriculture in Britain and North America is now more strictly controlled than it was during the early post-war decades, but such is the persistence of some of the residues that they are still present in many bird populations.

Although attempts have been made to deal with the problems arising from DDT and other early pesticides, the use of farm chemicals still gives cause for some concern. Some insect pests develop resistance, and increasing doses and new types of chemicals are required to achieve pest control. Although many modern pesticides affect a narrower range of species than the earlier ones, they may still be toxic to insect predators on the pest species as well as to the pest itself. With the loss of natural predators, the scale of pest outbreaks may increase, and the farmer may find himself on a treadmill, having to apply greater and greater quantities of pesticide in order to achieve control. Side effects on harmless species and on neighbouring areas result increasingly. Although many of the side effects of pesticides are impossible to quantify or to evaluate accurately, their annual cost in the United States has been estimated at a minimum of $839 million per annum (including $135 million for honey-bee poisoning and reduced pollination), and it may in fact be several times higher (Pimentel *et al.* 1980).

If the use of chemicals becomes impractical or even illegal as controls are imposed, new decisions may have to be made about land use as well as about land management. For example, the banning in 1972 of a poison used in Wyoming to control predation on sheep by coyotes meant that sheep farming was perceived to be no longer viable in some areas. Many sheep ranchers switched to cattle, and sheep farming shifted away from areas of high predation (Magleby and Gadsby 1979). Similarly, the banning of DDT in the same year created major problems for cotton producers in those areas of the American South where DDT still provided control over a broad spectrum of crops (Manners 1979).

Farm wastes

In many parts of Europe and North America, the production of crops and livestock was traditionally combined and integrated on the same farm. Animal feed was grown on the farm, and animal waste was returned to the land as farmyard manure. More recently, the trend has been for farms to specialise in a small number of enterprises so that economies of scale can be enjoyed. Many farms concentrate on either crops or livestock, and even if they do maintain both types of enterprise, the modes of animal production are often intensive, with the animals confined in buildings or feedlots. Large numbers of animals are accommodated in small areas, and problems of waste disposal arise. The production of animal waste is on a huge scale: it has been estimated that farm animals in the United States produce 10 times as much waste as the human population. Their pollution load is five times greater than that of the human population in the United States (Loehr 1970), and nearly three times larger in Britain (Royal Commission on Environmental Pollution 1979). A farmer with 250,000 chickens has a waste disposal problem equivalent to a city with 35,000 inhabitants (Alexander 1973).

Animal waste contains valuable plant nutrients, but the scale of production and its concentration in small areas, along with the nature of farming systems, means that this useful source of nutrients cannot always be used on the farm on which it is produced. Problems arise when waste material enters water courses, whether by leakages in slurry tanks, from surface drainage of feedlots, or from surface drainage from saturated or frozen land. When organic matter decomposes in the water courses, oxygen is taken up to the detriment of aquatic life. Nutrients such as nitrogen and phosphorus are added to the water, increasing the nutrient load and adding to the problems arising from artificial fertilisers. Many intensive livestock units are located near their markets in urban areas, and the smells generated by wastes and their disposal may be perceived as highly offensive. Work in Denmark has shown that if slurry is injected rather than just spread on the ground surface, run off is minimised, odours are greatly reduced and better yields are obtained (Dam Kofoed 1981), but injection is substantially more expensive than surface application. Grazing land on which slurry has been spread must remain unused for a number of weeks so that problems of disease transmission are minimised, and there is some danger of build-ups of concentration of metals (such as copper used as an additive to pig-feed, for example) to dangerous or undesirable levels in the soil.

Drainage

Drainage is an old-established technique of land improvement, and it dates back for at least 2000 years. It was not used extensively, however, until the nineteenth century, and its use has greatly increased during the last few decades when mechanical means of digging drains and ditches could be easily and cheaply employed, often with the encouragement of financial assistance by government. The annual area in which field drains were installed in England and Wales increased five-fold between 1950 and 1970 (Green 1976). On the North American prairies, numerous small marshy depressions or potholes have been drained, with the loss of habitats for waterfowl. Between 1936 and 1963, around 0.6 million ha of land was drained in the states of Minnesota and North and South Dakota alone (National Academy of Sciences 1970; Rounds 1981).

Drainage of agricultural land has a wide range of environmental impacts, as discussed by Hill (1976) and illustrated in Fig. 6.2.

These impacts affect soil properties such as structure and aeration, and may thus improve the land for purposes of crop growth, but other effects extend to stream discharge and water chemistry, and hence to neighbouring rivers and lakes.

Many areas of marsh or bog that previously defied drainage have now been tackled with the assistance of mechanical diggers. Many of these areas of wetland supported diverse communities of vegetation and wildlife, which were not present on the surrounding farmland. With the drainage of many of these wetlands, their distinctive habitats have been lost, and local ecological diversity has been reduced. This illustrates the general conclusion reached by Hill, namely that the greatest effects of land drainage result from schemes for the initial drainage of previously non-agricultural land, especially if carried out on a large scale. Thereafter, further improvements to existing drainage systems are likely to have lesser effects, with perhaps only minor impacts on local hydrology and water chemistry.

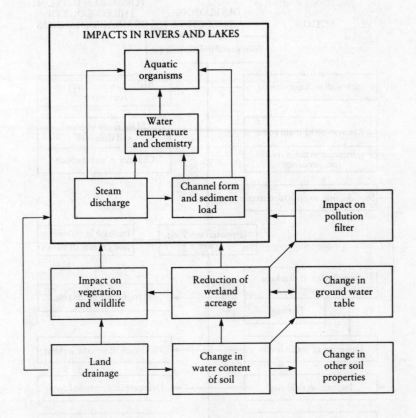

Fig. 6.2. Environmental impacts of agricultural land drainage.
Source: Hill (1976).

On the other hand, some drainage schemes are progressive, and instead of previously unused wetland being converted to arable land in one operation, there may be a sequence extending over several decades or even centuries. The drainage of the Monmouth Levels along the English-Welsh border has been described by Scotter *et al.* (1977). Although the beginnings of the drainage system date back to Roman times, major improvements date from the mid-1950s, when mechanical excavation began to be used to dredge and extend the reems or drainage channels, and herbicides were used to control vegetation on the channel banks. Arterial drainage is supplemented by underdrainage, and agriculture has developed. More intensive stocking became possible, and later arable farming was initiated. With each step of improvement in drainage, new types of effects on the ecology of the drainage channels resulted (Fig. 6.3).

157

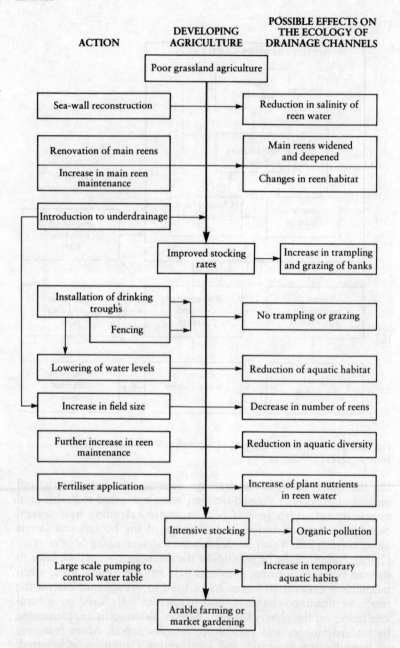

Fig. 6.3 Interactions between agriculture and the drainage system.
Source: Scotter *et al.* (1977).

The loss of diversity and the loss of habitats

Several forms of agricultural impact on the environment operate in the same direction, namely towards a loss of ecological diversity. The enlargement of fields by the removal of hedges and other boundaries, the drainage of wetlands, and the use of pesticides all tend to reduce diversity by eliminating habitats and species. At least 53 per cent of the Dutch flora have undergone a net loss in range during this century, and agricultural developments are believed to be responsible for a large proportion of these losses (van der Weijden *et al.* 1978). In Britain, four plant species have become extinct during the present century because of land drainage, and a further five have become very rare (Perring 1970).

Impacts may extend beyond plants to insects and animals. For example, the larva of the common blue butterfly (*Polyommatus icarus*) feeds on bird's foot trefoil (*Lotus corniculatus*). This plant disappears when pasture is ploughed or treated with herbicide, and with it disappears the butterfly (NCC 1977). Several other butterfly species have also shown a decline in population over the last few decades, as a result of agricultural changes (NCC 1984), as have also, for example, some species of dragonflies which have suffered from improvements of drainage for agricultural and other purposes. These are but a few examples of the changes arising from the changing nature of farming in many parts of the western world. As new agricultural techniques are employed and as farms are modernised, ecological effects result, and these frequently take the form of a loss of species or habitats.

Table 6.2 illustrates the contrast between numbers of species on modern and unmodernised farms in lowland England. With drainage, pasture treatments and new forms of field boundaries (usually around greatly enlarged fields), numbers of species of animals, birds and insects decline markedly (see, for example, Arnold 1983). While the modernised farm may be more efficient as an agricultural unit, its flora and fauna are greatly impoverished, and are increasingly so as the agricultural ecosystem is progressively manipulated.

Much concern has been focused in recent years on the rate of loss of certain semi-natural habitats in Britain as a result of agricultural development and other land-use change. An extreme case is the 31 per cent decrease in the area of lowland grasslands on chalk and limestone in England between 1967 and 1972, mainly by conversion to arable or improved grassland (NCC 1984). The loss of East Anglian fenland has been equally startling, with only 10 per cent of the area of fenland in 1934 surviving in that form in 1984 (NCC 1984). Munton (1983b) presents a useful tabulation of habitat loss

Table 6.2 Approximate number of species occurring in equivalent habitats in unmodernised and modern farms

Groups of animals	Unmodernised farms		Modern farms	
	Habitat	Number of species	Habitat	Number of species
	(a) Hedges* and semi-natural grass verges		(a) Wire fences with (i) sown grass (ii) semi-natural grass verges	
Mammals		20		(i) 5 (ii) 6
Birds		37		(i) 6 (ii) 9
Lepidoptera (butterflies only)		17		(i) 0 (ii) 8
	(b) Permanent pasture* (untreated)		(b) Grass leys†	
Lepidoptera (butterflies only)		20		0
	(c) Permanent ponds and ditches		(c) Temporary ditches and piped water	
Mammals (aquatic)		2		0
Amphibia		5		2
Fish		9		0
Odonata (dragonflies)		11		0
Mollusca (gastropods only)		25		

Source: Based on Nature Conservancy Council (1977).
* Includes hedgerow trees
† Includes grasslands on chalk

in Britain, compiled from a wide range of sources: he shows, for example, that ancient woodland in Britain decreased by between 30 and 50 per cent between 1947 and 1981. This loss resulted from the conversion of ancient woodland to farmland and from its replacement by commercial coniferous plantations.

Most of the habitats in question were semi-natural rather than natural: most of them had been created or modified by earlier land-use activities. Nevertheless, their loss is regretted because they were more natural than the habitats that replaced them, and their destruction meant the complete loss of some species from some areas. A feature of the loss of habitats is that strong regional dimensions are often involved, and some of the most distinctive features of local landscapes may disappear as land-use changes are introduced or changes in practices of land management are implemented.

Landscape effects

The effects of modern agriculture on the physical environment are reflected in the appearance of the landscape. As the nature of agriculture changes, the agricultural landscape is modified. New types of farm buildings appear, fields are enlarged so that combine harvesters and other machinery can be used more easily and efficiently; old field boundaries such as hedges are replaced by wire fences; and small marshes are drained and merged into the surrounding cropland. In landscapes such as those of lowland England, the patchwork of small fields enclosed by hedges has recently given way in places to more open, expansive landscapes better suited to modern cereal growing. Such changes are readily understandable. The new landscapes are functional, if less quaint and picturesque than formerly, and are related to modern types of farming in the same way that the older landscapes were related to contemporary farming practice. But the loss of ecological diversity following improvements such as drainage is paralleled by a tendency for the landscape to become less varied and rather more uniform and monotonous.

These landscape changes are apparent to many more people than are changes of a purely ecological nature, and much controversy has been engendered (Shoard 1980). In England, landscape change has a distinct spatial pattern, and has been much greater in the cereal-growing districts of the east than in the pastoral country of the west (Westmacott and Worthington 1974). In some districts, more than half of the hedges existing at the end of the Second World War had disappeared by 1970. In the mainly arable country of Huntingdonshire in eastern England, the number of mature or semi-mature trees per 40 ha fell from over 50 to under 5 between

1945 and 1983. In the more pastoral county of Herefordshire to the west, on the other hand, there had been a much smaller reduction from around 50 to about 30 per 40 ha (Westmacott and Worthington 1984).

A number of initiatives has been taken in response to disappearing hedgerows and trees; for example, the Countryside Commission offers grant aid for the planting of small woodlands for amenity purposes. However, the subject of landscape change and agriculture poses great problems for the philosophy of conservation as well as for its practice; these problems are discussed in Chapter 7.

Rangeland

On rangeland, the degree of environmental impact is usually lower than on arable land. Natural or semi-natural vegetation is grazed extensively by cattle, sheep or other animals, and inputs of capital and labour are small in comparison with those on cropping farms or intensive livestock units. Yet this does not mean that the environmental effects of land use are negligible. In some instances they are clearly marked, and have led to a distinct deterioration of the land for grazing or for other purposes.

Huge tracts of grassland in the semi-arid or sub-humid areas of the New World were brought into grazing use by European settlers in the nineteenth century. Fire was widely used in the management of the pastures to remove old growth and to promote the growth of younger and more palatable material. Repeated burning combined with grazing affected not only the vegetation, but also reduced or removed the litter layer of plant debris on the soil surface. This in turn affected the rates of infiltration of rainfall into the soil, and when vegetation cover became more open because of fire or over-grazing, then rates of soil erosion were further increased. In short, management for extensive grazing often led to a deterioration in the environment. Deterioration is reported from areas as diverse as South Africa (Christopher 1976b), Patagonia (Rey Balmaceda 1967) and New Zealand (O'Connor and Kerr 1978), as well as from the western part of the United States. In Colorado, an increase in erosion rates from 0.2 – 0.5 mm/annum of soil over the previous 300 years to 1.8 mm/ annum over the last 100 years has been attributed to the introduction of cattle (Carrara and Carroll 1979). In the South Island of New Zealand, excessive use of fire and overgrazing led to signs of deterioration within about 20 years of initial occupation in the mid-nineteenth century, and within 50 years the carrying capacity of some rangeland had fallen to one-third of its initial level (O'Connor 1980). It has been estimated that range productivity in the western United States had probably fallen by about 50 per cent by 1930 (Hadley 1977).

In more recent decades, erosion-control practices have been adopted and livestock numbers reduced in many areas. These changes in land use are thought to have been responsible for the 50 per cent reduction in suspended sediment loads in the Colorado River at the Grand Canyon during the period from 1942 to 1960 as compared with the preceding period from 1926 to 1941 (Hadley 1974). Nevertheless, much of the American range remains in a deteriorated condition (Vale 1979), and recovery is slow and incomplete. Most rangeland is in semi-arid areas and, even under natural conditions, it suffers moisture stress. When land-use stress in the form of fire and grazing is superimposed, the effects are severe and long-lasting, even although the intensity of land use is light.

It is not only in the New World and in areas settled by Europeans in the nineteenth century that deterioration of rangeland has occurred. In much of Africa and in parts of Asia, deterioration is proceeding apace at present (Barney 1980). Overgrazing results from both growth in population, with an accompanying growth in numbers of livestock, and from a wish to maintain as many livestock as possible as a sign of wealth. Rangeland in the Old World is often a common-property resource: the individual sees it in his interests to increase his flocks or herds, and the form of tenure fails to impose effective constraints. The result is that animal numbers exceed the carrying capacity of the land; eventually there is a loss of palatable species and of vegetation cover, and an increase in soil erosion. In severe cases, deterioration leads inexorably to desertification.

In Western Europe, conditions are usually less conducive to severe deterioration. There is usually less stress from aridity, and systems of land tenure are different from those in the New World or Africa. Nevertheless, there is a well established belief that extensive grazing of sheep on moorlands in Scotland, for example, has led to some deterioration in the quality of the grazings. The extent of this deterioration is certainly much less than in many semi-arid areas and disagreement exists as to its reality (Mather 1978c). If deterioration has occurred, it lends support to the suggestion of Darling (1956) that extensive grazing on rangeland or rough pasture *inevitably* causes a progressive deterioration of the habitat.

FORESTRY

Environmental consequences stem both from changes in land use involving forestry and from forestry management practices. While the large-scale effects of deforestation on the global climate remain rather speculative, the more local effects on streamflow and nutrient budgets have been more conclusively investigated, and both the removal and re-establishment of forest cover have significant consequences. Furthermore, the various operations involved in extracting timber and in preparing ground for planting may have noticeable effects.

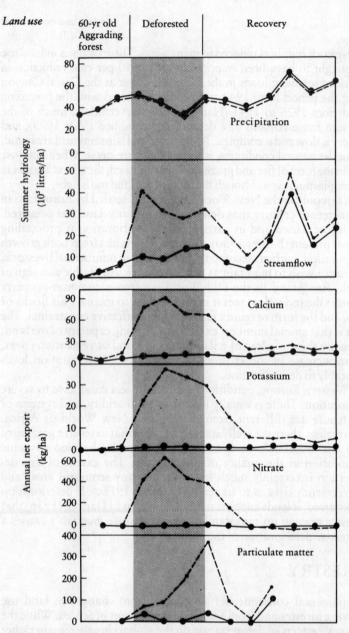

Fig. 6.4 Effects of deforestation on hydrology and biogeochemistry in an experimentally deforested northern hardwood ecosystem (open circles and dashed lines deforested ecosystem: solid circles and lines refer to forested ecosystem).

Source: Based on Likens *et al.* (1978).

164

The removal of forest

At this step, a natural ecosystem is replaced by a semi-natural or artificial one. Different forests have different ecological characteristics; for example, in the tropical forest ecosystem the bulk of the nutrients is in the vegetation rather than in the soil, and so when the forest is removed, there is a major loss of nutrients. In temperate humid forests, a greater proportion of the nutrients in the ecosystem is stored in the soil, and so the removal of the forest causes a correspondingly smaller direct loss. One of the most detailed investigations of nutrient budgets in forest ecosystems, and of the effects of deforestation, has been carried out over many years at the Hubbard Brook catchment in New England (Borman *et al.* 1974; Likens *et al.* 1978). An experiment was designed to measure the impact of removal of hardwood forest on runoff and water quality, and to establish the rate at which recovery proceeded. A control area of undisturbed forest was used for comparison. The study watershed was kept bare of vegetation for three years by the use of herbicides, so that the effects of uptake of nutrients by re-establishing vegetation would not complicate the budgets. The effects on the hydrology and on dissolved substances and nutrients lost from the deforested area are summarised in Fig. 6.4.

With the removal of the forest and hence a great reduction in transpiration, streamflow increased several-fold, as did the annual loss of particulate material and dissolved nutrients such as calcium and potassium. Loss of particulates increased by a factor of about 15 in the first three years. Minor increases in the first two years rose sharply in the third year as the breakdown of the humus layer of the forest soil increased its erodibility. Concentrations of dissolved substances in the drainage water increased because organic matter on the forest floor decomposed more quickly into its inorganic constituents in the absence of the forest, and there was also an absence of uptake of nutrients by vegetation. Clear differences in the loss of nutrients and particulate material and in streamflow persisted for several years after vegetation was allowed to regrow. Over a period of 10 years after deforestation, streamwater nutrient losses were more than 10 times higher for nitrate nitrogen in the deforested watershed than in the control area, and corresponding ratios were over three for calcium and about eight for potassium. Large proportions of the major nutrients previously stored in the ecosystem were lost. Several decades would be required for a full recovery from these nutrient losses to be achieved by weathering processes and inputs by precipitation. In the Hubbard Brook case, nutrient losses were perhaps unusually high because of the use of herbicides to suppress regrowth of vegetation. Examples of nitrate losses from forests subject to a variety of commercial harvesting treatments are quoted by Vitousek *et al.* (1979). Although lower than those in the Hubbard Brook experiment, they are all several times higher than in undisturbed control areas.

In the Hubbard Brook experiment, the felled trees were left *in situ*, and the ground was undisturbed. In commercially clear-cut forests, there would be greater nutrient losses through removals of timber, and greater losses of soil because of disturbance by road building and timber extraction. The Hubbard Brook study is valuable both in showing the nature and magnitude of effects following deforestation, and in producing results useful for the management of forests in similar settings. Clear cutting would be acceptable if carried out in rotations which allowed sufficient time for natural regenerative processes to run their course. Likens *et al.* (1978) concluded that the management of the timber harvest in the area on a 110–120 year rotation was compatible with these processes. Shorter rotations would result in progressive depletion of nutrients. They also suggested from their study that cutting should be limited to sites such as relatively fertile soils on modest slopes. It was shown on the deforested catchment (watershed) that most of the soil on some steeply sloping and rocky areas was lost by erosion, and so it was concluded that clear cutting on steep slopes and thin soils could lead to a long-term reduction in biological productivity. It was also concluded that a strip of uncut trees should be left along stream channels to give protection to the banks; that harvesting and extraction should be carried out with minimum disturbance and that roads and skid trails should be confined to a minimum. Another recommendation was that clear cuts should be kept small so that seed sources would be available for rapid revegetation, and that species with little timber value (such as pin cherry and elderberry) should be left as they play important roles in the recovery process by storing nutrients and reducing erosion. By implication, these conclusions and recommendations indicate the ways in which maximum damage can result from deforestation. Likens and his colleagues also drew attention to downstream effects which might be felt beyond the forest. Some eutrophication of rivers and lake may occur from the increased nutrient loadings, and the acidity of the drainage water may increase as organic material on the former forest floor decomposes. Clear cutting is unlikely to be the only cause of increased acidity (others may include emissions from power stations and other sources, and increased acidity of precipitation), but high acidity is toxic to many invertebrates and fish.

Unfortunately, the lessons from the Hubbard Brook study are not always heeded, and numerous instances of greatly increased streamflow and sedimentation following deforestation or logging have been reported from many parts of the world. Initial operations in native forests seem to have especially marked effects. In South Island, New Zealand, for example, a study of soil depths on steeply sloping mudstones clothed in virgin beech-podocarp forest showed that in areas logged two or three years previously, soil depths were 20 cm or less in 56 per cent of the sample sites, while in undisturbed forest they were 20 cm or less in only 33 per cent of observations. These differences in soil depths were attributed to disturbance from log extraction (Laffan 1979), and such indications of soil loss give rise to concern about the long-term well-being of the soil resource in such areas. In addition, the downstream effects may also be adverse. In the coastal waters of Marlborough Sound in New Zealand, increased sedimentation as a result of logging on nearby slopes affected marine life and fisheries (Johnston *et al.* 1981).

The amount of soil loss depends on a number of factors, including form of management and techniques of timber extraction. In a review of soil erosion from forest land in the eastern United States, Patric (1976) concluded that forest land *can* be managed with little or no increase in soil erosion, but on the other hand some types of management caused great increases in erosion rates. In sub-Arctic Canada, Aldrich and Slaughter (1983) found that while complete stripping of the vegetation in a forest increased rainfall erosion 16 times compared with the undisturbed forest, the removal of trees without disturbing the ground cover caused no significant increase. Similarly, a study of logging effects in broadleaf forest in Quebec showed that where logs were skidded across streams, sediment concentrations remained above 1000 mg/litre for the next four months, with peak values of 197,000 mg/litre. Where a buffer zone of standing trees and undisturbed soil was left along the streams, concentrations generally remained below 35 mg/litre, with a maximum value of 960 mg/litre (Plamoudou 1982). In a study set in the forests of Idaho, Megahan and Kidd (1972) found that logging operations alone, excluding roading, increased sediment production by a factor of about 0.6 over the 'natural' sedimentation rate. Roads associated with some logging systems increased sediment production by an average of about 750 times that of the 'natural' rate for the six-year period following construction.

Much of the sediment produced on deforestation or logging is derived from a few small source areas. McCashion and Rice (1981) concluded that about 40 per cent of the soil erosion in a 12,000 ha area of commercial timberland in north-west California was derived from the road system alone, and that of the erosion along the roads, 24 per cent could have been avoided if conventional engineering methods had been employed. Methods of erosion control on forest roads are well known but too often are not applied (Patric 1980).

The amount of soil disturbance varies greatly with the method of timber extraction, as well as with environmental factors such as slope. In a review of the comparative effects of different timber extraction methods on steepland in the Pacific Northwest, Swanston and Dyrness (1973) found that with the use of tractors for extraction, 35 per cent of the ground surface was bare soil and that 26 per cent of the area suffered soil compaction, whereas when extraction was by skyline (cables from which logs were suspended) the corresponding percentages were 12 and 3.

The magnitude of erosion effects appears therefore to depend on the actual techniques of management, in the forest as on the farm. Clear felling is likely to have greater effects than selective logging, and whole-tree harvesting is likely to have a greater effect on nutrient budgets than where 'slash' is left on site and its nutrients returned to the soil after burning.

Accelerated loss of soil is not, however, the only adverse effect of timber harvesting. Less obvious repercussions in water quality may also result from forest operations. A decline in water quality around Perth in Western Australia has been attributed to clear felling and the resulting redistribution of soluble salts (Conacher 1979). Of more direct and immediate concern to forest managers is the substantial reduction in timber growth that may result from the soil compaction caused by logging equipment and the skidding of logs. Froehlich (1979) reports a reduction of 12 per cent over a period of 16 years in the growth of Ponderosa pine on compacted soils on tractor skid trails, while according to Wert and Thomas (1981), the stand volume of Douglas fir on skid trails formed 32 years previously was only 34.1 m^3/ha compared with 128.9 m^3/ha on undisturbed control sites. While the amount of soil disturbance depends on the method of logging, the other key variable is slope angle (e.g. Bockheim *et al.* 1975). For a given logging method, disturbance increases rapidly with gradient – a specific example of how the effects of land use depend on the environmental setting as well as on the type of land use and land management.

Loss of soil and loss of timber growth are two consequences of deforestation or logging. A third effect, whose significance is perhaps less immediately obvious but which may be of the utmost importance in the long term, is the loss of species diversity. As virgin forest is removed, certain species are lost from the locality and some may be lost completely. Some tree species may be affected, but many more species of other plants, animals and invertebrates are at risk as their habitats are destroyed or modified. The number of tall tree species at risk is fairly small, but as many as 20,000–30,000 plant species (10 per cent of the flora) are estimated to be at risk of extinction, and each disappearing plant may take 10–30 other species with it (Green 1981).

Several parallels exist between forest removal and agriculture, and certain adverse effects are common to both land uses: accelerated soil loss, a potential reduction in the long-term usefulness of the land, and the loss of species diversity. In both land uses, careless or ill-considered management may heighten the adverse effects.

Afforestation

Forests are usually regarded as an ecologically 'sound' land use, and it might thus be expected that afforestation would generally be welcomed for its beneficial effects on the environment. Recent experience with afforestation, however, in Britain and some other countries suggests that afforestation can give rise to certain environmental disadvantages as well as advantages.

One consequence of the creation or restoration of forest on moorland or other open land is that stream flow is reduced. This was initially suggested by Law (1956) working on a small experimental catchment in West Yorkshire, and has since been corroborated (see Courtney 1981). The extent of loss of streamflow from a forest catchment in the west of Britain is of the order of one-fifth. Trees intercept rainfall, and the water which otherwise might have entered streamflow is lost by evaporation. This effect varies according to tree species. When deciduous hardwood was replaced by white pine in two experimental watersheds in the Appalachians, streamflow was reduced by about 20 per cent (Swank and Douglass 1974).

Recently the hydrological effects of coniferous forests have become a controversial issue in parts of Britain, where water from upland catchment is used for public supply, and in Scotland for generating hydroelectricity (Calder and Newson 1979, 1980). The value of water 'lost' through afforestation has to be set against the economic benefits of afforestation. The North of Scotland Hydroelectricity Board has calculated that the loss of revenue from the sale of electricity, which would result if extensive afforestation were to be carried out in the Scottish Highlands, would amount to £7–8 million annually (House of Lords, 1979–80). The preparation of land for afforestation also has its environmental consequences, such as accelerated soil erosion. Ditching and ploughing of hill land has been found in experimental catchments in North Wales and the north of England to lead to huge increases in both suspended sediment and total sediment yields. In some catchments, ditching led to increases of two orders of magnitude in sediment concentrations (Clarke and McCulloch 1979). Substantial changes in the supply of sediment are believed to continue after the ditches mature and undergo revegetation (Painter *et al.* 1974). The long-term effect, it has been estimated, is one of quadrupled sediment yields (Robinson and Blyth 1982). A resurgence in rates of sediment yield occurs once more during harvesting at the end of one rotation and replanting at the beginning of the next.

The effects of increased sediment yield can have various ramifications; for example, the scouring of stream beds and the redistribution of sediment can have damaging effects on the spawning beds of salmonid fish (Smith 1980). Some young forests in infertile moorlands are treated with fertilisers, and large quantities are washed from the land during the first year after application (Harriman 1978). In a setting of generally low nutrient levels, leaching of nutrients from fertilisers is unlikely to be detrimental to fish stocks, and in some situations could even increase stream productivity and so be beneficial. But the leaching of large quantities of nutrients into enclosed bodies of water could have undesirable effects, such as those outlined on page 153.

Afforestation has various other ecological effects on ground vegetation and on bird life. Under crops of spruce and fir, which generate heavy shade, vascular plants are almost completely eliminated at an early stage of tree growth, and they do not appear in quantity before clear felling, at least under the relatively short planting-felling rotations practised in Britain. Under the lighter canopies of pine and larch, a larger flora persists and there may be almost complete plant cover during the later stages of the rotation (Hill 1978). Bird life changes both in type and in quantity. Species of open moorland are replaced by those of woodland, and total songbird densities may be from four to six times greater in thinned plantations than on the open moor (Moss 1978). There may be distinct differences in fauna between plantations and native forests. In a study of *Pinus radiata* plantations and native eucalypt forests in Victoria, Friend (1982) found that species richness was lower and the proportion of introduced species was higher in the plantations, but the contrast was smaller around the edges of plantations alongside native forest, and where there was a mosaic of pine stands of various ages. The design of the plantations can therefore have a great effect on the fauna.

One of the basic questions about afforestation as it is carried out in Britain, Ireland and some other European countries is its long-term effects on soil and its fertility. Thirty years ago, Rennie (1955) concluded from work on Yorkshire moorlands that commercial forestry would cause soil degradation and a loss of productivity, but he did not include in his nutrient budgets inputs from weathering and precipitation, nor did he consider the possible effects of fertilisers. The problem of 'ecological sustention' was thoroughly reviewed by the House of Lords Select Committee on the scientific aspects of forestry (1979–80). The conclusion was uncertain. Most plantations are on sites that have never had a regular tree crop harvested from them, although they may have carried forest in the distant past. The full effects of production forestry on the soil and on future (or even second rotation) production are as yet unknown. Many of the soils in areas of afforestation in upland Britain are affected by waterlogging, and tree crops may remove or alleviate this problem and improve aeration (Pyatt and Craven 1978), but less is known about soil-chemical effects. Uncertainty is heightened by the variety of methods of ground treatment and harvesting. The problem is also complicated by the fact that different species of trees have different effects on the soil. The coniferous species (such as pine and spruce) that are most used in Britain are believed to make soils more acid. The reputation of birch as an improver of moorland and heathland soils has recently been confirmed by Miles and Young (1980), but the species is not at present used in commercial plantations in Britain. Unfortunately, definite research results on the pedological effects of plantation forestry will not be available for about 15 years (House of Lords 1979–80), though afforestation has proceeded apace in recent decades. Whether tree growth will be better or poorer in the second rotation is as yet unknown, although there are some instances of declining growth after the first rotation, for example in Radiata pine plantations in South Australia (Keeves 1966; Boardman 1978). The question is really two-fold: whether the production of timber on nutrient-poor soils depletes soil fertility so that timber growth is eventually impaired, and whether a significant loss of nutrients can be offset economically by the application of fertilisers.

RECREATION

While agriculture and forestry are old-established land uses, outdoor recreation has become a significant user of land only in the last few decades. Growth in outdoor recreation during the 1960s, often in areas previously used only very lightly if at all, soon gave rise to noticeable environmental effects. These in turn soon attracted the attention of researchers, and the volume of published research was, by the 1970s, sufficient to merit several literature reviews such as those of Speight (1973), Lucas (1978) and Wall and Wright (1977).

Outdoor recreaton takes numerous forms and takes place in a wide variety of settings. Some, such as golf courses, are intensively managed and are set in environments that have been deliberately altered to suit them for recreation. The level of use in such areas is often high, and active management is usually available to check signs of deterioration such as soil erosion. On the other hand, much of the growth in recreation over the last few decades has been in more

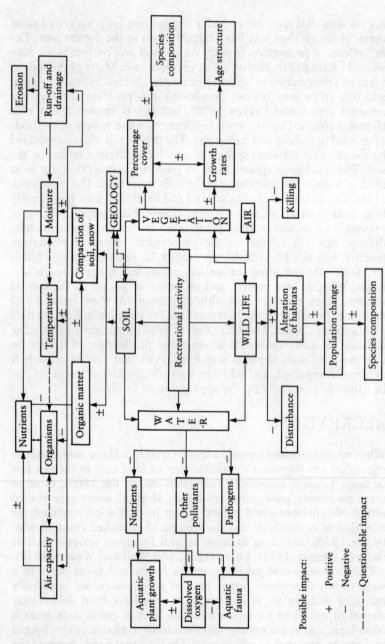

Fig. 6.5 Recreational impact inter-relationships.
Source: Wall and Wright (1977).

natural settings such as mountains or coastal areas. Although unattractive for forestry or agriculture because of adverse climates, soils
or slopes, many of these settings prove very attractive for informal
activities such as hiking or picnicking. By their very nature, many are
environmentally fragile: the same characteristics (such as thin soils or
adverse climates) that make them unattractive for agriculture mean
that their resilience in the face of new pressures from recreation is
low.

Recreational impacts on the environment are illustrated in
schematic form in Fig. 6.5. Major effects on soil, water, vegetation
and wildlife are the by-products of some types of recreation in some
environments, and effects may also extend, albeit less frequently, to
rocks and to the atmosphere. Initial impacts on individual environments may have secondary effects and may be transmitted
almost throughout the ecosystem. For example, trampling by the feet
of many recreationists can compact the soil and cause a loss of
vegetation and an increase in run-off and sediment yield. Its effects
can extend to soil microbiology, to the loss of habitats for wildlife,
and to water pollution.

Trampling effects take various forms and occur in association with
various other types of impact. One common form is around
campsites, especially in forests or in other back-country areas. Some
effects in a forest park in Ontario, for example, are reported by
James *et al.* (1979); intensive recreational use in campsites destroyed
surface organic horizons, resulting in soil compaction and decreased
infiltration rates. Growth of Jack pine was significantly reduced in
the high-impact areas of the campsite. Similarly, a reduction in
growth of between 20 and 40 per cent was found in stands of Scots
pine around a camping area in southern Finland. Here there was a
loss of soil humus and an increase in the exposure of tree roots, as
well as soil compaction (Nylund *et al.* 1980). In some respects,
therefore, the effects of recreation were similar to those of logging
equipment. In some back-country and wilderness areas, the impacts
of firewood gathering and the disposal of campers' wastes may also
be apparent. Around campsites in the Great Smokey Mountains
National Park, Bratton *et al.* (1982) found that trampling adversely
affected the regeneration of trees.

Linear damage by trampling occurs along paths or trails in many
mountainous areas used by large numbers of recreational visitors. In
the Cairngorm Mountains of Scotland, which rise to just over
1,000 m, the construction of a new access road and car park in the
early 1960s led to great increases in visitor numbers on the higher
slopes and tundra-like summit plateau. Within a very few years, a
system of paths had developed spontaneously. The widths of these
trampled paths were found by Bayfield (1973) to depend on a

number of characteristics. Path width increased with slope, wetness and local surface roughness, as hikers fanned out and sought alternative routes over difficult ground, but decreased with increasing roughness of the vegetation and terrain. Some of these relationships were also found by Dale and Weaver (1974) in the forests of central Montana and the adjacent part of Wyoming. They also found, like Bayfield, that trail width increased slowly with increasing traffic, there perhaps being a relationship between path width and the logarithm of the number of trail users. Trail depth, on the other hand, was found by Dale and Weaver (1974) to depend on the degree of compaction and erosion, and thus on variables such as climate, soil, and substrate type and slope, as well as on type of use and user (pedestrian, horse, motor cycle).

The use of off-road vehicles (ORVs) and their environmental effects have been investigated by numerous researchers. In arid and semi-arid areas in western USA, the use of ORVs has been found to increase the amount and frequency of run-off and erosion by increasing soil compaction and decreasing porosity. Iverson *et al.* (1981) concluded that denudation rates on desert hillslopes used by ORVs were commonly one or two orders of magnitude greater than natural erosion rates. On coastal sand dunes, which are sometimes even more sensitive than mountain environments to trampling by feet or vehicles, Hosier and Eaton (1980) found that both vegetation cover and number of plant species present on dunes and grassland at a North Carolina barrier beach were reduced on areas used by vehicular traffic. They concluded that a reduction in vegetation cover could increase the intensity of oceanic overwash, and that soil compaction in areas used by vehicles could increase the area of salt flats. In other words, the environmental effects were transmitted through vegetation and soil to landforms. In a comparable coastal environment in Australia, Gilbertson (1981) concluded that a short period of recreational use by ORVs had had a far greater effect on dune erosion and sand drift than the combined legacy of pre-European aboriginal land-firing and of European pastoralism.

Significant impacts on soils and vegetation may quickly be initiated by only modest levels of recreational use. Willard and Marr (1971) observed that plants adjacent to a new car-parking area constructed in a tundra environment at around 3,600 m in the Colorado Rockies showed signs of becoming wilted and matted within two weeks, by which time a network of paths had already become visible. After 12 weeks, the paths had become prominent and vegetation cover had fallen to 87 per cent. After two seasons of use, vegetation cover was down to 33 per cent of the original, and much of the ground surface consisted of sand and fine gravel from which the finer particles had been removed by the wind. In the Cairngorms, the sand and gravel exposed as vegetation was destroyed tended to move downslope, burying vegetation and extending damage beyond the trampled areas (Bayfield 1974).

Various attempts have been made to relate damage to general site characteristics. Willard and Marr (1970), for example, found that mountain tundra ecosystems with high soil-moisture contents were the most easily damaged in their study area in the Colorado Rockies. Liddle (1975), in attempting to generalise from published results of trampling experiments, suggested that a positive correlation exists between the primary productivity of vegetation and its vulnerability to damage by trampling. Timing and duration of visitor pressures are highly variable (for example, some are confined to a short, intensive spell in summer and others are more evenly distributed throughout the year), and it is perhaps questionable whether simple relationships such as those suggested by Liddle can ever be widely established as general rules, however, elegant they may be.

The environmental effects of recreation are, of course, not confined to trampling and its associated impacts on soil and vegetation. Recreationists may also have a direct or indirect effect on wildlife. The nature of this effect varies from species to species. It is possible, for example, that the breeding performance of some bird species sensitive to disturbance may be adversely affected, while numbers of other species may increase as a result of waste food dropped or dumped by visitors. At Cairngorm in Scotland, Watson (1979) found that snow buntings, pied wagtails, crows, gulls and rooks were more numerous in areas subject to disturbance than in other areas. Foin *et al.* (1977) reported big increases in a few species such as the mountain chickadee (*Parus gambeli*) around Yosemite campsites, but a decrease in the numbers of most other species. Bears and other animals may also be attracted by waste food, with consequent problems for visitors in some areas.

The dumping of wastes other than food may also have undesirable consequences: tin cans and other refuse buried in coastal campsites may be exhumed on dune erosion, for example, and in some settings refuse may be very long-lasting. Willard and Marr (1970) reported that tin cans dumped by construction workers on Rocky Mountain tundra in the 1930s were still intact with legible labels 40 years later. The vegetation below them had, of course, been destroyed.

In several respects, the environmental effects of recreation resemble those of agriculture and forestry. Species diversity often tends to be reduced, and rates of sediment yield are often increased. The sources and precise natures of the impacts may be different, but the general effects are broadly similar.

URBAN LAND USE

In urban areas, the degree of modification of natural ecosystems is usually much greater than in forestry, farming or recreation. Large areas are covered with roads, buildings and other impervious surfaces. Open spaces are maintained for recreational or ornamental purposes rather than for the production of food or timber, and so the ecosystem dynamics of the remaining 'green' areas of the city are usually quite different from those of the open countryside. The city is a prodigious producer of waste of various types – waste energy, human and domestic waste, and waste from the city's industries. Perhaps its production of waste is the most striking characteristic of the city's effects on the environment.

A city has its own distinctive climate (see, for example, Bach 1979). Temperatures are usually slightly higher in the city, because of waste heat from houses, transport and industry, as well as because of the thermal properties of the city's buildings and roads. Temperature differences between city and countryside are usually modest, averaging less than one degree centigrade, but occasionally rising to several degrees when urban, topographical and meteorological conditions are favourable for the urban heat-island to develop. Rainfall is also often higher in the city, by a margin of five to ten per cent, because of greater turbulence above urban areas and a high concentration of dust particles which can serve as nuclei for raindrops. On the other hand, average wind speeds tend to be lower, because of friction around buildings, and the duration of sunshine is often reduced because of air pollution.

Urban hydrology is perhaps even more distinctive. The impervious surfaces of the city mean that little infiltration can occur, and run-off is rapid. The drainage network is usually more efficient than in the countryside, because of the system of drains and storm sewers, and flood peaks are often increased by a factor of three or four (Walling 1979). When construction is in progress, with accompanying disturbance to the ground surface, sediment yield may rise several fold compared with previous levels under agriculture, but after building is complete and much of the land surface is sealed, rates fall to perhaps a tenth of their peak level, and to levels well below those experienced under agriculture. Nevertheless, sediment yields from the city are still usually higher than those under undisturbed natural vegetation, and urban land use is no exception to the general rule that human activity tends to increase sediment yields.

The effects of the city on vegetation and wildlife have been less extensively and systematically researched than those on climate and hydrology. Numerous accounts of plants and animals in individual cities have been produced, but comparatively little of a general, systematic nature has been written. Vegetation cover has obviously been partly replaced by paved surfaces, and exotic, ornamental plant species are extensively used in private and municipal parks and gardens. At first sight, the use of these species would suggest an increase in species diversity, and indeed in Britain introductions have increased ten-fold the 50–60 tree and shrub species found in the natural forest (Tittensor 1981). But many of these exotic species are very rare, and are confined to a very few localities: in practice, a limited range of species is usually employed.

The management of urban vegetation is usually very intensive. The two million hectares of lawns in the United States are estimated to have had $3 billion spent on them, at 1968 prices (Detwyler *et al.* 1972). Levels of use of fertilisers and pesticides per unit area are usually much higher than on agricultural land, with corresponding environmental effects. Species diversity is kept low by the ruthless pursuit of weeds and pests.

Evidence on the effects of urbanisation on wildlife is ambivalent. In a study of bird life in suburban neighbourhoods in California, Vale and Vale (1976) found that the number of species and individuals increased over time, especially in the first few years when young trees and shrubs in suburban gardens were maturing. On the other hand, in a study extending to a period of over 100 years, Walcott (1974) found that the number of nesting species in a residential area in Cambridge, Massachusetts, fell from 26 to nine.

Traditionally, city waste was dumped within the city itself. Over long periods of time, the combination of waste and rubble from demolished buildings led to a rise in ground level, at a rate estimated at one foot (0.3 m) per century in the case of London (Sherlock 1922). Human waste and some industrial waste are now normally removed in sewage systems. Treated sewage is eventually released into freshwater or seawater, with effects similar to those resulting from agricultural wastes. The addition of nitrates, phosphates and other constituent materials may cause eutrophication similar to that resulting from agricultural fertilisers. Many of the more celebrated cases of water pollution, such as the Great Lakes, were the product of both agricultural sources and sewage. Although arrangements for the disposal of human wastes are perhaps not yet ideal, they have improved enormously over the last century. Unfortunately, similar improvements have not yet been achieved in relation to wastes from the pets of the urban population. London is estimated to have a dog population of 700,000 and New York one of 500,000 (Schmid 1974), with polluting potentials which must be far greater than those of the human populations of many towns or of many agricultural feedlots.

Solid wastes are now usually dumped, with or without incineration, at sites around the edges of the city. Demand for land for dumping adds to the pressures affecting land use in the peri-urban zone (Ch. 5), but in some instances old quarries or gravel pits are used, and after infilling by dumping may be converted into parks or other recreation or amenity areas.

As in the case of the environmental effects of agriculture and other land uses, those of urban land use vary enormously. The severity of pollution, for example, varies both within and between cities. In a major study of American cities carried out for the US Environmental Protection Agency, Berry *et al.* (1974) concluded that urban form, expressing the urban land-use pattern, is directly related to the nature and intensity of environmental pollution. Urban regions with radial transportation networks and steep density gradients were found to have superior air and water qualities to those of more dispersed urban areas with less strongly focused transportation networks and more uniform population densities.

CONCLUSIONS

This brief review of the environmental effects of land use suggests a number of broad conclusions. Firstly, environmental effects vary with types and intensities of land use, and with management practices. In general terms, effects increase with intensity of use, but low intensities of use do not necessarily mean that side effects are negligible. Management practice is the key factor that complicates the relationship between intensity of land use and magnitude of environmental effect. A time-lag may intervene between a change in type or use or management and its environmental effect. For example, Trimble and Lund (1982) attribute the time-lag between land-use change, erosion and sedimentation in Wisconsin to the time required for the formation and growth of channels to carry additional run-off and sediment.

Secondly, similar types of effect can result from different types of land use. For example, the enrichment of a lake by phosphates can be caused by sewage effluents, from run-off from cropland, or even by soil erosion resulting from trampling on a recreational site, as Dickman and Dorais (1977) report from Quebec.

Thirdly, many types of land use have similar effects in terms of accelerated erosion and sediment yield. Sediment yield is usually one or more orders of magnitude higher under land use than under natural vegetation. Effects of erosion and sedimentation are probably of greatest magnitude at the time when a new land use is introduced, and thereafter they may slow down but they are unlikely to return to their original levels. Changes in technology and in management practice may be just as significant as changes in land use.

The use of land also usually brings about a loss of species diversity. While some species are promoted and indeed become the focus of land use and management, many are removed, either deliberately as weed or pest species or unintentionally through the alteration of habitats. These trends mean that fewer species of plants, animals or insects are to be found in a given area of land, and in some extreme cases species may become extinct. While extinctions for reasons unconnected with man are certainly not unknown in the natural world, there is little doubt that they can also be caused as a side effect of land use. Man in using land seems to increase the rate of extinctions, in the same way that he increases the rate of other natural processes such as erosion and the ageing of lakes by eutrophication.

The environmental effects of land use often tend to be cumulative and mutually reinforcing. For example, the Norfolk Broads in eastern England have been affected by agricultural, urban and recreational use (Moss 1979). The input of phosphates from agricultural land increased the growth of phytoplankton in the shallow waterways of the Broads, and increased algal growth on the surfaces of water plants. Low-growing water plants were replaced by taller, ranker weeds. More recently, sewage effluents from resident and recreational populations added to the process of eutrophication and promoted large crops of phytoplankton. The growth of water plants in the turbid waters was affected, and the water assumed an unpleasant appearance. Disturbance by boats was made worse by the lack of water weeds to dampen the energy of washes, which eroded channel banks and stirred up bottom sediment. At the same time, the amount of arable land in the catchment was increasing, so that there was an increased sediment input. The net effect was that sedimentation rates increased to between 10 and 100 times their pre-1800 levels, and some parts of the shallow Broads are filling with sediment at a rate of 1 cm/annum. Under conditions such as these, it is difficult to attribute damage to the individual land use responsible, and so it is also difficult to devise management strategies which will maintain adequate control. Furthermore, it seems that land users are often inaccurate in their perception of environmental damage. For example, Jackson (1977) reports that farmers in Utah tended to underestimate environmental damage resulting from irrigation. This inaccuracy may stem from a wish to deny or discount damage, or from genuine misperception. Whatever the reason may be, if a land user does not perceive damage, he is unlikely to adopt alternative methods of management that might reduce damage levels.

The significance of environmental effects obviously varies greatly. Some are of little significance from the viewpoint of the individual land user or of other citizens, while some, such as water pollution, may have adverse effects on other citizens but not on the land user directly responsible. Others, such as accelerated soil erosion, may threaten the continued use of land and may greatly reduce its productivity. Others again, such as loss of species diversity, may have long-term adverse effects on the population at large through a loss of genetic material, potentially useful for plant breeding. Some effects, such as trampling on a mountain trail, appear to have little direct economic significance in the sense of reducing the physical usefulness of the land, but can be likened to a scratch on a fine antique table. The function of the table is not affected by a small scratch, but most people would agree that its beauty and value are reduced.

Thus different types of significance, as well as different degrees, are attached to the environmental effects of land use. These differences ensure that the conservation of land resources, discussed in the next chapter, is a complex issue in terms of both its principles and its practice.

FURTHER READING

The literature on the environmental effects of land use is enormous, but fortunately several reviews have been produced and serve as useful introductions and guides.

Agriculture

Manners, I. R. (1974) The environmental impact of modern agricultural technologies.

Manners, I. R. (1978) Agricultural activities and environmental stress.

Friday, R. E. and **Allee, D. J.** (1976) The environmental impact of American agriculture.

Forestry

Blackie, J. R. *et al.* (1980) *Environmental effects of deforestation : an annotated bibliography.*

US Environmental Protection Agency (1976) *Forest harvest, residue treatment, reforestation and protection of water quality.*

Recreation

Speight, M. C. D. (1973) *Ecological change and outdoor recreation.*
Wall, G. and **Wright, C.** (1977) *The environmental impact of outdoor recreation.*
Lucas, R. C. (1978) Impact of human pressure on parks, wilderness and other recreational lands.

General

Warren, A. and **Goldsmith, F. B.** (eds) (1983) *Conservation in perspective.* Various chapters deal with the environmental effects of agriculture, recreation, and afforestation.

7

Land use and conservation

Conservation is rooted in the relationship between man and his environment, and in particular in man's attitude towards his environment. This relationship is examined in the monumental and scholarly work of Glacken (1967): for thousands of years man has seen his earthly home as the product of divine creation. He has seen this home as being both useful and beautiful; he has sought to exercise dominion over the earth and to use it for his own purposes, and he has felt a sense of stewardship and responsibility for his use of it. Obviously these concepts or beliefs have not been held with equal firmness by all men in every part of the world. In the west, for example, the balance between dominion and stewardship has fluctuated, and in the orient pantheistic views of god-in-nature prevailed in place of the western view of God-created nature. But in east and west alike, man had religious reasons for using land in a responsible manner. Whether he always did so is another matter, but his religion provided him with basic values from which responsible behaviour ought to have followed. To-day the main problem of conservation is in obtaining agreement on basic values, and in translating these values into frameworks for practical action. The technical means of conservation are not without their own problems, but as in so many other areas of life and society, the tools are better developed than the will to use them.

CONSERVATION MOVEMENTS AND THEIR ORIGINS

Although the roots of conservation lie in philosophy and religion, the first attempts to conserve land and its resources in modern times were decidedly practical in nature, and were concerned largely with protecting forests. Decrees aimed at protecting forest were issued in China as early as 1122 BC (Eidsvik 1980). In the medieval and subsequent centuries, in Britain and other north-west European countries, the native forest was becoming increasingly scarce. By the sixteenth and seventeenth centuries in Britain, the disadvantages of a poorly wooded country were being felt at the national level as well as in local areas, as timber for shipbuilding became increasingly scarce. Various enactments were made to preserve the surviving forests around the main shipbuilding ports. Such conservation, if conservation it can be called, was really no more than preservation, and it was motivated by purely practical, utilitarian concern quite uncomplicated by philosophical principles.

Interest in conservation of a more general nature was beginning to appear by the eighteenth century, when practical scientists began to look at issues such as the relationship between deforestation and erosion in the Alps, and attempts were made to stabilise coastal sand dunes along parts of the Atlantic, North Sea and Baltic coasts (Glacken 1956). The same period of the latter part of the eighteenth century and early nineteenth century also saw a number of other strands of thought about conservation beginning to emerge. New attitudes to nature emerged through the writings of Rousseau, Wordsworth and other members of the Romantic Movement, and the essays of Thomas Malthus on the relationship between population growth and resources marked the beginning of what may be regarded as economic conservation. Unfortunately, there was little if any synthesis between the practical, economic and philosophical strands. Some would argue that there still is insufficient integration.

In 1864 a partial synthesis appeared in the work of George Perkins Marsh entitled *Man and nature; or physical geography as modified by human action*. Marsh travelled extensively in Europe and the Near East, observing the obvious signs of soil erosion and other environmental damage around parts of the Mediterranean, and warned that similar damage would occur in the New World unless great care was taken in developing its land resources. His observations of what had happened and his warnings of what might happen were incorporated in a philosophical framework: creation was beautiful and useful, and man had a responsibility to keep it so.

Within two or three decades of the publication of Marsh's book, the symptoms of environmental malaise were becoming unmistakable in the United States: in at least some parts of the country, land resources were not being conserved. In response, a conservation movement was well under way by the early years of the twentieth century. It reached its zenith in 1908, when the President, Theodore Roosevelt, called a meeting of the governors of the states and territories to consider the conservation of natural resources. In their conference declaration, the governors recognised that the natural resources that constituted the material basis of the nation were threatened with exhaustion, and that conservation was an issue of 'transcendent' importance. They even agreed that 'land should be so used that erosion and soil wash shall cease' (van Hise 1910). A leading part in the growth of the movement was played by Gifford Pinchot, head of the US Forest Service and a close associate of the president, Theodore Roosevelt, with easy access to the president and some influence upon him (McConnell 1954; Steen 1976). Pinchot's view of conservation was practical and utilitarian rather than philosophical. It was concerned with efficient use rather than preservation (Hays 1959). To Pinchot, the first principle of conservation was the use of natural resources for the benefit of people now living. The second principle was the avoidance of waste, and the third – and perhaps key – principle was that resources should be developed for the benefit of the many and not merely for the profit of the few. During President Roosevelt's administration, about 100 million ha of federal land were made unavailable for private exploitation, the greater part being retained permanently as the property of the nation (van Hise 1910; see Dana and Fairfax 1980 for discussion on the movement, its antecedents and achievements).

If the first peak of the conservation movement was reached in 1908, a second high mark was attained during the 1930s (O'Riordan 1971). The Dust Bowl was an unmistakable sign that all was not well in the relationship between man and his environment in the United States of America, and that land use had caused serious damage to the land resource. Misuse of land, it seemed, had contributed to the misery of the Depression, and if the view of conservation in the 1930s was still practical and utilitarian rather than moral or philosophical, there was nevertheless a questioning about the nature of man's relationship to the land and to his use of it. The 1930s were a milestone in the evolving use of land in America. The Soil Conservation Service was established, the Tennessee Valley Authority was set up to rehabilitate an area suffering from socio-economic depression and environmental decay, and the Taylor Grazing Act was passed in an effort to curb further damage by private grazing on federal lands in the west.

The effects of this burgeoning environmental consciousness spread far beyond North America. Soil erosion was a principal focus of conservation in the United States in the 1930s, as forests had been in the earlier part of the century. As soil erosion was publicised in America, before long it was being perceived with heightened concern in various other countries, including Australia (Knowles 1978), New Zealand (Mather 1982) and Kenya (Moore 1979). Legislation and the setting up of a Soil Conservation Service in the United States was followed within a few years by similar developments in other lands. The freedom of a land occupier to use his land as he pleased was now beginning to be curtailed (at least in theory) by soil-conservation legislation. Land use was being seen, however tentatively, as a matter for the nation and not just for the individual land user.

If ripples from the American interest in conservation in the 1930s spread across the seas, they did so on an even grander scale during the rise of the environmental movement of the late 1960s and early 1970s. In Britain, for example, the number of new environmental interest groups formed during the ten years from 1966 was more than twice that of any earlier decade (Lowe and Goyder 1983), and new government environmental agencies were set up and new legislation enacted. In most western countries, environmental issues suddenly came to the forefront of public interest and concern, rivalling for a time the Vietnam War, crime, and almost all other issues as the principal subject of attention (e.g. Albrecht 1976).

The growth of the most recent conservation movement, like those of the two earlier phases, is not easily explained, and especially not in terms of simple or individual factors. Various contributory factors have been suggested; the publication of Rachel Carson's *Silent Spring*; spaceshot photographs of the earth, emphasising its finitude at a time of unprecedented growth in population and pressure on natural resources; reaction against the materialism of the post-war urban-industrial society. Perhaps it is inaccurate to talk of *an* environmental movement, for the one of the 1970s had many themes and many strands. Some were preservationist; some were mystical; some were pragmatic and utilitarian, reflecting fear that the growing pressure of the earth's resources could not be sustained.

If the themes of this movement were diverse, its effects were profound. Numerous countries passed new legislation governing the use of land, and set up new agencies and institutions to handle environmental and land-use issues. Existing agencies and institutions in many instances had to modify their policies, and new laws and agencies were superimposed on those dating from earlier peaks in the conservation movement. The history of conservation in the twentieth century suggests a wave-like pattern of growth and relative decline. Each phase of growth rises to higher levels, and manifestations such as soil-conservation legislation, once passed, are seldom repealed even if popular interest fades. If the effects of land use on the environment are greater now than ever before, then it is also true that the battery of control- and counter-measures is now stronger than at any time in the past.

WHAT IS CONSERVATION?

Any review of the history of conservation, even when in skeletal outline, clearly indicates that it has many meanings. Indeed during the 1970s conservation was a 'buzz-word' almost devoid of meaning; such meaning as it had was often equated merely with resource management. Imprecision in the use of the word merely reflected imprecision of thought about conservation and the management of resources. Before principles and techniques of conservation can be discussed, it is necessary to pause for reflection about its meaning.

The dictionary defines *conserve* as *keep from harm, decay or loss*; to conserve land is therefore to keep it from harm, decay or loss. Beyond this rather simplistic level, it is difficult to proceed, and even this elementary definition is not without problems and ambiguities. One concerns the definition or perception of harm, decay or loss. Although rates of physical processes such as soil erosion or the narrowing of species diversity can be measured objectively, their interpretation is much more subjective. A particular physical process may be perceived as undesirable by one individual and as a matter of no consequence by another. In other words, harm, loss or decay are largely subjective concepts over which unanimity of opinion is unlikely to be held. Different individuals have different standpoints from which they perceive loss, harm or decay, and these standpoints depend on the value system of the individual.

Conservation is often equated with saving. If this apparently simple meaning is taken, it opens up a new range of uncertainty. Does it mean to *save for*, or to *save from*? Is land being saved for future use, or is it being saved from harm or damage? The contention that, if land is being *saved from* harm, it is also being *saved for* future use does not really remove the problem of definition. Land could be saved from harm or decay not because of any real or potential usefulness, but rather for some perceived intrinsic value. *Saving from* damage is not necessarily related to *saving for* future use. The distinction between *saving from* and *saving for* leads to the basic question of whether conservation is based in ethics or pragmatism. If it is based on the pragmatism of protecting a resource so that it will be useful in the future as well as at present, it is equated with the avoidance of waste. This was the view of Gifford Pinchot during the first conservation movement. Equally pragmatic or utilitarian views

186

are sometimes still expressed. For example, Harley (1978) sees conservation as ensuring that land produces enough natural products for
human needs, and for the non-material benefits of recreation,
amenity and scientific study.

On the other hand, there were other strands of thought even
during the first conservation movement. John Muir in the second
half of the nineteenth century sought the preservation of parts of the
American West, not for efficient use in the future but because he
perceived that land (such as in the area of Yosemite, for example)
had an intrinsic value that ought to be conserved irrespective of any
practical usefulness. Conservation in this sense is akin to preservation, while conservation in the previous sense is concerned with
efficient, thrifty use. Simple popular definitions of conservation such
as wise use therefore tend to break down, because wisdom to one
man may be imprudence to another. In the absence of strongly held
values common to mankind, there can be no complete agreement on
what constitutes wisdom any more than there can be agreement on
loss, harm or decay.

A broad division can be made into nature conservation on the one
hand and resource conservation on the other. Nature conservation is
concerned mainly with the protection of parts of the environment for
their own sake (*saving from*), or for non-utilitarian values. Resource
conservation, on the other hand, is concerned more with the protection of the usefulness of the land (*saving for*). It is man-centred or
anthropocentric, while nature conservation is centred more on
nature itself; it is more biocentric. Different objectives, principles and
techniques apply in different branches of conservation. Some of these
differences can be illustrated by case studies of soil conservation as
practised in North America (as an example of resource conservation), and of nature conservation as practised in Britain. The
former is an obvious example of conservation for utilitarian and
material purposes. The latter is associated with conservation for
aesthetic and intellectual reasons (Ratcliffe 1977a), rather than for
material purposes. Landscape conservation fits neatly into neither
category, and raises a number of fundamental problems which are
worth considering in their own right as a separate study.

NATURE CONSERVATION IN BRITAIN

Nature conservation now has a firm legislative basis in Britain, and
has its own government agency in the form of the Nature Conservancy Council (see Blackmore 1974). Its roots extend back to the
nineteenth century when growing concern was felt about cruelty to
animals, both in activities such as cockfighting and in the widespread

slaughter of birds and animals in the name of sport. The Royal Society for the Prevention of Cruelty to Animals (RSPCA) was established in 1824, and later in the century the Royal Society for the Protection of Birds (RSPB) was set up, partly in response to the widespread collecting of birds' eggs and other activities of the growing band of amateur naturalists (Sheail 1976). The RSPCA succeeded in promoting a series of bills granting protection to certain forms of wildlife such as some bird species and seals, but much less progress was achieved in relation to plants (Sheail 1982). The list of protected species has been progressively extended since then, and species protection has become a major arm of conservation.

In 1895, the National Trust for Historic Sites and Natural Scenery was set up in England and Wales. This voluntary body acquired several properties of ecological interest, and in effect ran them as nature reserves. Within the National Trust a group known as the Society for the Promotion of Nature Reserves emerged and publicised the concept of the reserve. In 1929 the British Government set up the Addison Committee which reported in 1931. Its remit focused on national parks rather than on nature conservation *per se*, but it recommended that a series of national reserves should be established, where scenery and wildlife could together be conserved. But with the economic crisis of the 1930s, its recommendations were not implemented by government, and government action was delayed until the Second World War. Early in the war years, it became apparent that there would be major changes in post-war Britain, especially in the field of planning. Voluntary bodies renewed pressure for legislation for conservation, and drew up lists of areas suitable for nature-reserve status. The Society for the Promotion of Nature Reserves (SPNR), which had been formed in 1912, was especially active in this respect (Sheail 1976; Lowe and Goyder 1983). Government agreement in principle to the idea of nature reserves was forthcoming in 1942, but legislation was delayed until 1949. During the intervening years, much vital ground work was done, notably by the Huxley Committee in England and Wales, and the Ritchie Committee in Scotland (Ministry of Town and Country Planning 1947; Department of Health for Scotland 1947). Huxley laid the foundations of nature conservation in post-war Britain, setting out both its ends and means. The objectives of nature reserves were defined as follows (MTCP, 1947): 'to preserve and maintain as part of the nation's natural heritage places which can be regarded as reservoirs for the main types of communities and kinds of wild plants and animals represented in this country, both common and rare, typical and unusual'. These reserves were to be considered as a single system for preserving the principal types of the flora and fauna found in Britain. They expressed the key-area concept, or the notion that nature conservation could be achieved by the protection of a number of areas containing good examples of specific communities or features.

In this blueprint, the underlying purposes of conservation were not spelled out in detail. Maintenance (or preservation) was seen as an objective in its own right, without relation to more fundamental purposes, but it was also stated that the system of nature reserves would offer opportunities for research and experiment, education, and enjoyment by nature lovers.

Both the Huxley and Ritchie Committees listed areas suitable for designation as national nature reserves. These lists were drawn up by consensus among committee members, who in many cases had detailed knowledge of natural history. National nature reserves were to be both open-air laboratories and open-air museums, with careful management and protection of their scientific interest. After the enabling act of parliament was passed in 1949 (the National Parks and Access to the Countryside Act), the designation of National Nature Reserves (NNRs) began. Some areas were purchased by the Nature Conservancy, and in these cases complete control (within financial constraints) could be exercised. But in many cases the proposed NNRs listed by Huxley and Ritchie could not be acquired from their private owners. In some of these cases, NNRs were established by agreement with the landowners, who continued their previous land uses on them. These reserves, which were subject to Nature Reserve Agreements between their owners and the Nature Conservancy, were often used for farming, forestry or sport as well as for nature conservation, and the Nature Conservancy was not able to exercise complete control while the private land owners retained their interests.

The other designation proposed in the 1949 Act and by the preceding committees was that of the Site of Special Scientific Interest (SSSI). This designation, it was hoped, would contribute to a more satisfactory geographical spread of conservation areas. Most NNRs lay in the less densely populated areas of the north and west where human impact on the environment was weaker than in the south and east. SSSIs were to be notified to the local planning authorities, and thereafter the Nature Conservancy would have to be consulted about any planning application concerning them. This designation was of limited effectiveness: the advice of the Nature Conservancy did not have to be heeded where the planning application was decided, and many major changes of land use in any case required no planning consent (see Ch. 8). Consent was not required, for example, for the improvement of land by drainage or for the planting of trees on open land, although these operations could alter land radically and could fundamentally affect the interest and value of the land for nature conservation.

189

The main threats to nature conservation were seen at the time to come from urban and industrial developments rather than from farming or forestry. Indeed farming and forestry were excluded from planning controls on the tacit assumption that they were benign activities which posed no threat to the countryside or its wildlife. The Scott Committee (1942), whose report was one of the foundations of post-war planning policy in Britain, went so far as to say that prosperous agriculture was the key to maintaining a healthy and beautiful countryside. Farming was perceived in its pre-war form, and the effects of the radical changes in agriculture in the post-war period were not foreseen.

By the late 1960s and 1970s, it had become clear that the wartime foundation on which nature conservation was based was no longer adequate. It was now accepted that 'human impact in Britain is so universal and pervasive that no area of land or water is safe from developments destructive or deleterious to their nature conservation interest' (Ratcliffe 1977b). The Nature Conservancy Council (as it now was) thus embarked on a major survey to identify the most important sites while they were still identifiable. This major review required that more systematic and analytical thought be given to the identification of important sites than had been the case in the past (Ratcliffe 1971, 1977b). Within the broad objectives previously established by Huxley, a range of criteria were defined. These included diversity, 'naturalness', rarity, 'typicalness', fragility, potential value and recorded history. These criteria contain some internal contradictions as well as other problems; rarity and 'typicalness' are obvious examples. The wish to conserve a rare species approaching extinction is often stronger than the wish to conserve one which is still common, and the case for its conservation can be argued more forcefully. But on the other hand, the basic objective of conserving examples of all the main ecosystems found in Britain requires that the typical must be conserved as well as the rare. Another problem arises from 'naturalness'. Few areas in Britain are untouched by the hand of man, and some areas such as the Norfolk Broads are of great interest even although they are man-made. Nor could the criteria be easily quantified, and the survey on which the review was based could never become a completely objective process, although it was less subjective than the consensus method previously used to identify potential nature reserves.

Designation of the key sites as NNRs or SSSIs followed identification, and by the end of 1983 there were 193 NNRs and 4150 SSSIs (NCC 1984). Around 6.5 per cent of the land surface of Britain lies within SSSIs, and about 0.65 per cent in NNRs. All sites of major interest could not be designated as NNRs because of lack of finance and management capability. Those sites that were regarded as being of conservation value equivalent to NNRs were defined as grade 1 or grade 2 SSSIs. In the event of a local planning authority proposing to grant planning permission for a proposed development on a grade 1 or 2 SSSI, against the advice of the Nature Conservancy Council, then central government could intervene and decide on the planning application itself. In this way, decisions about changes in land use (or at least some changes in land use) on key sites would have a national as well as a local dimension. However, this procedure did not deal with the basic problem that the character of the land in an SSSI could be fundamentally altered by farming operations which required no planning consent. In their case-study area in south-east England, for example, Barton and Buckley (1983) found that SSSI status often failed to prevent damage to conservation interest arising from farming, urban development and forestry.

During the second half of the 1970s, the NCC was becoming increasingly concerned about the impact of land-use change on the environment. As discussed in Chapter 6, changing land-use practices and types have strong effects on some habitats. For example, many areas of wetland and heathland were converted to cropland or improved grassland, while many old woodlands were either cleared for agriculture or transformed into commercial plantations. From the viewpoint of nature conservation, this loss was serious, since many of these habitats, if not completely natural, were at least much less affected by man than were improved farmland or commercial forest plantations.

In an effort to reduce the severity of this impact, various measures were introduced, such as consultation between the Ministry of Agriculture and the Nature Conservancy Council before grant aid for land improvement in designated areas was offered, and valiant efforts were made by the NCC to offer advice to farmers and other land users on how to uphold the conservation value of their land while still using it for other purposes.

Eventually the issue came to a head when the Wildlife and Countryside Bill was promoted in 1980 and passed as an Act of Parliament, after long and sometimes bitter debate, at the end of 1981 (Cox and Lowe 1983). It is the most important piece of legislation since the 1949 Act, and although its provisions may not seem very radical, its passage saw the airing of a number of crucial issues relating to the use of land in a country such as present-day Britain. The Act extended and rationalised legislation relating to the protection of plant and animal species. Around 80 species and groups of species of birds, animals and plants are now protected against shooting, egg collecting, picking and uprooting. This section of the act was relatively uncontroversial compared to the one dealing with habitat protection.

Under the 1981 Act, the NCC is required to inform the owner and occupier of a SSSI of its location, feature(s) of special interest, and range of operations likely to be damaging to that interest. In return, owners and occupiers are required to inform the NCC of any intention to carry out a listed damaging operation. A period of three months must then elapse during which the NCC may seek to persuade the land user to modify his scheme or to enter into a management agreement. Under such an agreement, the owner or occupier can be compensated for the financial benefit foregone if he does not proceed with the scheme. Obviously this provision enables the NCC to become more closely involved with the management and protection of a SSSI than they were previously, but it raises two major problems. The first of these is financial. Compensation payments required to safeguard sites could far exceed funds available to the NCC at present. Adams (1984) estimates that the annual cost could amount to £40 million, or more than twice the total NCC budget. A more fundamental problem is that at the basis of the provision lies the notion of paying land users *not* to develop land or *not* to change their land use and management practices within the notified sites. This runs counter to the established principle in the British land-use planning system that planning permission is required *for* certain changes of land use. These and other problems arising from the Wildlife and Countryside Act have attracted a great deal of criticism, and at the time of writing the British government is reviewing the provisions of the Act. The situation is very fluid, and the debate has been widened to incorporate the relationship between grant aid for agriculture and forestry, habitat destruction and nature conservation. Grant aid from the Ministry of Agriculture has, in some instances, led to the loss of some habitats through, for example, the drainage of wetlands (e.g. Bowers 1983a, 1983b), while another government agency, the NCC, seeks to conserve such habitats by means of compensation payments. It is not surprising that such a state of affairs should give rise to calls for more harmonisation of government policies relating to the land. A significant change in agricultural grant policies was announced at the end of 1984: capital grant payments were to be reduced overall and withdrawn completely for land reclamation (except in Northern Ireland). On the other hand, grant aid for shelterbelts, hedges and walls built of traditional and local materials was to be increased. These changes illustrate something of the present fluidity of agricultural policies in Britain, under stress as they are both in relation to agricultural surpluses within the EEC and from conservation interests.

As the effects of agriculture and forestry on the environment have increased in the post-war decades, relationships between land users and conservationists (especially those in voluntary bodies and pressure groups, but also in some cases those in the NCC) have tended to become more strained. Underlying the key-area concept is the idea that existing features need to be preserved. Although advocates of conservation carefully avoid using the term, conservation is often equated with preservation by land users seeking to change their land use or land-management practices as economic and social conditions change. Resentment builds up in places, especially because areas of conservation interest are not evenly distributed but tend to be concentrated in certain parts of the country. In a study of farmers' attitudes towards conservation and conservationists in East Anglia, an intensively farmed area of lowland England, Newby *et al.* (1977, 1978) found that 60 per cent of a one-in-two sample of large farmers (with over 400 ha) and 40 per cent of all farmers in a group of 44 parishes were hostile towards environmental conservationists, although they expressed views that were generally sympathetic towards conservation. These views varied according to type of farmer, and their degree of direct involvement in husbandry and their extent of market orientation. Family farmers were generally more sympathetic towards conservation than other types of farmer.

Hostility towards conservationists stemmed from what was seen as inflexibility of attitudes and general resistance to change, which the farmers saw as unrealistic in times of changing economic and technological climate. Perhaps resentment, hostility and misunderstanding stem ultimately, however, from perceptions of conservation and its objectives. Little has been done in recent years to develop or elaborate the objectives originally set out by the Huxley Committee: basic, fundamental reasons for preserving and maintaining features as parts of the nation's heritage are rarely offered, although the objectives of maintaining fauna and flora for scientific study, aesthetic enjoyment and economic use have been affirmed (Ratcliffe 1977a). It has been suggested that the emphasis in conservation objectives has shifted in recent years towards aesthetic and recreational aims, and the enjoyment of wildlife as a largely spare-time activity by an essentially urban population (Ratcliffe 1981). This shift has not been confirmed by any official pronouncement, but if it has occurred then the implications are profound. They extend to the types of species to be conserved (birds are more popular than insects), to locational questions and perhaps also to economics. If conservation is for the enjoyment of the population, then conservation areas will need to be accessible and if the viewing of wildlife is a valued recreational activity, then why should it not be paid for? In other words, why should conservation land use not require at least some economic justification?

One significant and revealing discussion of the underlying philosophy of nature conservation as practised in Britain is that of

Ratcliffe (1976), who was chief scientist of the NCC and principal editor of the *Nature Conservation Review*. He concludes '. . .when all is said and done, this analysis of motives and attitudes [towards nature conservation] has a kind of aridity, for nature conservation and its meaning penetrates far beyond the rational and conscious into the emotional and unconscious. It touches the roots of human nature and is ultimately to do with being and feeling' (pp. 52–53). While many people would agree that wildlife is worth protecting for its own sake, irrespective of monetary values or usefulness to man at present or in the future, it is not difficult to understand why farmers and other land users sometimes become impatient with what seems to them to be obscure, vague and insubstantial objectives. But problems also arise in rather more concrete ways. What should be the immediate goals of management of key areas for purposes of conservation? Should it be the maintenance of the *status quo* indefinitely? How is change to be regarded in protected areas? (White and Bratton 1980). In a thoughtful paper, Tittensor (1981) argues that preservation is at odds with the history of continual change over a long period in many British ecosystems.

In Britain, it seems to many that nature conservation has become too closely associated with preservation, that it lacks sufficiently clearly defined objectives and a sufficiently robust philosophical foundation and that above all it has become divorced from active land use. The two ancient attitudes towards nature – that it should be both beautiful and useful – have lost their balance and complementarity, perhaps in the organisational structures of conservation as well as in its practice. On the other hand, nature conservation has in recent years become a much more popular interest. Approximately one in 10 of the British adult population belongs to an environmental interest group, and the combined membership of such groups (which incidentally has doubled since 1970) is now larger than any political party or trade union (Lowe and Goyder 1983). It is also much larger than the farming section of the population. This environmental movement has no single or precise concept of conservation, and the objectives of different component groups differ widely. Nevertheless, it is clear that environmental questions are now of increasing political importance. The views of one-tenth of the electorate cannot be lightly dismissed, and at least some environmental groups are highly skilled at publicising their messages and at conveying them to politicians and government officials. Furthermore, some environmental groups are active in acquiring and managing their own nature reserves, which now number several hundred and form a series parallel to that of the national nature reserves. Indeed the Royal Society for the Protection of Birds has in recent years spent more money in acquiring reserves than has the state conservation service, the Nature Conservancy Council (NCC 1984). Environmental interest groups therefore play a major role, both in campaigning for policies and legislation favourable to conservation (however defined) and in practical work such as the creation and management of nature reserves. Whatever philosophical problems are involved in defining conservation and its objectives, and whatever difficulties are encountered in relationships between conservationists and land users such as farmers and foresters, there is no doubt that conservation enjoys wide popular support.

SOIL CONSERVATION IN NORTH AMERICA

If nature conservation in Britain is based on the philosophical belief of preserving plants and animals for their own sake rather than for any pragmatic, utilitarian reason, the basis of soil conservation in the United States and Canada is quite different. The objective is to conserve the usefulness of the soil resource, so that it will be productive in the future as well as at present. Soil conservation is pursued on a very considerable scale in the United States. The Soil Conservation Service employs around 15,000 people (Troeh *et al.* 1980), and its annual budget runs at over $300 million (McConnell 1983). Between 1935 and 1980, cumulative conservation investments in agriculture amounted to $43 billion (1977 dollars) (Pavelis 1983). The Service is a product of the second conservation movement of the 1930s (see Simms 1970), although preliminary steps had been taken as early as 1917 when the first research on the relationships between erosion, run-off and crop types began on experimental plots at the University of Missouri. Such is the place of soil conservation in the American consciousness that these plots have now been designated as a National Historic Landmark by the National Parks Service. A Soil Erosion Service was set up as part of the temporary public works programme in 1933, shortly after F. D. Roosevelt came to power, and soil and water conservation projects were initiated as useful means of providing employment during the Depression. Labour, materials and technical assistance were supplied free of charge to private landowners, and public awareness of the problems of soil erosion greatly increased. Then in 1934 and 1935, two major dust storms on the Great Plains carried dust more than 2,500 km eastwards. Such was the magnitude of these storms that dust even filtered into government offices in Washington DC. At the time the head of the Soil Erosion Service, H. H. Bennett, was vigorously campaigning for the status of the Service to be changed from that of a temporary work programme into a permanent soil-

195

conservation agency. This was duly achieved in 1935, and a Soil Conservation Act was passed in the same year. The act declared that it was now the policy of Congress to seek to control and prevent soil erosion.

At the local level, the soil conservation effort is *directed* through the soil-conservation district. Each district, which typically corresponds to a county, has an elected governing body consisting of a few private citizens who are responsible for the planning and administration of soil conservation. The district provides the means by which the technical knowledge and expertise of the Soil Conservation Service is made available to individual farmers and other land users. By involving local citizens, it was hoped to bridge the gap between the government service and the individual land user, and so promote and encourage the use of technical advice supplied by the Soil Conservation Service. Demonstration farms are established to stimulate interest in soil conservation, and at the farm level, conservation plans are drawn up. Although many soil-conservation districts do have regulatory powers that in theory require vulnerable land to be retired from cultivation or that specific practices such as contour cultivation be employed, the significance of these powers has been small (Ciriacy-Wantrup 1968) and they are rarely employed. The use of compulsion has generally been avoided for fear that it might result in adverse reaction and in opposition.

While the Soil Conservation Service provides technical advice on soil conservation, much of the finance comes from the Agricultural Conservation Program (ACP) of the Agricultural Stabilization and Conservation Service. Under ACP, the federal government shares 50 to 75 per cent of the cost of approved practices (Halcrow *et al.* 1982).

The basis of the soil conservation effort is voluntary action by the farmer in seeking advice and assistance. This voluntary basis, which was also adopted in other countries such as New Zealand, has the advantage of avoiding the resistance that would follow if compliance were enforced compulsorily, but it means that the acceptance of advice depends on the characteristics of the land user as much as on the severity of soil erosion. Some users have been, and are, more ready to adopt conservation practices than others. Over the years, there has been some movement towards more compulsory compliance. For example, every occupier of land in New York State is now obliged by law to request a conservation plan from his soil conservation district (Troeh *et al.* 1980), and the state of Iowa in 1971 introduced a law providing for compulsory or mandatory adoption of conservation practices. Under the law, soil erosion can be declared a nuisance, and land occupiers are then required to limit soil losses to tolerable rates. In return, 75 per cent of the costs are available from government sources.

The evolution of soil conservation policy is discussed by Griffin and Stoll (1984), who consider it in the context of the processes of incrementalism and mixed-scanning reviewed in Chapter 2.

The Universal Soil Loss Equation (USLE)

One of the most widely used tools in work in soil conservation is the USLE. This equation was produced from empirical work on soil loss at experimental stations in the eastern half of the United States (Wischmeier and Smith 1965), and has been widely used in the design of conservation works and practices. The form of the equation is $A = R.K.L.S.C.P.$, where A is total annual loss of soil; R is an index of erosivity or erosive effect of rainfall and K of soil erodibility; L and S relate to slope length and steepness, while C and P are respectively indices of crop management and protective practices. Crop management includes various kinds of tillage, residue management and cover crops, while examples of factors included in P values would include contour cultivation, terracing and strip cropping. The erosivity of rainfall increases with its intensity, and R is therefore a function of rainfall intensity. K is the average soil loss per unit of R for a given soil on a standard plot of defined size, slope and management. L and S are usually combined in a single index (LS) which expresses the ratio of soil loss from a given slope to that from a slope of standard length and gradient. C is the ratio of soil loss under specified cover and management practices to that from fallow conditions, while P is the ratio of soil loss with supporting practices such as strip cropping to soil loss under straight-row cultivation up and down slope. In practice, values for these factors are obtained from tables in technical manuals. *Agricultural Handbook 282*, in which the equation was originally published, lists values for cropland in America east of the Rocky Mountains (Wischmeier and Smith 1965). USLE was originally devised for water erosion by sheetwash and rills on arable land in this area, and was based on many years of results from experimental plots. Within its original provenance, its predictive accuracy has been fairly high. Checked against 2,300 plot-years of data from 189 plots scattered throughout the area, the average prediction error was around 12 per cent (Wischmeier 1976).

Recent attempts have been made to extend its use to other areas and to other land uses. Wischmeier and Smith (1978), in an update and revision of their 1965 publication, present maps of R values for the whole of coterminous USA, and discuss applications on construction sites as well as in forest and rangeland, for which they list C factors. The equation has been employed in areas as diverse as California (Evans and Kalkanis 1977), rangeland in the arid

197

southwest (Osborn *et al.* 1977), and forest land in Alaska (Aldrich and Slaughter 1983). One of the main problems in USLE is in establishing accurate measures of rainfall intensity, especially in areas of poor networks of rain gauges and short records. Another is that different relationships between rainfall and erosion exist under different climates. The major difficulty, however, lies in establishing accurate values for the equation variables in areas beyond the original setting. This process will take time, but progress to date in areas such as California (Singer *et al.* 1977) and eastern Canada gives rise to confidence about the wider usefulness of the equation. As a step towards making the use of USLE in eastern Canada easier, rainfall erosion indices were published by Wall *et al.* (1983), and comparisons between measured erosion loss and loss predicted by USLE in southern Ontario have revealed no significant differences (van Vliet and Wall 1979).

While USLE is a useful tool that can be used in many settings, it is only a tool, and it cannot in itself solve problems of soil erosion. Nor does it obviate the making of decisions by the soil conservator. The first decision concerns what is an acceptable rate of soil loss. Ideally, the rate of soil loss should not exceed the rate of soil formation. If it does, then the soil is a wasting asset, and the rate of wastage depends on the relative rates of formation and loss. Rates of soil formation vary with parent material and climate, but are usually very slow in relation to soil loss under agriculture (see Ch. 6): rates of soil loss may be 10 times greater than those of soil formation. If the acceptable rate of soil loss were to be set at the rate of soil formation, it would be almost completely unattainable while the land was retained in arable use. A reduction in the rate of soil loss so that it matched the rate of soil formation is impracticable under agricultural use, and therefore a compromise value is sought. Soil conservation is thus usually not pursued in an *absolute* sense, as it would be incompatible with continued crop production. Instead, the aim is to achieve conservation in a relative sense, by slowing down rates of soil loss. If the rate of soil wastage means that most of the rooting depth is lost over a period of thousands of years, it is viewed with unconcern. If it means that the loss will take place over a very few decades, it is, of course, viewed with much greater concern.

Much attention was devoted to soil-loss tolerance values in the United States in the 1950s and 1960s (McCormack and Young 1981). A maximum *T* value of 11.2 tonnes/ha/year (5 tons/acre) was eventually agreed, with lower *T* values of as little as 2.2 being set for shallow soils with poor rooting depths. The maximum *T* value of 11.2 was selected for a number of reasons. Soil losses beyond that level mean that costs of sedimentation of waterways are usually very high, as are those of plant-nutrient losses. Excessive sheet erosion is usually accompanied by gullying which makes cultivation difficult as well as contributing large quantities of sediment to streams and ditches. Moreover, conservation practices are technically capable of keeping soil losses to under 11.2 tonnes/ha/year on most soils.

After a decision has been made on the *T* value for an area of soil, the next step is to devise a set of crop and conservation practices that will offer *C* and *P* values suitable for USLE to be satisfied or, alternatively, to modify the *LS* factor by terracing the land. Row crops with intervening bare ground normally give the highest rates of soil loss. Loss can be reduced by running the rows across the slope rather than in an up-and-down direction, and by using methods of cultivation which minimise the duration and extent of bare soil. For example, no-tillage methods involving the direct drilling of seed will normally give rise to much lower rates of soil loss than conventional downslope ploughing (soil loss from no-tillage systems of as low as 8 per cent of that from conventional tillage is reported by Moldenhauer 1979). Soil loss is also usually much lower when crop residues are left on or in the soil than when the crop is completely removed. Appropriate *C* factors for substituting in USLE are available in tables in technical manuals (along with values for *R* and *K*), and indicate the cultivation techniques and residue treatments required for a given *T* value. Alternatively, the *P* factor could be reduced by protective practices such as contour ploughing.

The adoption of soil conservation practices

The administrative machinery and practical techniques for soil conservation in the United States are well developed, and some notable successes have been achieved. In the Coon Creek Basin of Wisconsin, for example, rates of erosion and sedimentation have been reduced by as much as two orders of magnitude over the last 40 years, after having increased by around three orders during the first 80 years of European settlement (Trimble and Lund 1982). The basin had been selected as a demonstration area in the 1930s. In 1939, there were only 233 adopters of contour-strip farming in the state of Wisconsin, and almost all of them were in the Basin. By 1967, they numbered 6,402, and the practice had diffused throughout the state. Yet the problem of soil erosion has not been solved throughout the United States. Even the limited goal of reducing soil loss to the level of *T* values has not been fully achieved: soil loss is estimated to exceed the *T* value on 27 per cent of the cropland of the United States (McCormack and Young 1981). Furthermore, there are indications that soil loss has increased in recent years, at least in some areas such as Georgia (White *et al.* 1981) and Iowa (Alt and Heady 1977).

Increased soil erosion has occurred because continuous row-cropping is now more profitable than previously. Reductions in productivity as a result of soil loss have been masked by technological improvements such as improved hybrid varieties and inexpensive inputs of plant nutrients, pesticides and machinery (English and Heady 1980). The higher soil losses from continuous corn cropping in Ontario, for example, were not found to reduce yields over a few years, and Ontario farmers were reluctant to use conservation practices that required above-normal expenditure (Ketcheson and Webber 1978). Soil organic matter and soil physical properties could be improved by inserting forage crops in a rotation of row crops, and erosion losses would thereby be reduced, but farm income would be adversely affected (Ketcheson 1980). A loss of income in this way is a powerful disincentive to the adoption of conservation practice.

The time-scales and viewpoints of farmers may also discourage them from taking up conservation practices. These practices will usually give no significant increases in yield over the short term of a few years, and will often be more costly than the practices previously or currently employed. It has been suggested that farmers in Iowa would suffer a reduction of 10–15 per cent in net income if they were to adjust practices in order to reduce soil loss to T values (Boggers *et al*. 1979). Soil conservation may have long-term benefits in that it helps to ensure that the productivity of the land is maintained, and over a period of decades the extra costs of conservation practices may be insignificant in comparison with the additional production achieved. From the viewpoint of society, these long-term advantages may outweigh the costs, but from the point of view of the individual farmer there is much less apparent benefit in adopting better practices. A farmer in the Corn Belt would typically have to wait for 40–60 years before the benefits would match the costs (Seitz *et al*. 1979).

This contrast between the individual land user and society as a whole is further strengthened when the role of soil erosion in water pollution is considered. It is not necessarily in the farmer's interests to reduce sediment loss for this reason, although it would perhaps be in the interests of society for him to do so. This is partly reflected in the availability of cost-sharing and tax relief for conservation investment (Moore *et al*. 1979). The reluctance of the farmer to adopt conservation practices is therefore not necessarily irrational on his part, although it would benefit society as a whole, in the long term, if he were to do so.

While the different time-scales and viewpoints of the individual and the group are important factors in the attractiveness of soil conservation practices, they are not the only ones. Another significant factor is the rate at which future benefits are discounted. If the benefits of increased future yields are discounted at high rates, then the cost–benefit ratio of investment in conservation effort will tend to be unfavourable, as will the attractiveness of conservation practices. This applies at the national level as well as at the level of the individual land user, and in strictly economic terms it may raise doubts about government investment in conservation effort. Although the soil may be a wasting asset, if the costs or disbenefits are only to be felt in the distant future, and if their magnitudes seem to be small because of high discount rates, then conservation will not be seen as economically justified. From the restricted perspectives of economics, conservation will be justified only when the *computed* benefits exceed the costs.

The separation in time of costs and benefits may also be a powerful disincentive to tenant farmers. If the tenancy is insecure, or is likely to last only for a short time, then the tenant is unlikely to view investment in conservation very favourably. Napier and Forster (1982) state unequivocally that fewer soil erosion control practices are used on rented land than on owner-occupied land, and Easter and Cotner (1982) report that only 10 per cent of landlords who cash-leased their land on the Southern Plains between 1975 and 1977 made any conservation investment, while nearly 40 per cent of the owners who farmed or share-leased their land had done so. Other obstacles identified by Held and Clawson (1965) include high land prices and the physical layout of farms. When land prices are high, occupiers must maintain intensive land-use regimes in order to make adequate returns in order to service interest payments. This may inhibit certain shifts in land use which would assist soil conservation. Furthermore, when land prices are high in relation to returns from the land, most farmers are reluctant to invest further for objectives of soil conservation. The rectangular layout of farms in many parts of the United States (Ch. 3) may also be an obstacle, hindering the adoption of practices such as contour farming. The configuration of farms and fields may not be conducive to such practices, and problems of 'square farming' in 'round' country may arise.

The poor adoption of soil-conservation techniques combined with an apparently growing problem of soil erosion has encouraged research into the acceptance of conservation practices. In a study of Missouri farmers, Ervin and Ervin (1982) found that adoption was related to age and education. Younger and better educated farmers were more likely to be conservation-minded than their older and less-well educated counterparts. Younger and newer farmers were also found by Seitz and Swanson (1980) to be more likely to adopt conservation practices. On the other hand, Pampel and van Es (1977) in a study of farmers in Illinois found that distinct differences existed between the pattern of adoption of conservation practices and that of commerical innovations. The demographic variables normally regarded as significant in adoption research (Ch. 2) were less significant in relation to soil conservation practices. In an earlier piece of research on a sample of farmers in New York State, Prundeanu and Zwerman (1958) concluded that their 'high' conservation sub-group contained more farmers operating on a father-son partnership, and presumably intending to hand their farms on to their sons, than among the 'low' conservation group. More recently, Carlson and Dillman (1983) have reached a similar conclusion in the Palouse area of Washington and Idaho.

The social and psychological background factors to the adoption of conservation practices are complex. Seitz and Swanson (1980) report that many farmers perceive the existence of a problem of soil erosion and feel that they should do something about soil conservation, but relatively few farmers translate that perception into action. Furthermore, the Ervins' study in Missouri showed that farmers' decisions to co-operate with the Soil Conservation Service or to have a farm conservation plan drawn up were not significantly associated with either their perceptions of soil erosion or with increasingly severe physical erosion problems. On the other hand, a study of farmers in the Darling Basin of Australia showed that intention towards soil erosion was directly related to farm size, perception of soil erosion, increasing income over time, and higher educational levels (Earle *et al.* 1979). In this case intention and perception are clearly linked, but the relationship between intention and action was not investigated.

As this brief review indicates, much remains to be discovered about why some farmers adopt conservation practices and others do not. In their countrywide examination of the use of conservation practices in the United States in relation to easily measured owner characteristics such as age and type, Schertz and Wunderlich (1982) could find no clear correlation. Perhaps the answer lies in less easily measured characteristics such as personality.

While cost-sharing or government contributions towards the costs of implementing conservation practices is a major factor (and one which helps to bridge the gap between the interests of the individual and those of society), there remain deep-seated social obstacles to the introduction of new methods. Hagen (1977) gives an interesting account of the resistance to new contour-ploughing methods in Iowa in the 1930s. Although the symptoms of soil erosion were severe, farmers were very reluctant to employ new ploughing practices in place of straight-drill cultivation, which they saw as displaying their ploughing skills before the eyes of their neighbours and peers. More recently, it has been suggested that the 'trashy' appearance of fields where low-tillage systems are practised may deter farmers from adopting the practice. Although it requires less energy and causes less soil loss than conventional systems, and gives yields as high or higher

(Phillips *et al.* 1980), the low-tillage system may be perceived as inferior to more conventional systems with clean tillage and straight rows.

Several general points can be drawn from this brief review of soil conservation in North America. One concerns the voluntary system of adoption of conservation practices. This system depends on the initiative of the individual land user, and hence does not necessarily mean that technical and financial assistance are focused on the areas of greatest need. With a voluntary system, there is a problem of 'targetting' and of ensuring that assistance is given primarily in the areas where the problem is most acute, and not dissipated over other areas where there are receptive farmers but little problem of soil erosion.

At a more general level, the arguments for soil conservation seem convincing if not overwhelming. Soil erosion damages the land resource and makes it likely to be less useful in the future, and it also contributes to water pollution. Stated government policy is to control soil erosion, and a complex institutional structure has been set up to implement this policy. The technical means of soil conservation, such as contouring and low-tillage systems, are available, and are discussed in numerous textbooks (e.g. Troeh *et al.* 1980). Yet soil erosion proceeds at high rates in many parts of the country. Compared with nature conservation in Britain, the goals and methods of soil conservation in North America seem to be clearly defined and easily implemented. However, the problems encountered in extending these goals and methods to individual land users have been formidable. It is easy to argue that it makes sense to practise soil conservation, but it is much more difficult to encourage large numbers of individual land users that it makes sense to do so on their own land.

LANDSCAPE CONSERVATION

We may wish to conserve landscape for both pragmatic and philosophical reasons. Pleasant landscapes are often attractive settings for recreation, and they may support a tourist industry. Conservation of landscape can therefore seek to protect the resource base of an industry in much the same way in which soil conservation seeks to protect farmland. There are also more deep-seated and less material reasons for conserving beautiful scenery. Many people regard such scenery as valuable and worth protecting for its own sake, irrespective of any economic reasons. Many countries have designated areas for landscape conservation, either in national parks and wilderness areas where both scenery and wildlife are usually the objects of conservation, or in other designations such as areas of great landscape value, or of outstanding natural beauty. While designation reflects a wish to conserve or protect, it has, however, frequently proved difficult to translate that wish into specific management objectives and in turn to translate the objectives into specific management regimes. Landscape conservation is therefore of great interest in terms of both philosophical and practical problems.

The world's first national park was established at Yellowstone in the United States in 1872 (e.g. Runte 1979). Both conservation and recreation were defined as primary objectives, although preservation was not a pressing need in the early parks where the perceived economic potential was very low, and their location and remoteness meant that large numbers of visitors could not be expected.

Since the late nineteenth century, numerous national parks have been established both in North America and in other parts of the world, usually with the dual objective of conservation and recreation. The original park idea conceived of national or federal ownership and management of a large area of natural landscape. This idea was appropriate in its original area: much of North America was under federal ownership, and much of the landscape was largely free from human impact and totally free from the hand of the white man. This classical model of the national park, however, does not readily fit into the scene in many European countries, where almost all landscapes bear human imprint, and where there is less extensive government ownership of land. In England and Wales, for example, the national parks established after the Second World War are located mainly on privately owned land on semi-natural landscapes of moorlands and hills. In this setting, major problems emerge both in relation to the goals of conservation and in the means by which it is to be achieved. Should the goal be to conserve landscape as it was at the time of designation? Or, if the goal is not to 'freeze' landscape at one moment in time, how much change and what kinds of change are permissible? How can the goals be achieved when the land is occupied by numerous individual farmers and other land users, all pursuing their own goals, which are unlikely to coincide directly with those expressed by the nation in designating the park? These problems also arise even if individual land ownership is not involved. In Spain, for example, the first two national parks were located mainly on land owned by towns and villages, and the interests of the collective owners could not be readily reconciled with those of the state (de Viedma *et al.* 1976).

Although problems of landscape conservation are particularly difficult in the Old World, they are almost equally profound in the New. One fundamental question concerns natural change, and applies equally in landscape conservation and in nature conservation. Merely to protect an area of land from human impact does not necessarily ensure that no change occurs. On some of the National Seashores of the United States, for example, it has been clearly shown that erosion and deposition are natural processes (Hayden and Dolan 1974). The question then arises as to whether conservation management should seek to maintain the original *form* of the area, or rather maintain the natural *processes* which through time lead to changing form. On the US National Seashores, the latter goal is now pursued rather than the former. Similar problems apply, over longer time-scales and in less obvious ways, to some vegetation communities. Early park management sought to preserve objects such as large trees, geological phenomena and certain species of animals, and sought to exclude what were perceived as damaging phenomena such as fire (e.g. Bonnicksen and Stone 1982). The outcome was that forest invaded perennial grasslands in the Yosemite Valley, and white fir competed with the giant mountain redwoods of the Sequoia National Park (Rowntree *et al.* 1978). Broadly similar processes occurred in some Canadian parks (Nelson 1978). Natural fires had played important roles in the ecology of these areas, and helped to maintain the stability of the forest (Wright 1974). When fire was suppressed, ecological changes, and hence landscape changes, ensued.

A major turning point in national park policy in the United States came in 1963 with the publication of the Leopold Report on wildlife management in the national parks (see Leopold *et al.* 1963). The report acknowledged that contemporary man had allowed a rather artificial vegetation succession to develop by suppressing natural fire, and advocated that the policy of management should henceforth be to recreate and maintain the ecological conditions applying in the national parks when European man first discovered America. This concept of the *era* landscape contrasts with that of the *evolutionary* landscape: in the former the landscape of a particular era is preserved, while in the latter landscapes are allowed to evolve by the occurrence of fire, disease and fluctuations in animal populations and changes in vegetation (Nelson 1978). In practice, the conservation of both era and evolutionary landscapes is now sought in North America.

While the logical and philosophical basis of era landscape conservation may be questioned, it is in accord with the history of the early parks established in the nineteenth century, and its great attraction is that it is identifiable and definable. It is perhaps not applicable on seashores and other dynamic environments, but in general terms it is an achievable goal in much of America and in other parts of the New World. At a more basic level, the suggestion that man should not supply or divert significant amounts of materials or energy to or from park ecosystems can form another fundamental principle in the management of national parks (Houston 1971).

In the more humanised parts of the Old World, similar goals are less easily established. Some of the most valued landscapes are largely the product of man rather than nature. In countries such as England and Wales, there is a strong but ill-defined wish to conserve landscape, but specifically defined goals are conspicuous by their absence. National parks were established in England and Wales after 1949, when the National Parks and Access to the Countryside Act was passed. The objectives were to conserve landscape and to provide recreational opportunity.

It is difficult to conceive of definite goals for landscape conservation that could realistically be adopted in these parks. In some countries such as Nepal, for example, efforts have been made to resettle the inhabitants of designated parks outside the park boundaries, so that purely natural conditions can prevail within the park (Bjonness 1980b). It is doubtful whether residents in, for example, the Lake District National Park in England would take kindly to such resettlement, but even if such radical action were a practical proposition, serious problems would remain. The landscape of many parks would change markedly if all human pressure were to be removed. Grazing maintains many areas of heathland and moorland at the expense of forest, and the removal of cattle and sheep would bring about changes in the very qualities of landscape whose perceived value was reflected in the initial designation of the area. Furthermore, human impact in some national parks dates back for thousands of years, during which there have been changes in climate and natural vegetation. If re-establishment and maintenance of 'natural' environments were to be the goal of landscape conservation, decisions would have to be made on the question of *which* 'natural' landscape was to be selected (see MacEwen and MacEwen 1981, for discussion of the problems of these parks).

These fundamental problems in the philosophy of landscape conservation are matched by the practical and technical problems of how conservation can actually be achieved. In the national parks of the New World, government ownership and management mean that there are relatively few obstacles to the implementation of conservation policies. In many parts of the Old World, however, these policies cannot be implemented so directly. One favoured approach in national parks and other areas designated for landscape conservation in Britain is through strengthened policies of planning or development control (see Ch. 8). Planning powers are often applied more stringently in these designated areas, and house building, for example, may be permitted only if local natural stone is employed.

Strengthened or extended powers of development control are unsatisfactory in a number of ways. Firstly, they and their costs impinge on the residents of the designated areas, but not elsewhere. This may give rise to feelings of dissatisfaction and in some instances to conflicts between local interests and the interests of national conservation agencies. These feelings and conflicts extend to nature conservation as well as to landscape conservation, and to less densely populated countries such as Norway (Dalland 1978) as well as to countries such as Britain. The conservation of areas of any economic worth or potential is frequently opposed; ironically, areas perceived as having no economic worth can be much more easily designated as conservation areas, but by definition little protection from development is required in these areas.

A second unsatisfactory aspect is that powers of development control may apply only to certain types of land use (in the case of Britain normally *not* to farming and forestry) and hence to certain kinds of landscape change. Furthermore, these powers can prevent certain changes from taking place, but they cannot ensure that land uses are continued. For example, development-control powers cannot ensure that grazing is maintained on moorlands, although forest would begin to invade if it were discontinued. In short, development-control powers can only react to proposals for change, and other means are required if positive management is needed. As in the case of nature conservation, the idea of the management agreement has been used (as yet to a limited extent) in landscape conservation in Britain (e.g. Feist 1978; Curtis 1983; Leonard 1983). Under such an agreement, the land occupier agrees to manage an area of land in a certain way, and in return is compensated by the conservation authority for the income or profit which he loses by doing so. Unfortunately, the cost of management agreements of this type is likely to rise steeply as time goes by and pressures to change land use, and hence landscape, build up. The cost of perpetuating a particular type of land use or management regime will increase as changing economic and technological climates stimulate changes in land use and management. There is also the more fundamental problem that landscape conservation in using tools like this is tacitly seeking to preserve landscapes at one stage in their evolution, although the logical basis for doing so is flimsy.

Many of the problems of areas designated for landscape conservation apply also to designations for nature conservation. The concept of the protected area is now well established in conservation and land-use planning, but its effectiveness is difficult to assess. The criteria by which success may be gauged are often poorly defined. In an area designated as one of outstanding natural beauty, for example, designation does not necessarily indicate that landscape conservation should have priority over all other considerations, but rather that it should receive particular attention. The question of how special the attention should be has to be resolved in relation to individual cases and circumstances. Furthermore, the effectiveness of designation cannot be measured precisely, because the outcome or pattern of development if designation had *not* occurred cannot be known. A further possible weakness in the concept of the protected area in conservation is that it carries the risk that areas unprotected by special designations are regarded with impunity, and that little thought is given to conservation within them. Designations are undoubtedly useful in some settings and for some purposes, but as their relative extent increases, the credibility and defensibility of protected areas may decrease. This is acknowledged by bodies such as the Nature Conservancy Council in Britain. Their two-pronged approach to conservation combines the protection of key areas, on the one hand, with efforts to influence through advice and education the attitudes of land users and policy makers on the other (Ratcliffe 1977a). Designations alone cannot ensure that land is kept beautiful and useful.

ARE THERE GENERAL PRINCIPLES OF CONSERVATION?

These brief reviews of conservation in relation to wildlife, soil and landscape have revealed numerous problems at various levels ranging from the philosophical to the practical. Conservation can be motivated by ethical or pragmatic reasons, or by a mixture of both. In some cases, its goals can be defined precisely; for example, it may seek to reduce rates of soil erosion to given levels; but in other instances, goals are difficult to define sharply, and are even more difficult to make operational. Nevertheless, some general conclusions about conservation can be reached, with a broad if not general measure of applicability.

In 1980, a *World Conservation Strategy* (WCS) was published by the International Union for the Conservation of Nature, with the assistance of the United Nations Environmental Programme and the World Wildlife Fund (IUCN 1980). FAO and UNESCO were also involved in the project. Despite the general fuzziness of the concept of conservation and despite the varied interests of the sponsoring bodies, WCS was able to define three specific objectives: to maintain essential ecological processes and life-support systems, on which human survival and development depend; to preserve genetic diversity; and to ensure that species and ecosystems were used in a *sustainable* way. The stated primary reasons for preserving genetic diversity include plant and animal breeding in the future, and such preservation is also stated at the same time to be a moral principle.

Like Pinchot's principles of conservation almost a century earlier, the objectives of the WCS are largely pragmatic or utilitarian in tone, and seek to control development rather than to achieve strict pre-servation. Perhaps it may be concluded that strict preservation is unrealistic as an aim of conservation if it is to attract popular support, and it may also be unrealistic as a goal for the management of specific ecosystems or landscapes. In Britain, an inter-depart-mental committee made up of representatives of the conservation agencies and other agencies with interests in rural land use recently agreed on a compromise definition of the concept of conservation: change should be managed in such a way that scarce resources are conserved and adverse effects on the environment are minimised (Countryside Review Committee 1979). The wording may be more bland than that of WCS, but the acceptance and central role of change are significant.

A second general point emerges from the objective of preserving genetic diversity. Modern land use is threatening ecological diversity in many ways (see Ch. 6), but diversity is desirable for several reasons. It may be of value to mankind in the future in keeping options for future paths of development open, in plant and animal breeding, and in the production of drugs. It has moral and ethical connotations arising from a belief that species have a right to exist, irrespective of their usefulness to man. Diversity may also be related to ecological stability. A large body of literature is devoted to the relationship between diversity and stability, and focuses on the idea that high levels of diversity help to maintain stability (Elton 1958). Very simple ecosystems with only a few species at each trophic level are prone to violent fluctuations in the populations of their species, while more diverse ecosystems are usually more stable. Support is lent to this hypothesis by the practical examples of ecosystems simplified by the use of pesticides: predatory species are affected as well as the pest species, and thus subsequent pest outbreaks may increase in size and significance. On the other hand, it has been suggested that the hypothesis, if it is to be applied, for example, in crop management, needs to be qualified, as only certain forms of diversity are likely to promote stability (Murdoch 1975). Even if the validity of the hypothesis or its usefulness in practical land man-agement may be questioned, the maintenance of ecological diversity may be desirable for other reasons. Diverse, varied landscapes are usually more attractive than monotonous, uniform ones made up of only a few natural or manipulated ecosystems.

Several arguments encompassing various aspects of conservation, therefore, suggest that the maintenance of diversity is a desirable objective. These arguments are both pragmatic and ethical, and they apply to wildlife, soil and landscape to varying degrees. If there is a single principle of conservation, then it must be the maintenance of diversity. Indeed, conservationists such as Moore (1969) have argued that the maintenance of diversity should be the primary aim of conservation. But even if it is accepted, this principle is difficult to implement because one of the main effects of land use on the environment has been shown in Chapter 6 to be a reduction in ecological diversity.

At a more basic level, the goals or objectives of conservation, as of land use, must stem from man's values. For many centuries man has seen nature or the earth as both useful and beautiful, and this view has, to varying degrees, been balanced by a sense of stewardship or responsibility for its care. Black (1970) develops this theme of stewardship and utilisation in counterbalance: man is to exercise dominion over the earth and to use it for his own purposes, but he is to use it responsibly. When this sense of responsibility breaks down, according to Black, environmental damage is the inevitable result, and so also a reduction in usefulness and beauty. Although Passmore (1974) has objected that explicit Biblical references to stewardship in relation to the created world are scanty and unconvincing, it might still be claimed that a Biblical view of God, man and creation would lead to stewardship in the use of management of land. Even if man does not feel a sense of responsibility and stewardship towards God, then he may still do so towards future generations. A sense of stewardship implies a particular attitude to land: a prerequisite of conservation, therefore, would seem to be a particular view of land and its contents. With such a view, and with an objective of keeping the land both useful and beautiful, many of the uncertainties of conservation philosophy fade away. *Saving for* and *saving from* merge together. The practicalities nevertheless remain, for the pull of short-term gain and personal advantage is a powerful one against the less immediate and less tangible counterforce of stewardship. If the aim of conservation is to create, in the elegant words of Combes (1982), 'une harmonie dans les cacophonies des forces naturelles et des intérêts économiques', the form of the harmony and the relative roles of these factors are 'determined by the interaction of faith, reason, and immediate and ultimate values' (Price 1955).

FURTHER READING

Anonymous (1981a) *Bibliography on protection of the environment.*

Burton, I. and **Kates, R. W.** (eds) (1965) *Readings in resource management and conservation.* Chicago : University of Chicago Press.

Green, B. (1981) *Countryside conservation.*

Held, R. B. and **Clawson, M.** (1965) *Soil conservation in perspective.*

Nash, R. (ed.) (1976) *The American environment – readings in the history of conservation.*

Troeh, F. R., Hobbs, J. A. and **Donohue, R. L.** (1980) *Soil and water conservation for productivity and environmental protection.*

Warren, A. and **Goldsmith, F. B.** (eds) (1983) *Conservation in perspective.*

8

Land-use planning

Some form of planning is involved in most decisions about land use, but the term *land-use planning* usually refers to a scale greater than that of the individual land unit; it usually involves government at one level or another; and is usually concerned with reconciling the goals and objectives of individuals and groups in society. Land-use planning, as it is organised and conducted in the western world, reflects differences in goals between individual land users and the nation as a whole, or broad groups within it. The individual land user may, for example, be concerned to maximise his profit by selling his land for urban purposes, while the nation may perceive greater utility in retaining the land in agricultural use. Similarly, the individual land user may be content to manage his land in a fashion that does not maximise output or employment, while the nation seeks to use its land resources in such a way that output or employment is maximised. At one level, land-use planning is concerned with reconciling these conflicting objectives. At another level, land-use planning may seek to mediate or adjudicate between the objectives of interest groups (for example, nature conservationists and recreationists) and thereby to establish compromise goals for the management of government-owned land or to balance broad policies among the main land-use sectors.

The aims of planning, like the goals of land users, can be multiple, and the structures or institutions of planning are almost infinitely varied. Like its objectives and structures, the methods and techniques of planning are diverse. Nevertheless, a number of general techniques of classifying land and landscape has been widely used in land-use planning, and examples of these techniques will be reviewed briefly before our attention turns to planning systems.

PLANNING TECHNIQUES

Land classification

Land is almost infinitely variable in its physical characteristics, and the planning process is made easier if land can be classified into a manageable number of categories. These classes can be, and have been, defined in numerous ways, and numerous systems of classification are in use.

The USDA method

The type of land capability classification usually known as the USDA method is, indirectly, a product of the soil conservation movement of

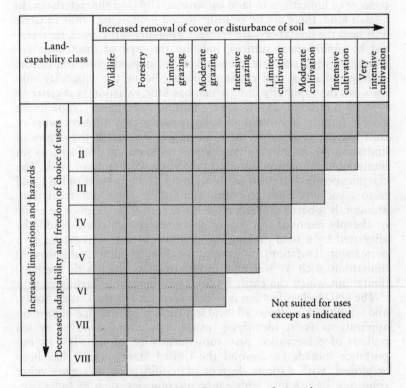

Fig. 8.1 USDA land capability classification: correlations between permanent land limitations and safe land use.

Source: Hockensmith and Steele (1949). (By permission of the Soil Science Society of America).

the 1930s. It was devised by the Soil Conservation Service of the US Department of Agriculture as a means of grading land for purposes of soil conservation. The method was first described by Hockensmith and Steele (1949), who identified a number of possible subsidiary applications such as in the field of agricultural credit and the planning of new routes. The primary purpose, however, was in the planning of soil conservation work on farms and ranches. The method was geared to producing farm-scale maps which graded land on the basis of the intensity of soil disturbance that was 'safe'. For example, very intensive cultivation was a 'safe' land use only on Class I land, and cultivation was 'safe' only on the top four land classes (see Fig. 8.1).

A full description of the method was first published in 1961 (Klingebiel and Montgomery 1961). The method is based on the concept of limitations to land use imposed by land characteristics. In Class I land, there are no or insignificant limitations, while in Class VIII land the limitations are severe. Capability sub-classes, represented by alphabetical suffices, indicate the type of limitations encountered within a class; they include wetness, climate, soil factors such as stoniness, and erosion hazards. Below the capability sub-class lies the capability unit, which has little variation in severity or type of limitation and which is suitable for similar crops under similar farming systems. It will be apparent that different types of soils may be grouped in the same capability class if the degree of limitation is constant; classification is based on the severity of limitation and hence not necessarily on the type of soil. The classification is concerned solely with physical attributes of land, and factors such as farm structure and location are not taken into account. It is based on permanent limitations which cannot be easily or cheaply removed (for example, wetness which could readily be alleviated by a field drainage scheme would not be regarded as a permanent limitation). It is also concerned more with physical limitations such as soil texture or stoniness than with chemical limitations which can easily be overcome by lime or fertilisers.

The USDA classification is widely employed in the United States, and is included in almost all local soil-survey reports. One of its main applications is in identifying prime agricultural land to which policies of preservation may subsequently be applied. But its importance spreads far beyond the United States, and it has been employed, with various degrees of modification, in many other countries. Its use in a wide range of countries, such as India, Australia and Venezuela, for example, is discussed by McRae and Burnham (1981).

Canada Land Inventory

One of the most ambitious attempts at land capability classification is the Canada Land Inventory, which was initiated following the Agricultural Rehabilitation and Development Act of 1961. The act provided for programmes of farm enlargement, farm improvement and adjustment of land use in response to rural poverty arising from limitations of farm size and infertility of the soil. As a foundation on which to rest these programmes, a comprehensive statement of the relative capability of land to support arable farming and alternative land uses was required. The entire settled area of Canada, extending to about one million square miles, was to be covered by the survey, and five assessments of land capability were to be made – for agriculture, forestry, recreation, wildlife (ungulates) and wildlife (waterfowl) (McCormack 1971). Each of these classifications bears a strong resemblance in its structure to the parent USDA system, although seven classes were employed in Canada instead of eight. The concept of limitations is basic to the classification. For agriculture, forestry and wildlife, these limitations are broadly similar to those in the USDA system although they differ in detail and number. For outdoor recreation, much greater modification was required. The basis here is the amount of use that may be generated and sustained under perfect market conditions. Class I recreation land has therefore both a high index of attractions and sufficient resilience to ensure that intensive use can be sustained without un- duly damaging the resource. Sub-classes in the recreation classification (shown as in the other classifications by alphabetical suffixes) relate to type of recreational attraction (for example A for angling, B for beach activities) rather than severity of limitation. Maps are prepared at a scale of 1:50,000 as working documents, and their contents are stored in data banks. Published maps are at a scale of 1:250,000.

Land capability classification in Britain

Progress in Britain has been much more modest than in Canada, and no national programme comparable to the Canada Land Inventory has been launched. The Soil Surveys of both Scotland and of England and Wales have adopted the USDA land capability classification and have employed it after modification. The original eight classes of the USDA scheme have been reduced to seven in Britain. Class V of the original scheme, which included land in flood plains and similar areas, was omitted. The original sub-classes are employed, with the addition of extra ones to denote limitations imposed by gradient (largely in relation to the use of machinery) and soil pattern. Whereas the sub-classes were defined qualitatively in the American system, quantitative definitions have been introduced in Britain. For example, class 3 land is defined as land with gradient not exceeding 11°, lying below 1,250 ft (381 m), with mean daily temperature maximum above 14 °C, rainfall not more than 300 mm greater than evapotranspiration and rooting depth than 10 inches (25.4 mm) (Bibby and Mackney 1969).

Only parts of England and Wales and of Scotland have been covered by this classification. Maps are published at a scale of 1:25,000 in England and Wales and 1:50,000 (formerly 1:63,360) in Scotland. An extract of the map of the area around Edinburgh is shown in Fig. 8.2.

The three main aims of land use capability classification (LUCC), as it is entitled in Britain, are to simplify soil maps, to provide a basis for farm planning and to aid land-use planning (Mackney 1974).

Use has been made of the classification in planning work, especially in the planning of urban expansion and new routeways, and in Scotland some use is made in property markets where information on land class is sometimes included in descriptions of farms offered for sale. Some use has also been made at the level of farm planning, and Hooper (1974) has concluded on the basis of a case study that LUCC can be a valuable aid at this level also. Nevertheless, little use has been made for this purpose. The scale of mapping has been too small, especially in Scotland, for useful application at the level of the farm or field. There may also be more fundamental obstacles to applying the classification at this level. A study in Northern Ireland showed that the profitability of farming was not directly related to soil units as defined by the morphology of the soil profile (Cruickshank and Armstrong 1971). Since the classification was largely based on the mapping of these units, its usefulness in agricultural planning appeared to be undermined. But a subsequent re-interpretation of the same data by Webster and Beckett (1973) led to a claim that the soil map had 'some' value for predicting the profitability of farming. In Canada, good correlations between yields and returns on the one hand, and land capability class on the other, have been reported from Ontario (Patterson and Macintosh 1976) and Alberta (Peters 1977).

Planners have also tried to use LUCC in development planning. It was a basic input into a development plan for the Island of Mull in the Scottish Highlands (Smith and Sutherland 1974; HIDB 1973). Only small parts of the island are arable or potentially arable, and most of the land is moorland. In this setting, the emphasis of the classification on arable land classes was inappropriate. Most of the land was of a type falling within one of the three non-arable classes, and this classification was rather too coarse to accommodate the variations in quality or type of moorland and to provide a useful

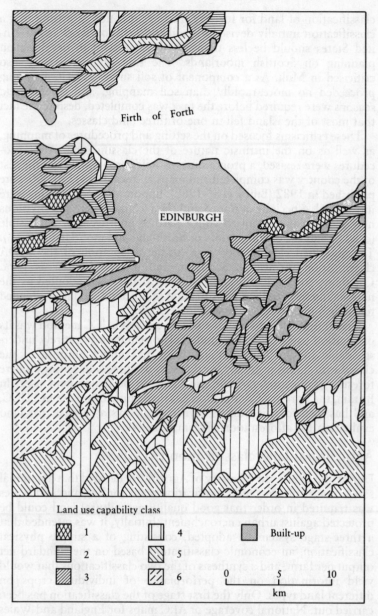

Fig. 8.2 Land use capability classification in the Edinburgh area, Scotland.
Source: Based on material published by the Soil Survey of Scotland: reproduced by permission of the Macaulay Institute for Soil Research and the map authors.

classification of land for forestry. Perhaps it is not surprising that a classification initially devised for soil conservation work in the United States should be less than wholly successful in development planning on Scottish moorlands. The rate of survey was also criticised in Mull. As a component of soil survey, LUCC mapping proceeded no more rapidly than soil mapping, and several field seasons were required before the task was completed, despite the fact that most of the island fell in one of three land classes.

These criticisms focused on the setting and procedures of mapping, as well as on the intrinsic nature of the classification. After procedures were revised, a programme of rapid, broad survey in the rest of the country was completed and maps at a scale of 1:250,000 were published in 1982 (Bibby *et al.* 1982). Important modifications were introduced, especially in class 5 and class 6 land, where sub-divisions now indicate the extent to which pasture improvement is possible (class 5) and the grazing values of heathland and moorland (class 6). This modified classification is a further adaptation of the USDA classification for use in Scotland, and is now known as Land Capability for Agriculture, or LCA. LCA has been adopted as the national method of land classification in Scotland, and it is intended to publish map sheets at a scale of 1:50,000.

One of the weaknesses of the USDA-derived LUCC method was its orientation towards arable land. This orientation is entirely understandable in the light of the history and initial purpose of the classification, but it greatly weakens its usefulness in settings where forestry or pastoral farming are likely to be major land uses. In Britain, the Forestry Commission has made little or no use of LUCC, and has instead relied on its own soil surveys as a basis for land evaluation for afforestation (Toleman 1974).

Agricultural land classification (ALC)

During the 1960s, the Ministry of Agriculture decided that a national series of agricultural land classification maps for England and Wales was required in order that good quality agricultural land could be protected against urban encroachment. Initially, it was intended that a three-stage system be adopted, consisting of a simple physical classification, an economic classification based on the standard net output per farm, and a synthesis of the two classifications that would yield information on the performance of individual crops on different land types. Only the first stage of the classification has been carried out. National coverage of ALC maps for England and Wales has been published at a scale of 1:63,360. The classification consists of five grades of agricultural land, classified according to the degree to which physical characteristics impose long-term limitations on agricultural use. Limitations operate in several principal ways: range of crops; yield (level and/or consistency); and inputs required (Morgan 1974). Grade I land is very tightly specified (Table 8.1) and is confined to only 3 per cent of the land area. On the other hand, the 'average' quality of land ranked as Grade 3 extends to about 50 per cent of England and Wales. In addition to five grades of agricultural land, two other classes relate respectively to non-agricultural land in the form of forest and built-up areas.

Table 8.1 Agricultural land classification (ALC)

Grade 1	Land with very minor or no physical limitations. Deep, well-drained, easily cultivated soils on gentle slopes, with no major climatic limitation.
Grade 2	Land with some minor limitations, often connected with the soil (e.g. texture or depth). These limitations may hinder cultivation or harvesting, leading to lower yields or less flexibility of cropping, but a wide range of agricultural and horticultural crops can be grown.
Grade 3	Land with moderate limitations which restrict the choice of crops, timing of cultivations or level of yield. There may be soil defects or altitude, slope or rainfall may be limiting factors (e.g. land over 400 ft [122 m] with more than 40 in rainfall is not normally graded above Grade 3).
Grade 4	Land with severe limitations due to adverse soil, relief, climate or a combination of these. For example, land over 600 ft [183 m] with over 50 in rainfall is not generally graded above Grade 4. (A high proportion is under grass with occasional fields of oats, barley or fodder crops.)
Grade 5	Land with very severe limitations, including very steep slopes, excessive raininess or exposure, shallow soil or extreme stoniness. Land over 1,000 ft [305 m] with more than 60 in rainfall is generally not graded above Grade 5. Grade 5 land is usually under grass or rough grazing.

Source: Summarised and paraphrased from Morgan (1974).

ALC is useful in highlighting the limited areas of prime agricultural land, and to this extent the map series is useful. But two factors have limited the usefulness of the maps as planning tools. The first of these is the scale and method of survey. The survey is only reliable for land units of 80 or more hectares, but the great majority of planning proposals for residential developments, for example, relate to smaller areas of land (e.g. Gilg 1975a). The usefulness of the maps is therefore limited by their scale. A second weakness concerns Grade 3 land. As might be expected in a class that comprises one-half of the land area, there is considerable internal variation in land quality within this grade. It was decided in 1976 to sub-divide Grade 3 land into sub-classes a, b and c (MAFF 1976). Some Grade 3 land is very serviceable and valuable for agriculture, but it has proved difficult to defend such land against planning proposals because of its third-class connotation. An attempt has recently been made to deal with this problem by the simple expedient of renumbering the classes; the Secretary of State for the Environment proposed that land in Grades 1, 2 and 3 should all become Grade 1 land, sub-divided into 1a, 1b and 1c (Anonymous 1981b).

Over the last two decades, considerable progress has been achieved in land classification and land capability classification in Britain, and in other countries. (Indeed, a national system of land classification based on the rating of soils on a 100-point scale with the base (100) relating to the best farmland in the country was introduced as early as 1934 in Germany; see Weiers 1975.) Perhaps the main and most successful application has been in identifying good agricultural land with a view to retaining it in agricultural use, but problems persist in this application, and others are encountered in fields such as development planning. One fundamental difficulty in Britain has been in organisation and administration, and the simultaneous use of two systems (ALC and LUCC) seems inefficient. In some situations, a good case can be made for using different systems of agricultural land classification concurrently. In a study in Yolo County, California, marked differences in the definition of prime agricultural land emerged when three different classifications were used. This prompted the suggestion that a definition of prime land should be based on two or more systems, and if this were done much less variability would result (Reganold and Singer 1979). But ALC and LUCC are probably too similar, at least in their higher land grades, for this purpose. Furthermore, little progress has been made in classifying land on the basis of its relative capability for different purposes, and work is largely confined to individual sectors such as agriculture, with little interaction taking place between sectors (see Thomas and Coppock 1980).

Few countries have succeeded in implementing integrated land classification surveys, and even when sound methodologies and general practicability can be demonstrated, the ability of governments to employ the results in land-use planning may be called into question (e.g. Laut 1979). For example, it has been suggested that land classification maps of ALC do not appear to have had a major effect on development control in one study area in Devon, as little difference in the success rates of planning applications on different classes of land is evident (Gilg 1975b). The application, as well as the method, of land classification presents problems and difficulties, but these problems and weaknesses fade into relative insignificance when the focus switches to landscape classification.

Landscape classification

Over the last 20 years there has been a great growth of interest in landscape classification or evaluation. The first systematic methods were developed during the late 1960s, but landscape evaluation, without the benefit of ostensibly systematic techniques, is much older. The national parks in England and Wales, for example, were selected on the basis of consensus within committees, without recourse to 'scientific' techniques. The growth of planning in Britain and the growth of outdoor recreation and concern for amenity in the United States prompted the development of techniques of landscape evaluation, which were allegedly more objective than those relying solely on the preferences of planners or committee personnel. Since the late 1960s, numerous techniques have been devised. Some are relatively simple and elegant; some are of great statistical complexity; some are weird and wonderful (including one based on the principle that the pupil of the human eye dilates when a pretty sight is seen, and hence that scenic beauty can be 'measured' by measuring the pupil diameters of viewers (Wenger and Videbeck 1969). This technique has not yet caught on). The proliferation of techniques for assessing landscape beauty is itself a reflection of the inherent difficulty of measuring beauty, which exists in the eye of the beholder. The enthusiasm for systematic techniques of landscape evaluation, which flourished in the early 1970s, has now partly faded, perhaps as a result of the sheer intractability of the problem and of the failure of numerous techniques of evaluation to deal satisfactorily with it.

Purposes of landscape evaluation

As in the case of physical land classification, the purpose of landscape evaluation is several fold (e.g. Penning-Rowsell 1975). The most frequent purpose is simply as a basis for landscape preservation. Landscape evaluation may be used to define areas of landscape where particular planning policies are to be pursued in an effort to conserve landscape quality. The great growth of landscape evaluation during the late 1960s and early 1970s coincided with the advent of structure planning in Britain, and was in part a response to it. Another purpose is in recreation planning. Here, the alternatives are: either the high quality landscapes, as defined by evaluation

221

techniques, can be identified and protected from recreational developments (as from other types of development) or, and more usually, these high quality landscapes may be regarded as prime areas for developments which will offer high quality outdoor recreation. A third application for landscape evaluation is in identifying the worst landscapes so that landscape improvement schemes can be set in motion. A few local authorities in England have used landscape-evaluation techniques for this purpose, but far more are concerned with identifying the 'best' areas. It follows that most techniques have been devised with the 'best' end of the landscape continuum in mind rather than the 'worst' end.

Examples of techniques of landscape evaluation

One possible classification of techniques is into those which are user-dependent, and those which are user-independent, or those which are based on the preferences of large numbers of users of the landscape, and those which are carried out by planners or other technical experts. Perhaps a better grouping is into analytical types and preference types. The former breaks the landscape down into the constituent parts thought to influence or determine landscape quality. These constituent parts are then measured and the measurements are used to compile landscape scores. In preference techniques, the landscape is not analysed in this way. Instead, people are asked to rank or score entire landscapes, either in the field or from photographs.

In analytical techniques, three basic problems arise. Firstly, which landscape elements should be used? Which physical properties of landscape determine its scenic quality? Secondly, how should these elements be measured? Thirdly, how should the elements and measurements be weighted and scored? How important is relief compared with vegetation, for example? One influential example of an analytical approach is that of Linton (1968). Linton assumed that landscape quality was principally determined by two variables, landform and land use. He therefore defined a number of classes for each category, and proceeded to award scores for each class. He assumed that mountains were more attractive than lowlands or plateaux, and awarded scores of 8, 0 and 3, respectively. He also assumed that wild landscapes and 'richly varied farmland' were attractive and awarded them 6 and 5 points respectively, while urbanised and industrialised landscapes were unattractive and merited −5 points. By adding scores for the landform and land-use landscapes, a composite assessment of the landscapes of Scotland was obtained (Fig. 8.3).

If it is accepted that landform and land use are key variables, the next problem concerns the choice of weights to be ascribed to each

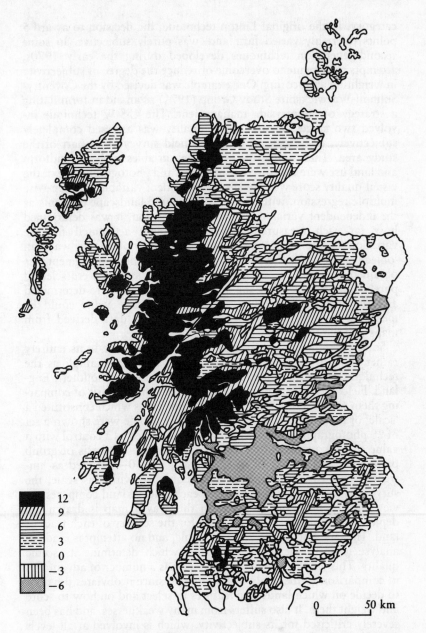

▨	12
▧	9
☰	6
	3
	0
▥	−3
▦	−6

0   50 km

Fig. 8.3 The scenic resources of Scotland: a composite assessment using the
Linton method.
Source: Linton (1968).

category. In the original Linton technique, the decision to award 5 points to 'richly varied farmland' was purely subjective. In some second-generation techniques developed during the early 1970s, attempts were made to overcome or reduce the degree of subjectivity in weighting and scoring. One example was devised by the Coventry-Solihull-Warwickshire Study Group (1971) as an aid in formulating a strategy of countryside management. The C-S-W technique involved two stages. Firstly, visual quality was assessed completely subjectively, on a scale of 0–26, by field surveyors in part of the study area. Then numerous landscape variables such as landform and land use were measured, using maps and photographs. Next, the visual-quality score was used as the dependent variable in a step-wise multiple regression, with the set of measured landscape elements as the independent variables. From this regression, it was determined how far each measured landscape element accounted for the variation in the subjective visual-quality score. In this way, an 'objective' set of weights to be applied to each landscape element was obtained, whereas the weights in the Linton system were selected purely subjectively. After the appropriate weights were determined and the technique thereby calibrated, landscape value could be measured 'objectively' by measuring landscape data derived from maps and photographs.

Some techniques have tried to assess the landscape in its entirety rather than to measure its component parts. An example is the technique devised by Fines (1968) in East Sussex in southern England. Field surveyors scored landscape tracts on the basis of comparing them with a series of pre-scored photographs which constituted a 'scale' of landscape quality. A group of 45 people were shown a set of 20 photographs, one of which was pre-selected as a control with a value of 1. A numerical value was obtained on the basis of group preference, and a scale of 0–32 devised, with 0–1 defined as 'unsightly' and 16–32 as 'spectacular'. Equipped with this scale, the surveyor goes into the field, and for each tract of land compares the view against his standard scale. In this way a map is drawn up, depicting a numerical value or score for the scenery of each tract of land. The landscape is viewed as a whole, and no attempt is made to analyse it or to identify the features which determine its scenic quality. This whole-landscape approach has a number of advantages in comparison to the analytical approach, since it obviates the need to decide on which landscape features to select and on how to score and weight them. It also suffers from many weaknesses, and has been severely criticised for its subjectivity, which is involved at all levels from choosing the photographs for setting the scale to comparing the field view with the scale photographs.

The techniques outlined here are representative examples of a wide range of landscape-evaluation techniques. Like all existing techniques in this field they contain conceptual or methodological weaknesses. The basic problem of how to measure the elusive quality of scenic beauty remains unsolved. In the early 1970s, when interest in systematic techniques was high, the Countryside Commission for Scotland commissioned a firm of consultants to devise a suitable method for classifying the scenic resources of Scotland (Land Use Consultants 1971). But the method developed by the consultants was not adopted by the Commission, and prime landscape areas were eventually identified by a small number of field surveyors relying on their judgement rather than on 'scientific' methods. In England and Wales, the Countryside Commission funded a research project at Manchester University (Robinson *et al.* 1976) to develop a manual of landscape evaluation for use by local planning authorities. The original intention was not fulfilled, however, and the manual was not published. The increasing statistical sophistication of techniques devised in the first half of the 1970s, as compared with the comparative simplicity of first-generation techniques such as those of Linton and Fines, did not solve all the problems inherent in the earlier methods, and their complexity was itself a major disadvantage. More recently, much of the remaining effort in landscape evaluation has focused on 'preference' techniques (Penning-Rowsell 1981, 1982). These techniques seek to measure preferences for whole landscapes rather than persisting in the search for ways of measuring landscape elements as surrogates for landscape quality.

One major advantage in the 'preference' approach is that the landscape is evaluated as a whole, and there is no need to break the landscape down into its elements in order to identify those contributing most strongly to landscape quality, nor to judge the relative contributions from the various elements. On the other hand, preference studies may be difficult to conduct, especially if they involve large numbers of people. It is much easier to use photographs of landscapes in these studies than the actual landscapes in the field. The use of photographs, however, itself involves problems, the most basic of which is the extent to which a photograph can accurately represent a landscape. Photographs are convenient to use, but there is a suspicion that they may not accurately represent, for purposes of evaluation, the landscapes that they depict. Nevertheless, a number of comparisons of preferences of photographs and landscapes have shown high degrees of correlation (e.g. Dunn 1976), suggesting that the use of photographs as surrogates is valid. Another point of controversy relates to the nature of the people expressing preferences. In particular, the possibility exists that professional personnel concerned with landscape may have different preferences from those of the public. On the basis of responses to a set of colour slides

225

of Virginian mountain scenes, Buhyoff *et al.* (1978) concluded that the personal preferences of landscape architects did not correspond to those of a group of their clients. On the other hand, Zube *et al.* (1975) found a high degree of correspondence between experts and non-experts. Preference techniques are obviously much more practicable if they can be used simply with small numbers of professional personnel rather than with large numbers of the public.

Perhaps concern about the possibility of inter-group differences in preferences has obscured a more profound issue. If the function of planning is to help to achieve societal goals in the use of land, then landscape evaluation should be based on the preferences of the general public rather than on those of experts (assuming for the moment that differences exist between 'landscape' professionals and the public). Yet in other fields of aesthetics, the 'best' is not usually the same as the most popular, and Turner (1975) argues that public preferences, even if they could be established, should not be the criteria on which landscape planning is based.

This controversy is one aspect of a broader feature of landscape evaluation, and perhaps even of land-use planning in a wider sense. More effort has been devoted to the mechanics or techniques of landscape evaluation than to broad questions of the purposes of evaluation and the goals of landscape conservation. When the techniques of landscape evaluation were receiving so much attention during the 1970s, the purposes for which the tools should be used were sometimes overlooked. Unfortunately, this tendency to concentrate on the means and neglect the ends applies also in some other aspects of land-use planning.

PLANNING SYSTEMS AND ISSUES

Different systems and structures of land-use planning have been devised in different parts of the world. These differences are related to the prevailing political philosophies, to the prevailing views and concepts of land, and to the various pressures and demands to which land is subjected. Two case studies will be considered: Britain and the United States (with some reference to Canada). These studies are intended to illustrate some of the basic problems that land-use planning has addressed in the respective areas, the approaches employed and the difficulties encountered. The intention is not to attempt to portray the totality of land-use planning in the respective areas, but rather to focus on certain aspects with a view to illustrating specific issues and problems.

Town and country planning in Britain

Planning in Britain dates largely from the 1940s. The forerunners of modern planning legislation appeared in the mid-nineteenth century (geared to maintaining public health rather than to the efficient use of land), and further acts dealing with urban areas were passed in the early twentieth century. During the Second World War, a number of major committees of inquiry investigated topics such as the distribution of population and industry, and the use of land in rural areas. Their reports became the basis for the Town and Country Planning Act of 1947, which is the foundation on which the modern planning system rests. Three major sections relate respectively to development control, to development plan, and to betterment and compensation. Betterment and compensation relate to the thorny question of the financial and fiscal implications of planning controls. Land on which houses and factories can be built with planning permission is usually much more valuable than land remaining in agricultural use. The granting or refusal of planning permission can have a strong effect on land values generally and on specific sites in particular, and the question arises as to whether the landowner should be allowed to enjoy the full benefit or to suffer the full loss resulting from the public action of granting or refusing planning permission for changes in land use. During the last few decades, the original legislation on compensation and betterment has frequently been altered, not least in accordance with the political philosophy of the government of the day.

Development control is concerned with applications for planning permission. Development in this context broadly means the making of material change in the use of land or buildings. Types of development are defined in General Development Orders, which are periodically modified and revised. Planning permission is automatically granted, without application, to minor built developments of less than certain defined sizes, and also for land uses connected with agriculture and forestry. Various other forms of development carried out by highway authorities and other public bodies are also treated in this way. A point of the utmost importance is that the major rural land uses of agriculture and forestry are, in effect, outside the system of development control, although certain types of buildings related to these uses may be subject to control.

For developments or changes in use which are subject to development control, the developer must apply to the local planning authority for planning permission. The elected members of the local authority will then grant permission (perhaps subject to certain conditions) or turn down the application. In practice, powers may be delegated to planning officials to deal with straightforward planning applications on which clear guidelines have been established by the local authority. If the applicant is dissatisfied with the outcome, he may appeal to the planning minister, who can over-rule the local authority. In practice, planning permission is granted by the local authority unless there is a clear reason for refusal. Refusal rates vary according to type of development, but overall are usually under 20 per cent. The overall refusal rate in England and Wales from 1966 to 1981 was 16.3 per cent (Brotherton 1982). In designated areas such as Areas of Outstanding Natural Beauty (AONBs) and National Parks, development-control policies are usually more stringent. The assessment of these designations is difficult, since it is not known how development would have proceeded if no designation had occurred, and identical 'control' areas with which the designated areas may be compared are not available. Perhaps the problem of assessment explains the conflicting opinions held about the effects of designations of AONBs, for example. Blacksell (1979) and Blacksell and Gilg (1977) concluded that designation in East Devon made no material difference, and that refusal rates were higher outside the AONB than within it. However, in East Sussex, Anderson (1981) reached the opposite conclusion, and concluded that AONB designation could be used successfully to withstand urban encroachment in a scenic rural area. Brotherton (1982) found that the refusal rate for planning applications in National Parks was, at 25.5 per cent, substantially higher than the national average, and he expressed the belief that planning controls were slowing down the rate at which the parks were becoming developed, especially in the areas under the greatest pressures.

Changes have occurred in the General Development Orders and in the details of development-control procedures since the system was first introduced, but the essential structure of development control remains unchanged. More substantial changes have been wrought in the development-plan system. For the first 20 years after the Town and Country Planning Act was passed in 1947, local authorities were required to produce development plans. These plans, expressed in maps at a scale of 1:10,560 in urban areas and 1:63,360 in rural areas, defined the areas that were to remain undeveloped, to be developed (and with what land uses), or to undergo change during the currency of the plan. The development plan was based on a development survey carried out by the local authority, and was supported by written statements about the development programme. The development plan required ministerial approval before it was implemented. On implementation, it became the foundation on which development-control policies were based, and it was intended that it would also become the basis of action by the local authority in developing housing, industry and other land uses.

By the late 1960s, the inadequacies of the development-plan system had become obvious. Growth in population and in the economy had been faster than expected, and the development plan was seen as a tool too static and rigid for effective use. It also tended to emphasise physical aspects of planning rather than economic or social considerations. In 1968, therefore, a substantial change was introduced in the passing of a new Town and Country Planning Act in England and Wales, and a similar act was introduced soon afterwards in Scotland. Under these acts, structure plans, local plans and subject plans replaced the old development plans. The structure plan is a written statement setting out the local authority's policy towards development in its area and its own proposals for development. It must be approved by the planning minister before it can be adopted and implemented. After approval, it becomes the basis for strategic planning, and may set out policies such as the preservation of prime agricultural land, for example. It is complemented by several local and subject plans, dealing in detail with a small area or a single subject such as recreation.

The British planning system is sometimes regarded as one of the most comprehensive in the world, but it is not without its weaknesses, conflicts and irrationalities. Two main features are worthy of comment. The first concerns the relative roles of local and national government. Structure planning, local planning and development control are functions of local government, but central government retains a powerful influence through its powers to require that structure plans be modified before approval, and also in its ability to hear appeals arising from local-authority decisions about development control. It also exerts an influence by issuing circulars or guidelines to local planning authorities dealing with subjects such as green belts or the release of agricultural land for house-building. The duality of central and local government involvement has the great advantage of allowing national and local interests to be considered simultaneously, but it can also mean some conflict, especially if the political complexions of the two levels of government are different. This problem can also arise in the different levels of local government. Difficulties in the relationships between various levels of government are, of course, not confined to Britain (nor to planning matters). In a study of planning and the preservation of agricultural land in the rural-urban fringes of Ontario, Gayler (1982) refers to imperfect relationships between tiers of government, and makes the point that difficulties arise especially when new levels of government are introduced. This accords closely with the experience in Britain.

The second feature is more basic and more profound. The British planning system has its roots in the slums of the Victorian industrial cities. Historically, planning has meant town planning, and a strong urban bias has survived to the present, although it has weakened in recent years. During the formative period of the Second World War, Britain was faced with a serious food shortage, and it is not surprising that the containment of urban areas became a primary objective so that farmland could be preserved. Indeed, the Scott Committee in 1942 recommended that agriculture should have a prescriptive right over land currently used for agriculture. It argued that the presumption should be that land should remain in agricultural use unless it could be proved that the prospective new use was to the advantage of the nation. At the same time it was assumed that agriculture was a benign land use, and that all that was required for the countryside to remain healthy and attractive was that agriculture should remain prosperous. Planning controls were therefore not extended to agriculture (or to forestry), but they were applied vigorously to the transfer of agricultural land to urban uses. One consequence was that high densities were achieved in housing developments, and the rate of transfer of agricultural land was almost certainly far slower than it would have been if the planning system had not been in operation.

The urban bias of the planning system has meant that it has been largely ineffectual in controlling rural land uses. Planning authorities have been able to exercise control only over the types of development for which planning permission is required, and the local-authority planners in the rural areas have had to confine their activities to topics such as recreation or village development, while the landscape has been transformed by changes in agriculture or forestry. Although the planning system was widened by the introduction of structure planning, it remains largely impotent in the face of major changes of land use such as open heathland to forest, while it strictly controls relatively minor changes such as alterations to houses. This apparent inconsistency and illogicality, rooted in the history of the planning system, has been the subject of much attention, and there have been frequent calls for agriculture and forestry to be brought under stricter planning control. These calls have been strenuously opposed by the powerful lobby of farmers and landowners, and have repeatedly been rejected by government.

At a more basic level, the question of the purpose of the planning system arises. If the objective of land-use planning is to reconcile the goals of society and those of individual land owners, the extent to which the British statutory planning system has been successful is debatable. The preservation of agricultural land may have been an important and indeed vital goal during the troubled times of the Second World War, but it is of less obvious importance 30 years later when agricultural output has increased to the extent that some

commodities are in surplus. The high urban densities that have
resulted from policies of preserving agricultural land might be argued
by some to have been too high a price to pay. However, there has
been little debate on the basic purposes of the planning system, and
its objectives have become obscured by the mechanics and the
practice of planning. The goals of society, composed as it is of such
varied sections, cannot be easily specified or defined, and they cannot
be readily translated into policies or objectives for land-use planning.
If societal goals cannot be accurately defined then, what is the point
and purpose of land-use planning? These goals constitute the
ultimate context of land-use planning, and should provide the
framework within which techniques such as land capability
classification are employed. If the goals are clearly defined, then it
should be possible to identify the areas of importance for particular
land-use activities and the critical areas where there is little flexibility
of use, and without which the defined goals cannot be achieved
(Flaherty and Smit 1982). But all too often attention has been
focused on the techniques *per se*, rather than on the purposes for
which they are required.

Perhaps paradoxically, some societal goals that have been defined,
albeit loosely and imprecisely, have been incapable of achievement
by the statutory planning system. This system, based on the Town
and Country Planning Acts, is much more successful in preventing
certain types of development or changes in land use than in promoting change or development. It is usually regarded in negative
rather than positive terms, although increasing attention has focused
on management agreements in recent years. Under these agreements,
the planning authority pays or compensates a landowner for using
his land in an agreed way for *not* carrying out a certain change of
land use. In this way the positive ability of the planning authority has
been increased, at least to some extent, although management
agreements pose their own problems of cost. As yet, the few examples of positive land-use planning that have been attempted in
Britain have not been outstandingly successful.

One interesting example is that of the Highlands and Islands
Development Board in drawing up land development plans (outside
the statutory planning system) for the Strath of Kildonan and the
Island of Mull in Scotland (HIDB, 1970, 1973). The HIDB in seeking
to increase the productive use of land in these areas, and to increase
land-based employment, drew up plans for land development, using
tools such as land capability survey. These plans in all probability
accurately reflected the views and objectives of the local communities, and were technically sound and robust. They could not be
implemented, however, because the owners of the land were content
to maintain their existing land-use regimes, and had no wish to adopt

the proposals set out in the land development plans. This in a nutshell illustrates the imbalance of land-use planning in Britain, and in a more general sense illustrates the problem of land-use planning in western democracies. Land owners may be prevented from making certain changes in land use, but they usually cannot be forced to use land positively and efficiently.

Issues in land-use planning in North America

The second case study, which illustrates different approaches and issues from those in Britain, is set in North America. It does not seek to give a comprehensive account of land-use planning and land-use control in any part of the continent (for such an account see, for example, Jackson 1981), but instead concentrates on two themes that illustrate some of the major contemporary issues and problems of land-use planning in North America. One relates to attempts to control the flow of privately owned agricultural land into urban and other non-agricultural uses, while the other is concerned with recent developments in land-use planning on the Forest Service portion of the federal lands, which collectively extend to about one-third of the area of the United States.

The preservation of agricultural land

The concept of public controls on private land use in the United States is not a new one: zoning ordinances based (theoretically) on a comprehensive plan have been in use since the early years of this century (see Ch. 3). In recent years, however, concern about the loss of good farmland has given rise to a number of new approaches. Although the rate of loss of agricultural land is surrounded by uncertainty and confusion because of inadequacies of data (Ch. 4), it is viewed with sufficient concern for policies of land preservation to have been devised and implemented in many parts of the continent.

In the United States, there is no national system of planning comparable to that in Britain. Responsibility for devising methods for preserving privately owned agricultural land rests primarily with the state governments. Different responses have been forthcoming in different areas, depending on the perceived severity of problems and the political complexion of state governments. The various approaches and measures adopted in relation to the preservation of agricultural land are reviewed by a number of writers including Keene (1979), Duncan (1984), and Rose (1984). The distribution of measures adopted in North American states and provinces is shown in Fig. 8.4.

The most widely used methods developed to protect farmland and

	Differential tax assessment	Circuit breaker taxation	Centralised land use policies	Agricultural land banking	Transfer of development rights	Exclusive agricultural zoning	Agricultural districting	Executive powers actions	Waiver of urban infrastructural assessment
Canada									
Alberta	●		●						●
British Columbia	●	●	●			●			●
Manitoba			●						
New Brunswick	●		●						●
Newfoundland	●		●			●			●
Nova Scotia	●		●						
Ontario	●		●						
Prince Edward I.	●		●	●			●		●
Quebec	●		●	●					●
Saskatchewan	●		●	●					
United States									
Alabama	●								
Alaska	●				●				
Arizona	●								
Arkansas	●								
California	●		●		●				
Colorado	●								
Connecticut	●				●				
Delaware	●								
Florida	●								
Georgia									
Hawaii	●		●	●					●
Idaho	●								
Illinois	●							●	
Indiana	●								
Iowa	●								
Kansas	●								
Kentucky	●								
Louisiana	●								
Maine	●								
Maryland	●					●	●		●
Massachusetts	●			●	●				
Michigan		●							
Minnesota	●						●		●
Mississippi									
Missouri	●								
Montana	●								
Nebraska	●								
Nevada	●								
New Hampshire	●				●				
New Jersey	●								
New Mexico	●								
New York	●						●		
North Carolina	●								
North Dakota	●								
Ohio	●								
Oklahoma	●								
Oregon	●		●			●			●
Pennsylvania	●			●					
Rhode Island	●								
South Carolina	●								
South Dakota	●								
Tennessee	●			●					
Texas	●								
Utah	●								
Vermont	●								
Virginia	●						●		●
Washington	●			●					
West Virginia	●								
Wisconsin		●	●			●			●
Wyoming	●								

Fig. 8.4 Farmland protection mechanisms in Canada and the United States.
Source: Furuseth and Pierce (1982).

open space is based on property tax levels. By 1974, 31 states had adopted some form of property tax relief aimed at preserving farm land (Lapping 1977), and by the end of the decade the number had grown to 48 (Furuseth and Pierce 1982). If land is assessed on the basis of its existing use, rather than on market value as would normally be the case, then one of the pressures that might otherwise encourage the farmer to sell his land for non-agricultural purposes is relieved (Hady 1970). The market value of land for residential purposes is, of course, much higher than the use-value under agriculture. There may be a straightforward differential tax assessment or, alternatively, there may be a penalty element, with the farmer enjoying use-value assessment, but having to pay a tax penalty if the use of the land is changed to another form which is incompatible with the program. In New York State, for example, the concept of 'agricultural districts' has been introduced (Conklin and Bryant 1974). If farmers apply for their land to be included in agricultural districts, their land is assessed for property tax on the basis of use-value, but if they then convert the land to other unacceptable uses, they are subject to a fine equivalent to five years of exempted taxes (Lapping 1975). Previous attempts to use state powers to preserve agricultural land had failed to gain much support, but the agricultural district program was viewed more favourably, probably because the initiative lay with the farmers themselves in seeking inclusion within an agricultural district. Around one-quarter of New York State's farmland now lies in agricultural districts (Furuseth and Pierce 1982).

Although the program may help to relieve some of the pressures for land-use change in states such as New York, differential-assessment policies are not without their problems. General evaluations of policy measures based on differential assessments suggest that their effectiveness is limited (e.g. Furuseth and Pierce 1982). In California, for example, as much as 35 per cent of the state's farmland was included in the preferential tax assessment program by 1974, after the program was introduced in the California Land Conservation Act (the Williamson Act) of 1965 (Lapping 1977). But much of the land under contract was remote from the main pressure areas, and while landowners may have benefited from lower property tax assessments, the extent to which the objectives of the policy were efficiently achieved is debatable. The highest rates of participation were found not in the areas of greatest urbanising pressures, close to the urban fringe, but in areas where pressures were weaker (Hansen and Schwartz 1975; Carman 1977; Gustafson 1979). In areas of keen demand for urban land, the farmer still has a strong incentive to sell his land for non-agricultural purposes, and urban-fringe pressures may be too great for differential assessment to offer an effective incentive for him to retain his land in agriculture. Keene (1979) reaches the general conclusion that differential tax measures have the greatest effect in areas where the demand for land for alternative uses is only moderate, where agriculture is reasonably profitable, and where the farmer is middle-aged or younger, or has family members who wish to continue farming.

Other measures used to restrain the flow of agricultural land to urban uses include the transfer of development rights, although the area thus protected is at present very small. Under the concept of transferable development rights (TDR), owners of land in designated conservation areas may sell their rights to develop (which they are not permitted to exercise) to owners in designated development areas. Development in these areas which, like the conservation areas, are delineated on a master plan, requires the possession of a number of development rights. The rationale behind this measure is obviously to ensure that landowners in the conservation zones do not suffer financially by foregoing development. Another variant is the purchase of development rights by a government agency: the land-owner is then no longer able to develop the land himself. Suffolk County in New York State has the longest experience with this measure. Under it, landowners of farmland submit offers to sell their development rights to the county and, if accepted, the right to convert the land to urban or other unapproved uses passes from the private owner. Although this measure involves high costs, it has met with support from both farming and non-farming residents in the county, where there is a keen wish to keep the landscape rural and attractive (Lapping 1977). A broadly similar measure has been in use in Massachusetts since 1980: a farmer can offer to sell his development rights and, if his offer is accepted (which will depend on factors such as soil quality and degree of threat of urbanisation), then a deed restriction runs with the property (Storrow and Winthrop 1983).

An even more expensive variant is for a government body to purchase land outright from farmers, and then lease it back to them as farming tenants. Such land banking has been used, for example, in British Columbia and Saskatchewan. The zoning of land for agriculture is another measure used in an attempt to preserve agricultural land (usually in combination with preferential assessment), but Lapping (1977) concludes that it has not been very successful. A basic weakness is that the zoning of land for agriculture does not in itself ensure continuing agricultural use any more than zoning for other uses ensures that these other uses will occur.

The strongest and most comprehensive measures have been adopted in Oregon. In 1973, a state Land Use Planning Act was passed, making local planning mandatory (Patterson 1979;

Gustafson *et al.* 1982) and setting up a Land Conservation and Development Commission, which the following year adopted a set of 'Planning goals and guidelines' after public hearings. One major goal was the preservation of agricultural land, and to this end the concept of exclusive farm use (EFU) was introduced. All prime or valuable farmland, as defined by land capability classes, had to be zoned for EFU and, furthermore, all land transactions which would create parcels of less than 4 ha required consent, which would be granted only if consistent with the state agricultural land-use policy. In this way, sub-division of land for 'ranchettes' and hobby farms was to be controlled.

These restrictions were complemented by a number of positive benefits to farmers. Assessment of land for purposes of property tax was to be based on use-value rather than market value; state inheritance tax was also to be based on use-value, and local governments were to be prohibited from enacting laws or regulations which would unreasonably restrict farm operators.

Participation in Oregon, unlike most states, is mandatory, and the measures are generally more stringent than in other parts of North America. Yet there appears to have been strong popular support for the measures, reaching a level of 90 per cent of respondents in one county poll (Furuseth 1980). Evidence has been reported that in most regions of the state, agricultural land-use is proving more resistant to conversion to urban and suburban development, even at a time when there was dramatic economic and population growth. In other circumstances, this growth might have been expected to result in rapid conversion rates (Furuseth 1981). The rate of loss of agricultural land in metropolitan areas has slackened. Broadly similar measures, involving exclusive agricultural zoning as well as differential assessment, have been adopted in British Columbia, and there are signs that they are beginning to be effective in that province also (Furuseth and Pierce 1982; Pierce 1983). It is perhaps significant that both Oregon and British Columbia have relatively small areas of arable land, on which development pressures are strongly concentrated. Stringent measures involving exclusive agricultural zoning have been acceptable there, but not as yet in other areas such as California and Ontario, where development pressures are as great or greater, but where the arable area is less restricted.

The state of Oregon is unusual in the rigour of its land-use planning policies, but the general trend in many other states (and Canadian provinces) is similar. This is part of what Bosselman and Callies (1972) describe as the 'quiet revolution' in land-use control, and coincides in time with the environmental movement of the early 1970s. Awareness on the effects of land-use decisions made by individual land owners on the environment and on other citizens has greatly heightened during the last two decades, and the degree of public control over private land use has increased. This element of control is not confined solely to agricultural land in urbanising areas, but is rather more general. In the state of Maine, for example, of which 90 per cent is under forest, a Land Use Regulation Commission was set up in 1972 to plan and zone one-half of the state, consisting of land lacking a local-government structure and lying mainly under the ownership of the forest industry. The Commission consists of elected members, supported by a small team of officials, and has drawn up a comprehensive plan that guides decisions on permission for development (Pidot 1982). Lands are classified in zones for protection (28 per cent), development (2 per cent) and management (70 per cent). Attempts have been made in some states to influence or control the type of management as well as the type of use. In California, for example, the Forest Practice Act of 1973 imposed standards and rules that combined environmental objectives such as control of soil erosion (see page 167) with efficient timber production. These standards and rules laid down specifications for road construction, for the harvesting of stream-side trees, and for many other practices (Dana and Fairfax 1980).

The experience in Maine reported by Pidot highlights one of the main features of land-use planning in areas dominated by private ownership. Landowners may resent and resist attempts to reduce their freedom of choice in making decisions about how to use and manage land, and problems of enforcement may arise, depending on the strength of the planning powers and the degree of popular support lying behind them. This illustrates the basic truth that land-use planning is a political process as well as a technical one. Understandably, the training of planners may emphasise the technical aspects, but planning cannot be free from political influences since it is concerned with the distribution and exercise of power and the definition and attainment of societal goals. Unless a plan is politically acceptable both in its goals and in the measures and powers that it involves, it will not be implemented. The history of land-use planning is littered with plans which may have been technically sound or even excellent, but which failed to be implemented because they lacked political acceptability or the political-legal means of implementation.

A general point arising from planning for the preservation of agricultural lands in North America concerns the basic validity and acceptability of the primary objective. As is discussed in Chapter 4, the rates of land transfer from agriculture to urban and similar uses are not known with great accuracy or precision. Objectives of land preservation therefore rest on weak factual foundations and, furthermore, the extent to which they reflect the concerns of the public, as opposed to planners or legislators, is uncertain. There is also an apparent paradox between the problem of accumulating agricultural surpluses on the one hand and the perceived problem of loss of agricultural land on the other: if agricultural production exceeds demand for agricultural products, why should there be concern about the loss of agricultural land? Policies and programs for preserving agricultural land at a time of growing agricultural surpluses may be justified in terms of probable *long-term* growth in demand for agricultural products, but the extent to which they are seen as justified in the short term is perhaps debatable. One of the few instances where there has been direct public involvement in defining objectives in land-use planning is in California, where in 1972 a proposition to preserve and protect the coastal zone, arising from public initiative, was supported by a majority of the electorate (e.g. Anderson 1973; Mogoluf 1975). As a result, the California Coastal Zone Conservation Act of 1972 was passed, providing for the preparation of a comprehensive plan for conservation and management of the coastal zone, and controlling development in a 1,000 yard (914 m) coastal strip by means of a permit system. Around 90 per cent of permit applications have, in fact, been granted, but in many instances conditions have been written in or modifications made to the original application (Jackson 1981).

Land-use planning in the US Forest Service lands

Some other issues and problems in land-use planning can be illustrated by outlining some recent trends in land-use planning on federal land in the United States and, in particular, on land controlled by the Forest Service. At first sight many of the problems of land-use planning encountered in areas under private land ownership, as discussed in the preceding section, should be absent in public lands. Public land agencies are at the same time planner and owner, and plans can be implemented without the fundamental problem of landowner resistance. Land-use planning in areas dominated by private ownership is concerned with reconciling individual and public interest in land. This concern does not apply in the same way on public lands, where the emphasis lies more on achieving efficient use and satisfying the sometimes conflicting demands of the various sections of the general public.

As in land-use planning in a more general sense, the 1970s saw a number of significant developments in planning on the federal lands in the United States (e.g. Culhane and Friesema 1979; Clawson 1975, 1983). In 1974, the Forest and Rangeland Renewable Resources Planning Act (RPA) was passed, and two years later the trend was further emphasised by the National Forest Management Act

(NFMA) and the Federal Lands Policy and Management Act (FLPMA). The FLPMA serves as the basic act for the Bureau of Land Management (BLM) (one of the major federal land holding agencies) and provides for land-use planning on land under the control of the BLM, while the two former acts relate to the Forest Service.

Under the RPA of 1974, the US Forest Service was required to prepare an assessment of renewable resources of forest and range-land, and a recommended programme for its activities. Assessment involved an inventory of demands on forest resources. The act required that an assessment be prepared by the end of 1975, and that it be updated during 1979 and each 10th year thereafter. It had to contain analyses of present and anticipated use of the renewable resources of forest and range, and of trends in demand and supply. Price trends had to be included, and the 'international resource situation' had to be considered. An inventory of present and potential renewable resources was also required, and opportunities for improving the yield of goods and services had to be included. These assessments were duly published in 1977 and 1981 (USDA Forest Service 1977, 1981). The projections show that demands for forest and range products are likely to increase faster than supplies over the next few decades, but that current production was below potential.

Within the RPA planning process, national goals and directions for forest and range resources had to be defined, alternative Forest Service programmes had to be identified and evaluated, and plans selected for each resource area. Under NFMA, this planning process was extended to include comprehensive land-use planning for all local administrative units. The land-use plan was to be the primary policy document for multiple-use management of Forest Service land.

Land-use planning in this context seems to be no more and no less than formal, rational decision-making, in which objectives are defined and alternative means of achieving them evaluated, all within the context of survey and inventory of resources. The introduction of this system of rational, rigorous and comprehensive land-use planning would, apparently, replace the old pattern of incremental and fragmented decision-making (Ch. 2). It does indeed set out the assumptions and projections on which decisions are made in a much more explicit and comprehensive fashion than existed previously, or than exists in the public sectors of most other countries to-day. It also serves as a foundation on which planning may be based, but there are limitations to the extent to which this planning system is rational in the classical sense.

One limitation is the role and form of public involvement. RPA provided for public participation, and it is obviously important that the public should be involved directly in planning about the use of public lands, and that it should be consulted about objectives and preferred plans. Major questions arise, however, about the form that public involvement should take. Identifying goals and using them to guide public programmes is acknowledged in the 1975 assessment to be a difficult and an inexact science. Goals expressed by legislators, interest groups or organisations are usually couched in rather general statements, and are difficult to translate into blueprints and quantitative targets, especially when different interest groups have conflicting goals. If goals cannot be specified precisely, decision-making cannot be fully rational in the classical sense. Furthermore, the behaviour of the public in the participation process may be no more 'rational', in the classical sense, than that of individual land owners. In public participation, there is a greater likelihood for the preferences of particular interest groups to be favoured than for all alternatives to be evaluated systematically. However desirable public participation may be in the planning of the use of public lands, it does not always fit perfectly within frameworks of rational decision-making.

There are various other factors which limit the extent to which the land-use planning system introduced in much of the federal land area in the 1970s can be comprehensive and purely rational in the formal, classical sense. These are reviewed by Cortner and Schweitzer (1981), and prominent among them is the nature of the public agency itself. A fundamental feature of a public bureaucracy is its wish to ensure its own survival. To survive, the agency must attract and maintain political support and funding. It may therefore be reluctant to embark on a course of action that would endanger that support and funding, and it follows that certain plans, although perhaps technically feasible, are not seriously considered. Even alternatives such as no action or maintaining the *status quo* may not be seriously evaluated as they would fail to enhance the agency's prestige. Similarly, alternatives that would fall outside its own powers or that would benefit another agency might not be fully evaluated. At another level, the agency is perhaps unlikely to consider scenarios that assume or imply the failure of national policies in, for example, employment or the economy, and it can hardly assume radical changes in international relations and hence in trading patterns. Many assumptions about future conditions simply involve an extrapolation of current conditions, and positive trends in prosperity are likely to be assumed. Future conditions are almost infinitely variable in any case, and no agency can hope to identify all the possibilities, even if it wished to do so. It follows that all alternatives cannot be identified or considered, and hence that decision-making cannot be fully rational.

At another level, further limitations arise from the time-scale of planning. Although a long-term perspective is required in the management of forest resources, politicians operate on a relatively short time scale, and will often favour solutions with immediate or short-term payoffs. A related problem is that the five-year planning period under RPA is not synchronous with the presidential term of four years. The 'feasibility' of a plan may therefore depend, in the view of the agency, on how it related to the policies of the main contenders for the presidency, given the aim of the agency to survive and flourish. In short, legislation in the United States may provide for comprehensive and rational land-use planning on federal and especially on Forest Service land, but the extent to which it may actually be achieved is questionable. In recent years, a definite provision for rational land-use planning has become available, but it is not without its ambiguities. Above all, it may seem to give the impression that land-use planning can be a purely technical, value-free process. In practice, however, it is also a political activity, on both public land and on private.

CONCLUSION

Ultimately, land-use planning depends on how political power is distributed and exercised. It cannot be simply a technical, 'value-free' exercise, although it has technical aspects such as land classification and the systematic evaluation of alternative strategies. Perhaps there has been too great an emphasis on such technical issues, and too little on the broad objectives of planning. Professional planners can contribute some of the means of planning, but the ends or objectives are highly political in nature. They depend, in the final analysis, on how land is perceived by society: on whether its use should be dictated by market forces and by the pursuit of profit by its owner; on whether it should be regarded as a common-property resource like air or water; and on whether it is an inheritance to which an obligation of stewardship is owed to future generations.

Systems of land-use planning in many western countries are the embodiment of compromises. They impose curbs and constraints on the extent to which the private owner can use his land as he pleases. The political pressures leading to these compromises reflect the social values from which they arise, and give expression to the belief that land should not be seen *merely* as private property or as a factor of production. Such a belief is, of course, not new, as was indicated in the opening chapter, but it has perhaps been re-affirmed in the light of the consequences of misery and devastation that have sometimes flowed from unbridled private property rights in land. The rights of the individual to acquire and use land as he pleases have to be set alongside the safeguarding of the beauty and usefulness of that land, and the well-being of his neighbours in society.

The compromises represented by land-use planning in many western countries are dynamic rather than static. The strengthening view of the social value of land is reflected in the growing controls on private land use that are imposed by planning systems, but even the ultimate step in this direction, namely the acquisition and management of land by government bodies, is no panacea for the problems that arise from the use of land. There is little evidence that public control of this kind guarantees that the usefulness and beauty of the land will be maintained, and different groups within society still seek different goals for the use of land whether that land is under public or private control. No system of land ownership or control as yet devised by man has been wholly successful on criteria of equity, efficiency and conservation, but some systems have failed more dramatically than others. Perhaps the failure has been most conspicuous when a narrow view has been taken of land and land use (for example, *just* as private property and *only* as economic activity). The theme of plurality or multiplicity pervades this book – there are different concepts of land, there are different aspects of the usefulness of land, and there is a great variety of influences on the use and management of land. It is the hope of the writer that this book can, in its small and limited way, help to foster a catholic view of land and its use.

FURTHER READING

Cullingworth, J. B. (1979) *Town and country planning in England and Wales.*

Davidson, D. A. (1980) *Soils and land-use planning.*

Jackson, R. H. (1981) *Land use in America.*

Penning-Rowsell, E. C. (1981) Fluctuating fortunes in gauging landscape value.

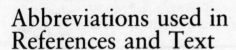

Abbreviations used in References and Text

ADAS	– Agricultural Development and Advisory Service
AONB	– Area of Outstanding Beauty
HIDB	– Highlands and Islands Development Board
IUCN	– International Union for the Conservation of Nature
MAFF	– Ministry of Agriculture, Fisheries and Food
MTCP	– Ministry of Town and Country Planning
NALS	– National Agricultural Lands Study
NCC	– Nature Conservancy Council
OECD	– Organisation for Economic Cooperation and Development
RICS	– Royal Institute of Chartered Surveyors
smd	– standard man day
USCEQ	– United States Council for Environmental Quality
USDA	– United States Department of Agriculture

References

Adams, W. M. (1984) Sites of Special Scientific Interest and habitat protection: implications of the Wildlife and Countryside Act 1981, *Area*, **16**, 273–80.

ADAS (1973) *Agriculture in the urban fringe : a survey of the Slough/Hillingdon area*, Ministry of Agriculture, Fisheries and Food Tech. Rep. 30.

ADAS (1976) *Agriculture in the urban fringe: a survey in the Metropolitan county of Tyne and Wear*, Ministry of Agriculture, Fisheries and Food Tech. Rep. 30/1.

Albrecht, S. L. (1976) Legacy of the environmental movement, *Environ. Behav.*, **8**, 147–68.

Aldrich, J. W. and **Slaughter, C. W.** (1983) Soil erosion on subarctic forest slopes, *J. Soil & Water Conserv.*, **38**, 115–18.

Alexander, M. (1973) Environmental consequences of increasing food production, *Biol. Conserv.*, **5**, 15–19.

Alonso, W. (1960) A theory of the urban land market, *Pap. & Proc. Reg. Sci. Ass.*, **6**, 149–58.

Alonso, W. (1964) *Location and land use : toward a general theory of land rent.* Cambridge, Mass. : Harvard U.P.

Alston, R. M. and **Freeman, D. M.** (1975) The natural resources decision-maker as political and economic man : towards a synthesis, *J. Environ. Manag.*, **3**, 167–83.

Alt, K. F. and **Heady, E. O.** (1977) *Economics and the environment : impacts of erosion restraints on crop production in the Iowa River Basin.* Ames, Iowa : Iowa State University CARD Report 75.

Anderson, E. A. Jr. (1973) A case-study in conservation politics : California's coastline initiative, *Biol. Conserv.*, **5**, 160–2.

Anderson, J. R. (1977) Land use and land cover changes – a framework for monitoring, *J. Res. US Geol. Surv.*, **5**, 143–53.

245

Anderson, J. R. *et al.* (1976) A land use and land cover classification system for use with remote sensing data, *Prof. Pap. US Geol. Surv.* 964.

Anderson, M. A. (1981) Planning policies and development control in the Sussex Downs AONB, *Town Plan. Rev.*, 52, 5–25.

Andreae, B. (1981) *Farming, development and space*. Berlin and New York : Walter de Gruyter.

Andrews, R. N. L. (1979) *Land in America : commodity or natural resource?* Lexington : Lexington Books.

Anonymous (1981a) Bibliography on protection of the environment, *Europ. Commun. Document. Bull.*, B/11.

Anonymous (1981b) Agricultural land classification, *J. Plan. Environ. Law*, 548.

Armstrong, A. M. and **Mather, A. S.** (1983) *Land ownership and land use in the Scottish Highlands*, Aberdeen : Univ. of Aberdeen O'Dell Mem. Monogr. 13.

Arnold, G. W. (1983) The influence of ditch and hedgerow structure, length of hedgerows and area of woodland and garden on bird numbers on farmland, *J. Appl. Ecol.*, 20, 731–50.

Bach, W., Pankrath, J. and **Kellogg, W.** (eds) (1979) *Man's impact on climate*. Amsterdam : Elsevier.

Bachrach, P. and **Baratz, M. S.** (1962) Two faces of power, *Am. Pol. Sci. Rev.*, 56, 947–52.

Bahre, C. J. and **Bradbury, D. E.** (1978) Vegetation change along the Arizona-Sonora boundary, *Ann. Ass. Am. Geog.*, 68, 145–65.

Baltensperger, B. H. (1983) Agricultural change among Great Plains Russian Germans, *Ann. Ass. Am. Geog.*, 73, 75–88.

Barlowe, R. (1978) *Land resource economics* (3rd edn). Englewood Cliffs, N. J. : Prentice Hall.

Barney, G. O. (1980) *The Global 2000 Report to the President of the US : entering the 21st century*, Washington: US Council for Environmental Quality, and Oxford: Pergamon.

Barton, P. M. and **Buckley, G. P.** (1983) The status and protection of notified Sites of Special Scientific Interest in south-east England, *Biol. Conserv.*, 27, 213–42.

Bayfield, N. G. (1973) Use and deterioration of some Scottish hill paths, *J. Appl. Ecol.*, 10, 635–44.

Bayfield, N. G. (1974) Burial of vegetation debris near ski lifts on Cairngorm, Scotland, *Biol. Conserv.*, 6, 246–51.

Bayliss-Smith, T. P. (1982) *The ecology of agricultural systems*. Cambridge : Cambridge U.P.

Belding, R. (1981) A test of the von Thünen locational model of agricultural land use with accountancy data from the European Economic Community, *Trans. Inst. Brit. Geog.*, 6, 176–87.

Berry, B. J. L. *et al.* (1974) Land use, urban form and environmental quality, *University of Chicago Department of Geography, Research Paper 155.*

Berry, D. (1979) The sensitivity of dairying to urbanization : a study of north-eastern Illinois, *Prof. Geog.*, 31, 170–6.

Best, R. H. (1978) Myth and reality in the growth of urban land. In A. W. Rogers (ed.) *op.cit.*, 2–15.

Best, R. H. (1979) Land-use structure and change in the EEC, *Town Plan. Rev.*, 50, 395–411.

Best, R. H. (1981) *Land use and living space.* London : Methuen.

Best, R. H. and Ward, J. T. (1956) *The garden controversy.* Ashford, Kent : Wye College Dept. Agric. Economics.

Bibby, J. S. and Mackney, D. (1969) Land use capability classification, *Soil Surv. Tech. Monogr.* 1, Rothamsted.

Bibby, J. S. *et al.* (1982) *Land capability classification for agriculture.* Aberdeen : Macaulay Institute for Soil Research.

Birch, T. W. and Dennis, D. F. (1980) The forest-land owners of Pennsylvania. Broomall, Pennsylvania: *USDA For. Serv. Res. Bull.* NE–66.

Bjarnason, J. (1978) Erosion, tree growth and land regeneration in Iceland. In M. W. Holdgate and M. J. Woodman (eds) *The breakdown and restoration of ecosystems.* NATO Conference Series 1 Ecology, 3, Plenum Press, pp.241–6.

Bjonness, I.-M. (1980a) Animal husbandry and grazing : a conservation and management problem in Sagarmatha (Mt. Everest) National Park, Nepal, *Norsk Geog. Tids.*, 34, 59–76.

Bjonness, I.-M. (1980b) Ecological conflicts and economic dependency on tourist trekking in Sagarmatha (Mt Everest) National Park, Nepal, *Norsk Geog. Tids.*, 34, 119–38.

Black, J. N. (1970) *The dominion of man.* Edinburgh : Edinburgh U.P.

Blackie, J. R. *et al.* (1980) Environmental effects of deforestation : an annotated bibliography, *Freshwater Biol. Ass. Occ. Publ.* 10.

Blackmore, M. (1974) The Nature Conservancy : its history and role. In A. Warren and F. B. Goldsmith (eds) *Conservation in Practice.* *op. cit.*, pp.423–36.

Blacksell, M. (1979) Landscape protection and development control : an appraisal of planning in rural areas of England and Wales, *Geoforum*, 10, 267–74.

Blacksell, M. and Gilg, A. W. (1977) Planning control in an area of outstanding natural beauty, *Soc. Econ. Admin.*, 11, 206–15.

Blair, A. M. (1980) Urban influences on farming in Essex, *Geoforum*, 11, 371–84.

Boal, F. W. (1970) Urban growth and land value patterns : government influence, *Prof. Geog.*, 22, 79–82.

Board, C. (1968) Land use surveys : principles and practice. In *Land use and resources.* Sp. Publ. 1, Inst. Brit. Geog. pp.29–42.

Boardman, R. (1978) Maintenance of productivity in successive rotations of *Radiata* pine in South Australia. In E. D. Ford *et al. op. cit.*, pp.543–53.

Bock, C. A. (1974) The expanding public interest in private property, *J. Soil Water Conserv.*, 29, 109–13.

Bockheim, J. G., Ballard, T. M. and Willington, R. P. (1975) Soil disturbance associated with timber harvesting in south-western British Columbia, *Can. J. for. Res.*, 5, 285–90.

Boels, D., Davies, D. B. and Johnston, A. E. (1982) Soil degradation, *Proc. Land Use Seminar on Soil Degradation*, Wageningen, 1980, Rotterdam : A. A. Balkema.

Boggers, W. *et al.* (1979) Farm-level impacts of alternative soil loss control policies, *J. Soil Water Conserv.*, 34, 177–80.

Bonnicksen, T. M. and Stone, E. C. (1982) Managing vegetation within US National Parks : a policy analysis, *Environ. Manag.*, 6, 109–22.

Borman, F. H. *et al.* (1974) The export of nutrients and recovery of stable conditions following deforestation at Hubbard Brook, *Ecol. Monogr.*, 44, 255–77.

Bosselman, F. P. and Callies, D. (1972) *The quiet revolution in land use controls.* Washington : US CEQ.

Bourne, L. S. (1976) Urban structure and land-use decisions, *Ann. Ass. Am. Geog.*, 66, 531–47.

Bowen, M. J. (1974) Outdoor recreation around large cities. In J. H. Johnson (ed.) *Suburban growth : geographical processes at the edge of the western city.* London and New York : John Wiley, pp.225–48.

Bowers, J. K. (1983a) Cost-benefit analysis of wetland drainage, *Environ. Plan. A*, 15, 227–35.

Bowers, J. K. (1983b) Economics and conservation : the case of land drainage. In A. Warren and F. B. Goldsmith (eds) *op. cit.*, pp.375–89.

Bowers, J. K. and Cheshire, P. (1983) *Agriculture, the countryside and land use : an economic critique.* London and New York : Methuen.

Bowler, I. R. (1979) *Government and agriculture : a spatial perspective.* London and New York : Longman.

Bradley, M. D. (1973) Decision-making for environmental resources management, *J. Environ. Manag.*, 1, 289–302.

Brandow, G. E. (1973) Conflicts and consistencies in the agricultural policies of the United States and Canada, *Am. J. Agric. Econ.*, 55, 778–84.

Brasch, E. (1979) Peri-urban agriculture in the areas of Kristianstad and Eslov. In OECD (1979) *op. cit.* pp.451–81.

Bratton, S. P., Stromberg, L. L. and Harmon, M. E. (1982) Firewood gathering impacts in backcountry campsites in Great Smoky Mountains National Park, *Environ. Manag.*, 6, 63–71.

Bray, C. E., del Castillo, A. M. and Bjornlund, E. (1979) Farm structure policy in other countries, *USDA Agric. Econ. Rep.* 438, 290–305.

Brigham, E. F. (1965) The determinants of residential land values, *Land Economics*, 41, 325–35.

Brotherton, I. (1982) Development pressures and control in the national parks 1966–1981, *Town Plan. Rev.*, 53, 439–59.

Brown, H. J., Phillips, R. S. and Roberts, N. A. (1981) Land markets at the urban fringe : new insights for policy makers, *J. Am. Plan. Ass.*, 47, 131–44.

Brown, J. A. (1975) Implications of government land banks and residency requirements for agricultural land use. In *Proc. 1975 Workshop of the Canadian Agricultural Economics Society*, Banff, Alberta, pp.90–108.

Brubaker, S. (1977) Land – the far horizon, *Am. J. Agric. Econ.*, 59, 1037–44.

Brun, A. (1978) Land ownership and the farm unit, *Europ. Rev. Agric. Econ.*, 5, 277–98.

Brunn, S. D. and Raitz, K. B. (1978) Regional patterns of farm magazine publication, *Econ. Geog.*, 54, 277–90.

Bryant, C. R. (1973) The anticipation of urban expansion : some implications for agricultural land use practices and land-use zoning, *Geog. Polon.* 28, 93–115.

Bryant, C. R. (1976) Some new perspectives on agricultural land use in the rural-urban fringe, *Ontario Geog.* 10, 64–78.

Bryant, C. R., Russwurm, L. H. and McLellan, A. G. (1982) *The city's countryside*. London and New York : Longman.

Bryant, R. W. G. (1972) *Land : private property, public control*. Montreal : Harvest House.

Bryden, J. M. and Houston, G. (1976) *Agrarian change in the Scottish Highlands*. London : Martin Robertson.

Buchanan, M. E. (1976) Immigrant tobacco growers in Southern Queensland, *Aust. Geog. Stud.*, 14, 182–9.

Buhyoff, G. J. *et al.* (1978) Landscape architects' interpretations of peoples' landscape preferences, *J. Environ. Manag.*, 6, 255–62.

Burgess, E. W., (1925) The growth of the city : an introduction to a research project. In R. E. Park, E. W. Burgess and R. D. Mackenzie (eds) *The city*. Chicago : University of Chicago Press, pp.47–62.

Burns, J. H. and Hart, H. L. A. (1970) *The collected works of Jeremy Bentham : an introduction to the principles of morals and legislation*. London : University of London Athlone Press.

Busby, R. J. N. and Grayson, A. J. (1981) *Investment appraisal in forestry*. London : Forestry Commission.

Buys, C. J. (1975) Predator control and ranchers' attitudes, *Environ. Behav.*, 7, 81–98.

Calder, I. R. and Newson, M. D. (1979) Land-use and upland water resources in Scotland – a strategic look, *Water Resources Bull.*, 15, 1628–39.

Calder, I. R. and Newson, M. D. (1980) The effects of afforestation on water resources in Scotland. In M. F. Thomas and J. T. Coppock (eds) *op. cit.*, 51–62.

Callies, D. L. (1980) The quiet revolution revisited, *J. Am. Plan. Ass.*, 46, 135–44.

Carlson, J. E. and Dillman, D. A. (1983) Influence of kinship arrangements on farmer innovativeness, *Rural Sociol.*, 48, 183–200.

Carman, H. F. (1972) Taxloss agricultural investments after tax reform, *Am. J. Agric. Econ.*, 54, 627–34.

Carman, H. F. (1977) California landowners' adoption of a use-value assessment program, *Land Economics*, 53, 275–87.

Carrara, P. E. and Carroll, T. R. (1979) The determination of erosion rates from exposed tree roots in the Piceance Basin, Colorado, *Earth Surface Processes*, 4, 407–17.

Carroll, M. (1979) Rural land use control in Great Britain, *Nat. Resources J.*, 19, 145–60.

Carter, H. (1972) *The study of urban geography*. London : Edward Arnold.

Carter, L. J. (1977) Soil erosion : the problem persists despite the billions spent on it, *Science*, 196, 409–11.

Carty, J. A. (1978) Report to the HIDB on methods of compulsory purchase of rural land . . . in Western Europe. In *Proposals for changes in the Highlands and Islands Development (Scotland) Act 1965*. Inverness : HIDB, pp.31–53.

Casebow, A. (1980) Human motives in farming, *Agric. Prog.*, 55, 119–23.

Chassagne, E. (1979a) Community control of land use : historical development and limitations corrective mechanisms (*sic*) : the French system as an example. In OECD (1979) *op. cit.*, pp.659–97.

Chassagne, E. (1979b) Peri-urban agriculture in the plain of the Ain (Region of Lyons). In OECD (1979) *op.cit.*, pp.113–52.

Chicione, D. L. (1981) Farmland values at the urban fringe : an analysis of sale prices, *Land Economics*, 57, 353–62.

Chisholm, M. (1962) *Rural settlement and land use*. London : Hutchinson.

Christopher, A. J. (1971) Colonial land policy in Natal, *Ann. Ass. Am. Geog.*, 61, 560–75.

Christopher, A. J. (1976b) *Southern Africa*. Folkestone : Dawson.

Christopher, A. J. (1982) *South Africa*. London and New York : Longman.

Christopher, A. J. (1983) Official land disposal policies and European settlement in Southern Africa 1860–1960, *J. Hist. Geog.*, 9, 369–83.

Ciriacy-Wantrup, S. V. (1968) *Resource conservation : economics and policies* (3rd edn). University of California Division of Agricultural Sciences.

Clark, G. (1982a) Institutions and rural development. In R. Flowerdew (ed.) *Institutions and geographical patterns*. London and Canberra : Croom Helm, pp.75–102.

Clark, G. L. (1982b) Rights, property and community, *Econ. Geog.*, 58, 120–38.

Clark, R. T. and McCulloch, J. S. G. (1979) The effect of land use on the hydrology of small upland catchments. In G. E. Hollis (ed.) *Man's impact on the hydrological cycle in the United Kingdom*. Norwich : GeoAbstracts, pp.71–78.

Clawson, M. (1971) *Suburban land conversion in the United States : an economic and governmental process*. Baltimore and London : Johns Hopkins Press.

Clawson, M. (1975) Economic and social conflicts in land-use planning, *Nat. Resources J.*, 15, 473–90.

Clawson, M. (1983) *The federal lands revisited*. Washington, D.C.: Resources for the Future.

Cochrane, W. W. (1958) *Farm prices – myth and reality*. Minneapolis : University of Minnesota Press.

Coffman, G. W. (1979) Entry and exit : barriers and incentives, *USDA Agric. Econ. Rep.* 438, 116–20.

Colbert, C. F. and O'Brien, T. (1975) Land reform in Ireland, *Univ. of Cambridge. Dept. of Land Econ., Occ. Pap. 3*.

Coleman, A. (1976) Is planning really necessary? *Geog. J.*, 142, 411–37.

Coleman, A. (1978) Agricultural land losses : the evidence from maps. In A. W. Rogers (ed.) *op.cit.*, pp.16–36.

Coleman, A. and Maggs, K. R. A. (1962) *Land use survey handbook*. Berkhampsted: Geographical Publications.

Coleman, A., Isbell, J. E. and Sinclair, J. (1974) The comparative statics approach to British land use trends, *Cart. J.*, 11, 34–41.

Combes, F. (1982) Réflexions sur les problèmes d'erosion dans les Alpes de Haute-Provence, *Rev. For. Fran.*, 34, 61–76.

Conacher, A. J. (1977) Conservation and geography : the case of the Manjimup woodchip industry in Southwestern Australia, *Aust. Geog. Stud.*, 15, 104–22.

Conacher, A. J. (1979) Water quality and forests in Southwestern Australia : review and evaluation, *Aust. Geog.*, 14, 150–9.

Conklin, H. E. and Bryant, W. R. (1974) Agricultural districts : a compromise approach to farmland preservation, *Am. J. Agric. Econ.*, 56, 607–13.

Conzen, M. P. (1971) *Frontier farming in an urban shadow*. Madison: State Historical Society of Wisconsin for Dept. of History, Univ. of Wisconsin.

Cook, K. A. (1980) The National Agricultural Lands Study : in which reasonable men may differ, *J. Soil Water Conserv.*, 35, 247–9.

Coppock, J. T. and Gebbett, L. F. (1978) Land use and town and country planning, *Royal Statistical Society and SSRC Reviews of UK Statistical Sources* 8. Oxford : Pergamon Press.

Cortner, H. J. and Schweitzer, D. L. (1981) Institutional limits to national public planning for forest resources : the Resources Planning Act, *Nat. Resources J.*, 21, 203–22.

Countryside Review Committee (1976) *The countryside : problems and policies. A discussion paper*. London : HMSO.

Countryside Review Committee (1977) *Leisure and the countryside : a discussion paper*. Topic Paper 2. London : HMSO.

Countryside Review Committee (1978) *Food production in the countryside*. Topic Paper 3. London : HMSO.

Countryside Review Committee (1979) *Conservation and the countryside heritage*. Topic Paper 4. London : HMSO.

Courtney, F. M. (1981) Developments in forest hydrology, *Prog. Phys. Geog.*, 5., 217–41.

Coventry-Solihull-Warwickshire Planning Study Group (1971) *A strategy for the sub-region : supplementary report No. 5 Countryside*. Coventry : Coventry Council.

Cox, G. and Lowe, P. (1983) A battle not the war : the politics of the Wildlife and Countryside Act. In A. W. Gilg (ed.) *Countryside Planning Yearbook 1983*. Norwich : Geo Books, pp.48–76.

Cox, P. (1976) Fertiliser use on rented land, *Ir. J. Agric. Econ. Rur. Soc.*, 6, 147–54.

Cozzens, A. G. (1943) Conservation in German settlements of the Missouri Ozarks, *Geog. Rev.*, 33, 286–98.

Crosson, P. R. and Brubaker, S. (1982) *Resource and environmental effects of US agriculture*. Washington, D.C. : Resources for the Future.

Cruickshank, J. G. and Armstrong, W. J. (1971) Soil and agricultural land classification in County Londonderry, *Trans. Inst. Brit. Geog.*, 53, 79–94.

Culhane, P. J. and Friesema, H. P. (1979) Land use planning for the public lands, *Nat. Resources J.*, 19, 43–74.

Cullingworth, J. B. (1979) *Town and country planning in England and Wales*. London : Allen and Unwin.

Curtis, L. (1983) Reflections on management agreements for conservation of Exmoor moorland, *J. Agric. Econ.*, 34, 397–406.

Dale, D. and Weaver, T. (1974) Trampling effects on vegetation of the trail corridors of North Rocky Mountain forests. *J. Appl. Ecol.*, 11, 767–72.

Dalland, O. (1978) Preservation of nature and local economic activity – conflict or mutual interests? Norwegian examples. In J. G. Nelson, R. D. Neeham and D. C. Mann (eds) *op.cit.*, pp.453–94.

Dam Kofoed, A. (1981) Water pollution caused by run off of manure and fertilisers. In J. C. Brogan (ed.) *Nitrogen losses and surface run off from land-spreading of manures*. Hague : Martinus Nijhoff/Dr. W. Junk (Publishers for EEC).

Dana, S. T. and Fairfax, S. K. (1980) *Forest and range policy*. New York : McGraw-Hill.

Darin-Drabkin, H. (1977) *Land policy and urban growth*. Oxford: Pergamon.

Darling, F. F. (1956) Man's ecological dominance through domesticated animals in wild lands. In W. L. Thomas, Jr. (ed.) *Man's role in changing the face of the earth* 2. Chicago and London : University of Chicago Press, pp.778–87.

Davidson, D. A. (1980) *Soils and land use planning*. London and New York : Longman.

Davis, M. B. (1976) Erosion rates and land-use history in Southern Michigan, *Environ. Conserv.*, 3, 139–48.

Denman, D. R. (1957) *Estate capital*. London : Allen and Unwin.

Department of Health for Scotland (1947) *National parks and the conservation of nature in Scotland*. Cmd 7235. London : HMSO.

Detwyler, T. H. *et al.* (1972) *Urbanisation and environment : the physical geography of the city*. Belmont : Duxbury.

Diamond, S. and Lee, J. (1972–3) Farm size in Ireland with particular reference to grazing livestock production, *Ir. J. Agric. Econ. Rur. Soc.*, 4, 25–33.

Dickenson, J. (1982) *Brazil*. London and New York : Longman.

Dickinson, G. C. and Shaw, M. A. (1978) The collection of national land-use statistics in Great Britain : a critique, *Environ. Plan. A*, 10, 295–303.

Dickman, M. and Dorais, M. (1977) The impact of human trampling on phosphorus loading to a small lake in Gatineau Park, Quebec, Canada, *J. Environ. Manag.*, 5, 335–44.

Dorling, M. J. and Barichello, R. R. (1975) Trends in rural and urban land uses in Canada. In *Proc. 1975 Workshop of the Canadian Agricultural Economics Society*, Banff, Alberta, pp.33–63.

Dorner, P. (1972) *Land reform and economic development*. Harmondsworth : Penguin.

Downing, P. B. (1973) Factors affecting commercial land values : an empirical study of Milwaukee, Wisconsin. *Land Economics,* 49, 44–56.

Dragonvich, D. (1980) Government assistance and the changing distribution of dairy farming in Australia, *Geoforum,* 11, 147–56.

Duckham, A. N. and Masefield, G. B. (1970) *Farming systems of the world.* London : Chatto and Windus.

Duerr, W. A., Teeguarden, D. E., Christiansen, N. B. and Gultenberg, S. (1979) *Forest resource management : decision-making principles and cases.* Philadelphia : W. B. Saunders.

Duffield, J., Boehlje, M. and Hickman, R. (1983) *Impacts of foreign and absentee investment in U.S. farmland on U.S. farms and rural communities. Results from surveys in California, Iowa and Mississippi.* Ames, Iowa : Iowa State Univ. CARD Report 114.

Dumanski, J., Brittain, L. and Girt, J. L. (1982) Spatial association between agriculture and the soil resource in Canada, *Can. J. Soil Sci.,* 62, 375–86.

Duncan, M. L. (1984) Toward a theory of broad-based planning for the preservation of agricultural land, *Nat. Resources J.,* 24, 61–136.

Dunn, M. (1976) Landscape with photographs : testing the preference approach to landscape evaluation, *J. Environ. Manag.,* 4, 15–26.

Earle, T. R., Rose, C. W. and Brownlea, A. A. (1979) Socio-economic predictors of intentions towards soil conservation and their implications in environmental management, *J. Environ. Manag.,* 9, 225–36.

Easter, K. W. and Cotner, M. L. (1982) Evaluation of current soil conservation strategies. In H. G. Halcrow *et al.* (eds.) *op.cit.,* pp.283–301.

Eckholm, E. P. (1976) *Losing ground : environmental stress and world food prospects.* New York : Norton.

Eckholm, E. P. (1982) *Down to earth : environment and human needs.* New York : Norton.

Edwards, A. M. and Wibberley, G. P. (1971) *An agricultural land budget for Britain 1965–2000.* Ashford, Kent : Wye College.

Eichers, T. R., Andrilenas, P. A. and Anderson, T. W. (1978) Farmers' use of pesticides in 1976, *USDA Agric. Econ. Rep. 418.*

Eidsvik, H. K. (1980) National parks and other protected areas : some reflections on the past and prescriptions for the future, *Environ. Conserv.,* 7, 185–90.

Eisgruber, L. M. (1973) Managerial information and decision systems in the USA : historical developments, current status and major issues, *Am. J. Agric. Econ.,* 55, 930–7.

Elson, M. J. (1979) Land use and management in the urban fringe, *The Planner*, 65, 52–54.

Elton, C. S. (1958) *The ecology of invasions by land animals and plants*. London : Methuen.

Ely, R. T. and **Wehrwein, G. S.** (1964) *Land economics*. Madison : University of Wisconsin Press.

English, B. C. and **Heady, E. O.** (1980) *Short and long-term analysis of the impacts of several soil loss control measures on agriculture*. Ames, Iowa : Iowa State Univ. CARD Report 93.

Ervin, C. A. and **Ervin, D. E.** (1982) Factors affecting the use of soil conservation practices : hypotheses, evidence, and policy implications, *Land Economics*, 58, 277–92.

Ervin, D. E. and **Fitch, J. B.** (1979) Evaluating alternative compensation and recapture techniques for expanded public control of land use, *Nat. Resources J.*, 19, 21–41.

Etzioni, A. (1967) Mixed-scanning : a 'third' approach to decision-making, *Publ. Admin. Rev.*, 27, 385–92.

Evans, R. and **Nortcliff, S.** (1978) Soil erosion in North Norfolk, *J. Agric. Sci. (Camb.)*, 90, 185–92.

Evans, W. R. and **Kalkanis, G.** (1977) Use of the universal soil loss equation in California. In Soil Conservation Society (1977) *op.cit.*, 31–40.

Eyre, S. R. (1978) *The real wealth of nations*. London : Edward Arnold.

Farquharson, J. E. (1976) *The plough and the swastika : the NSDAP and agriculture in Germany 1928–45*. London and Beverly Hills : SAGE Publications.

Feist, M. J. (1978) *A study of management agreements*. Cheltenham : Countryside Commission.

Fellman, J. D. (1957) Pre-building growth patterns in Chicago, *Ann. Ass. Am. Geog.*, 47, 59–82.

Fielding, G. J. (1964) The Los Angeles milkshed : a study in the political factor in agriculture, *Geog. Rev.*, 54, 1–12.

Fielding, G. J. (1965) The role of government in New Zealand wheat growing, *Ann. Ass. Am. Geog.*, 55, 87–97.

Fines, K. D. (1968) Landscape evaluation : a research project in East Sussex, *Reg. Stud.*, 2, 41–55.

Firey, W. W. (1960) *Man, mind and land*. Glencoe, Illinois : Free Press.

Fischel, W. A. (1982) The urbanisation of agricultural land : a review of the National Agricultural Lands Study. *Land Economics*, 58, 236–59.

Flaherty, M. and **Smit, B.** (1982) An assessment of land classification techniques in planning for agricultural land use, *J. Environ. Manag.*, 15, 323–32.

Fløystrup-Jensen, J. and **Dyreborg-Carlsen, B.** (1981) *Factors influencing ownership, tenancy, mobility and use of farmland in Denmark.* Information on Agriculture No. 73.

Foin, T. C. *et al.* (1977) Quantitative studies of visitor impacts on environments of Yosemite National Park, California, and their implications for park management policy, *J. Environ. Manag.,* 5, 1–22.

Ford, E. D., Malcolm, D. C. and **Atterson, J.** (eds) (1978) *The ecology of even-aged stand plantations.* Edinburgh : Proc. Internat. Union For. Res. Org.

Fornari, H. D. (1979) The big change : cotton to soybeans, *Agric. Hist.,* 53, 245–53.

Fotheringham, A. S. and **Reeds, L. G.** (1979) An application of discriminant analysis to agricultural land use prediction, *Econ. Geog.,* 55, 114–22.

Found, W. C. (1971) *A theoretical approach to rural land use patterns.* London : Edward Arnold.

Frawley, J., Bohlen, J. M. and **Breathnach, T.** (1975) Personal and social factors related to farming performance in Ireland, *Ir. J. Agric. Econ. Rur. Soc.,* 5, 157–81.

Frey, H. T. (1979) Major uses of land in the United States : 1974, *USDA Agric. Econ. Rep.* 440.

Friday, R. and **Allee, D.** (1976) The environmental impact of American agriculture. In J. W. Watson and T. O'Riordan (eds) *The American environment : perceptions and policies.* London and New York : John Wiley, pp.213–40.

Friend, G. R. (1982) Mammal populations in exotic pine plantations and indigenous eucalypt forests in Gippsland, Victoria, *Aust. For.,* 45, 3–18.

Froehlich, H. A. (1979) Soil compaction from logging equipment : effects on growth of young Ponderosa pine, *J. Soil Water Conserv.,* 34, 276–8.

Furuseth, O. J. (1980) The Oregon Agricultural Protection Program : a review and assessment, *Nat. Resources J.,* 20, 603–14.

Furuseth, O. J. (1981) Update on Oregon's agricultural protection program : a land-use perspective, *Nat. Resources J.,* 21, 57–70.

Furuseth, O. J. and **Pierce, J. T.** (1982) A comparative analysis of farmland preservation programmes in North America, *Can. Geog.,* 26, 191–206.

Gaffney, M. (1977) Social and economic aspects of foreign investment in United States land, *Nat. Resources J.,* 17, 377–93.

Garst, G. and **Miller, T. A.** (1975) Impact of the set-aside programme of the US wheat acreages, *Agric. Econ. Res.,* 27, 30–7.

Gasson, R. (1966) *The influence of urbanisation on farm ownership* *and practice*. Ashford, Kent : Wye College, Studies in Rural Land Use Report 7.

Gasson, R. (1973) Goals and values of farmers, *J. Agric. Econ.*, 24, 521–42.

Gayler, H. J. (1982) Conservation and development in urban growth: the preservation of agricultural land in the rural-urban fringe of Ontario, *Town Plan. Rev.*, 53, 321–41.

Genovese, E. D. (1961) *The political economy of slavery*. New York: Pantheon Books.

Gersmehl, P. J. (1978) No-till farming : the regional applicability of a revolutionary agricultural technology, *Geog. Rev.*, 68, 66–79.

Gilbertson, D. D. (1981) The impact of past and present land use on a major coastal barrier system, *Appl. Geog.*, 1, 97–119.

Gilg, A. W. (1975a) Agricultural land classification in Britain, *Biol. Conserv.*, 7, 73–7.

Gilg, A. W. (1975b) Development control and agricultural land quality, *Town Country Plan.*, 43, 387–9.

Gillmore, D. A. (ed.) (1979) *Irish resources and land use*. Dublin : Institute of Public Administration.

Gilson, J. C. (1973) A Canadian view of conflicts and consistences in the agricultural policies of Canada and the United States, *Am. J. Agric. Econ.*, 55, 785–9.

Glacken, C. J. (1956) The origins of conservation philosophy, *J. Soil Water Conserv.*, 11, 63–66.

Glacken, C. J. (1967) *Traces on the Rhodian Shore (nature and culture in western thought from ancient times to the end of the 18th C.)*. Berkeley and Los Angeles : University of California Press.

Golledge, R. E. (1960) Sydney's metropolitan fringe : a study in urban and rural relations, *Aust. Geog.*, 7, 243–55.

Gómez-Ibáñez, D. A. (1977) Energy, economics and the decline of transhumance, *Geog. Rev.*, 67, 284–98.

Goodall, B. (1970) Some effects of legislation on land values, *Reg. Stud.*, 4, 11–23.

Goodenough, R. (1984) The great American crop surplus : 1983 solution, *Geography*, 69, 351–3.

Gordon, D. S. (1978) Motivations of farmers in South West Scotland, *Landowning in Scotland*, 172, 5–8.

Gordon, S. I. (1980) Utilising LANDSAT imagery to monitor land-use change : a case study in Ohio, *Remote Sensing of environment*, 9, 189–96.

Green, B. (1981) *Countryside conservation*. London : George Allen and Unwin.

Green, F. H. W. (1976) Recent changes in land use and treatment, *Geog. J.*, 142, 12–25.

Greenland, D. J. (1977) Soil damage by intensive arable cultivation : temporary or permanent?, *Phil. Trans. Roy. Soc. (Lond) B*, **281**, 193–208.

Griffin, D. W. and **Preston, R. E.** (1966) A restatement of the 'transition zone' concept, *Ann. Ass. Am. Geog.*, **56**, 339–50.

Griffin, E. (1973) Testing the von Thünen theory in Uruguay, *Geog. Rev.*, **63**, 500–16.

Griffin, R. C. and **Stoll, J. R.** (1984) Evolutionary processes in soil conservation policy, *Land Economics*, **60**, 30–39.

Grigg, D. B. (1974) The growth and distribution of the world's arable land 1870–1970, *Geography*, **59**, 104–10.

Grotewold, A. and **Sublett, M. D.** (1967) The effect of import restrictions on land use, *Econ. Geog.*, **43**, 64–70.

Gustafson, G. C. (1979) Land-use policy and farmland retention : the United States experience. In OECD 1979, *op.cit.*, pp.699–732.

Gustafson, G. C., Daniels, T. L. and **Shirack, R. P.** (1982) The Oregon Land Use Act : implications for farmland and open space protection, *J. Am. Inst. Planners*, **48**, 365–73.

Hadley, R. F. (1974) Sediment yield and land use in southwest US. In *Symposium on the effects of man and the interface of the hydrological cycle with the physical environment.* IAHS Publication No. 113, pp.96–98.

Hadley, R. F. (1977) Evaluation of land-use and land-treatment practices in semi-arid western United States, *Phil. Trans. Roy. Soc. (Lond.) B*, **278**, 543–54.

Hady, T. F. (1970) Differential assessment of land in the rural-urban fringe, *Am. J. Agric. Econ.*, **52**, 25–32.

Hagen, W. R. (1977) Problems of implementing erosion control. In *Proc. Nat. Symp. Soil Erosion and Sedimentation by Water, Chicago, Illinois.* St. Joseph, Mich. : Am. Soc. Agric. Engineers, pp.116–24.

Hagenstein, P. R. (1972) One third of a nation's land – evolution of a policy recommendation, *Nat. Resources J.*, **12**, 56–75.

Haig, R. M. (1926) Towards an understanding of the metropolis, *Quart. J. Econ.*, **40**, 421–3.

Halcrow, H. G., Heady, E. O. and **Cotner, M. L.** (eds) (1982) *Soil conservation policies, institutions and incentives.* Ankeny, Iowa : Soil Conservation Society of America.

Hall, A. (1976) Management in the urban fringe, *Countryside Recreation Rev.*, **1**, 8–13.

Hall, P. (1966) *Von Thünen's isolated state.* London : Pergamon Press.

Hammond, K. A., Macinko, G. and **Fairchild, W. B.** (eds) (1978) *Sourcebook on the environment.* Chicago and London : Univ. of Chicago Press.

Hansen, D. E. and **Schwartz, S. I.** (1975) Landowner behaviour at the urban-rural fringe in response to preferential property taxation, *Land Economics,* 51, 341–54.

Hansen, J. A. (1981) A land-use study of Canada, the U.S. and Britain c.1951–71, *Area,* 13, 169–71.

Harley, J. L. (1978) The objectives of conservation, *Unasylva,* 30, 25–28.

Harper, W. M. and Eastman, C. (1980) An evaluation of goal hierarchies for small farm operators, *Am. J. Agric. Econ.,* 62, 742–7.

Harriman, R. (1978) Nutrient leaching from fertilised forest watersheds in Scotland, *J. Appl. Ecol.,* 15, 933–42.

Harris, C. D. and Ullman, E. L. (1945) The nature of cities, *Ann. Am. Ac. Pol. Sci.,* 242, 7–17.

Harris, P. E. (1980) Land ownership restrictions on the mid-western states : influence on farm structure, *Am. J. Agric. Econ.,* 62, 940–5.

Harris, R. C. (1966) *The seigneurial system in early Canada.* Quebec: Laval University Press.

Harrison, A. (1972) *The financial structure of farm businesses.* Univ. of Reading Dept. Agric. Econ., Misc. Stud. 53.

Harrison, A. (1975) *Farmers and farm businesses in England.* Univ. of Reading Dept. Agric. Econ., Misc. Stud. 62.

Harrison, A., Tranter, R. B. and Gibbs, R. S. (1977) *Landownership by public and semi-public institutions in the U.K.* Univ. of Reading, CAS Paper 3.

Harrison, C. (1981) A playground for whom? Informal recreation in London's Green Belt, *Area,* 13, 109–14.

Harrison, C. (1983) Countryside recreation and London's urban fringe, *Trans. Inst. Brit. Geog.,* 8, 295–313.

Hart, J. F. (1968) Loss and abandonment of cleared farm land in the Eastern United States, *Ann. Ass. Am. Geog.,* 58, 417–40.

Hart, J. F. (1972) The Middle West, *Ann. Ass. Am. Geog.,* 62, 258–82.

Hart, J. F. (1976) Urban encroachment on rural areas, *Geog. Rev.,* 66, 1–17.

Hart, J. F. (1977) The demise of King Cotton, *Ann. Ass. Am. Geog.* 67, 307–22.

Hart, J. F. (1978a) Cropland concentrations in the South, *Ann. Ass. Am. Geog.,* 68, 505–17.

Hart, P. W. E. (1978b) Geographical aspects of contract farming, with special reference to the supply of crops to the processing plants, *Tidj. Econ. Soc. Geog.,* 69, 205–15.

Hartke, W. (1956) Die 'Sozialbrache' als Phänomen der geographischen Differenzierung der Landschaft, *Erdkunde,* 10, 257–69.

Harvey, D. W. (1963) Locational change in the Kentish hop industry and the analysis of land use patterns, *Trans. Inst. Brit. Geog.*, **33**, 123–44.

Hayden, B. and **Dolan, R.** (1974) Management of highly dynamic coastal areas of the National Park Service, *Coastal Zone Manag. J.*, **1**, 133–9.

Hays, S. P. (1959) *Conservation and the gospel of efficiency : the progressive conservation movement 1890–1920*. Cambridge, Mass. : Harvard University Press.

Healy, R. G. (1976) *Land use and the states*. Baltimore : John Hopkins University Press for Resources for the Future.

Healey, R. G. and **Short, J. L.** (1979) Rural land : market trends and planning implications, *J. Am. Inst. Planners*, **45**, 305–16.

Heaton, T. B. (1980) Metropolitan influence on United States farmland use and capital intensity, *Rural Sociol.*, **45**, 501–8.

Heft, F. E. (1977) Political, social and economic aspects of soil erosion and sediment control programs. In *Proc. Nat. Symp. Soil Erosion and Sedimentation by Water, Chicago, Illinois*. St. Joseph, Mich.: Am. Soc. Agric. Engineers, pp.23–30.

Held, R. B. and **Clawson, M.** (1965) *Soil conservation in perspective*. Baltimore : Johns Hopkins University Press for Resources for the Future.

Hewes, L. (1967) The Conservation Reserve of the American Soil Bank as an indicator of regions of maladjustment in agriculture, *Wiener Geog. Schr.*, **24/29**, 331–46.

Hewes, L. (1972) The Kansas-Colorado Dust Bowl as suitcase farming country, *Proc. Ass. Am. Geog.*, **4**, 126.

HIDB (Highlands and Islands Development Board) (1970) *Strath of Kildonan : proposals for development*. Inverness : HIDB Sp. Publ. 5.

HIDB (Highlands and Islands Development Board) (1973) *Isle of Mull*. Inverness : HIDB Sp. Publ. 10.

Hill, A. (1976) The environmental impacts of agricultural land drainage, *J. Environ. Manag.*, **4**, 251–74.

Hill, A. R. (1975) Ecosystem stability in relation to stresses caused by human activities, *Can. Geog.*, **19**, 206–19.

Hill, M. O. (1978) The development of a flora in even-aged plantations. In Ford *et al.* (eds) *op.cit.*, pp.175–92.

Hockensmith, R. D. and **Steele, J. G.** (1949) Recent trends in the use of the land capability classification, *Proc. Soil Sci. Soc. Am.*, **14**, 383–8.

Holden, A. V. (1976) The relative importance of agricultural fertilisers as a source of nitrogen and phosphorus in Loch Leven. In *Agriculture and water quality*. Ministry of Agriculture, Fisheries & Food Tech. Bull. 32, pp. 306–14.

Hoole, A. (1978) Public participation in park planning : the Riding Mountain case, *Can. Geog.,* **22,** 41–50.

Hooper, L. J. (1974) Land use capability in farm planning. In D. Mackney (ed.) *Soil type and land capability. Soil Survey Tech. Monog. 4, Harpenden,* pp.135–49.

Horvath, R. J. (1969) Von Thünen's isolated state and the area around Addis Ababa, Ethiopia, *Ann. Ass. Am. Geog.,* **59,** 309–23.

Hosier, P. E. and Eaton, T. E. (1980) The impact of vehicles on dune and grassland vegetation on a south-eastern North Carolina barrier beach, *J. Appl. Ecol.,* **17,** 173–82.

House of Lords (1979–80) *Scientific aspects of forestry.* Report of Select Committee on Science and Technology (House of Lords). HL Paper 381.

Houston, D. B. (1971) Ecosystems of national parks, *Science,* **172,** 648–51.

Howard, G. (1979) *Scientific evidence relevant to South Island high country policies for Class VIII and severely eroded Class VII lands.* Wellington : MoWD.

Howell, D. L. (1978) *Land and people in nineteenth-century Wales.* London: Routledge and Kegan Paul.

Hoyt, H. (1939) *The structures and growth of residential neighbourhoods in American cities.* Washington, D.C. : US Federal Housing Administration.

Huffman, W. E. (1974) Role of education in decision making, *Am. J. Agric. Econ.,* **56,** 55–97.

Hurd, R. M. (1903) *Principles of city land values.* New York : The Record and Guide.

Ilbery, B. W. (1977) Point-score analysis : a methodological framework for analysing the decision-making process in agriculture, *Tidj. Econ. Soc. Geog.,* **68,** 61–6.

Ilbery, B. W. (1978) Agricultural decision-making : a behavioural perspective, *Prog. Hum. Geog.,* **2,** 448–66.

Ilbery, B. W. (1979) Decision making in agriculture, *Reg. Stud.,* **13,** 199–210.

Ilbery, B. W., (1983) Goals and values of hop farmers, *Trans. Inst. Brit. Geog.,* **8,** 329–41.

Ironside, R. G. (1979) Land tenure, farm income and farm practice in Southern Ontario, Canada, *Ontario Geog.,* **14,** 21–39.

IUCN (International Union for the Conservation of Nature) (1980) *A world conservation strategy.* Morgas, Switzerland : IUCN.

Iverson, R. M., Hinckley, B. S., Webb, R. M. and Hallet, B. (1981) Physical effects of vehicular disturbances on arid landscapes, *Science,* **212,** 915–7.

Jackson, R. H. (1977) Perception of environmental damage associated with irrigation, *J. Environ. Manag.*, **5**, 115–26.

Jackson, R. H. (1981) *Land use in America.* London : J. H. Winston and Sons and Edward Arnold.

Jacoby, E. H. (1971) *Man and land : the fundamental issue in development.* London : Andre Deutsh.

James, T. D. W. *et al.* (1979) Effects of camping recreation on soil, jack pine and understorey vegetation in a northwestern Ontario park, *For. Sci.*, **25**, 333–49.

Johnson, B. B. (1974) Farmland tenure patterns in the United States, *USDA Agric. Econ. Rep. 249.*

Johnson, H. B. (1976) *Order upon the land : the US rectangular land survey and the upper Mississippi country.* New York : Oxford U.P.

Johnston, A., Mace, J. and **Laffan, M.** (1981) The saw, the soil and the sounds, *Soil and Water*, **17**, 4–8.

Jonasson, O. (1925) Agricultural regions of Europe, *Econ. Geog.*, **1**, 277–314.

Jones, G. E. (1963) The diffusion of agricultural innovations, *J. Agric. Econ.*, **15**, 387–409.

Jones, G. E. (1967) The adoption and diffusion of agricultural practices, *World Agric. Econ. Rur. Soc. Abs.*, **9**, 1–34.

Josling, T. E. (1974) Agricultural policies in developed countries : an overview, *J. Agric. Econ.*, **25**, 229–63.

Just, R. E. (1973) A methodology for investigating the importance of government intervention in farmers' decisions, *Am. J. Agric. Econ.*, **55**, 441–52.

Just, R. E., Schmitz, A. and **Zilberman, D.** (1979) Technological change in agriculture, *Science*, **206**, 1277–80.

Kaiser, E. J., Massie, R. W., Weiss, S. F. and **Smith, J. E.** (1968) Predicting the behaviour of predevelopment landowners on the urban fringe, *J. Am. Inst. Planners*, **34**, 328–33.

Kates, R. W. (1962) *Hazard and choice perception in flood plain management.* Univ. Chicago Dept. Geog., Research Paper 78.

Keene, J. C. (1979) A review of governmental policies and techniques for keeping farmers farming, *Nat. Resources J.*, **19**, 119–44.

Keeves, A. (1966) Some evidence of loss of productivity with successive rotations of *Pinus radiata* in the south-east of South Australia, *Aust. For.*, **30**, 51–63.

Kerridge, K. W. (1978) Value orientations and farmer behaviour – an exploratory study, *Quart. Rev. Agric. Econ.*, **31**, 61–72.

Ketcheson, J. W. (1980) Long-range effects of intensive cultivation and monoculture on the quality of Southern Ontario soils, *Can. J. Soil Sci.*, **60**, 403–10.

Ketcheson, J. W., and **Webber, C. R.** (1978) Effects of soil erosion on yield of corn, *Can. J. Soil Sci.*, 58, 459–63.

Kingsley, N. P. and **Birch, T. W.** (1980) The forestland owners of Maryland, *USDA For. Serv. Res. Bull.*, NE-63.

Kislev, Y. and **Shchori-Bachrach, N.** (1973) The process of an innovation cycle, *Am. J. Agric. Econ.*, 55, 28–37.

Klepper, R. *et al.* (1977) Economic performance and energy intensiveness on organic and conventional farms in the Corn Belt : a preliminary comparison, *Am. J. Agric. Econ.*, 59, 1–12.

Klingebiel, A. A. and **Montgomery, P. H.** (1961) Land capability classification, *USDA Soil Conserv. Service, Agricultural Handbook No. 210.*

Knowles, G. H. (1978) Erosion assessment and control techniques in Australia. In *Proc. Conf. Erosion Assessment and Control in New Zealand.* Christchurch : NZ Ass. Soil Conservators, pp.349–62.

Kobayashi, S. (1975) A ranching system in Japan, *Geog. Rep. Tokyo Met. Univ.*, 10, 25–42.

Kollmorgen, W. M. (1941, 1943) A reconnaissance of some cultural-agricultural islands in the South, *Econ. Geog.*, 17, 409–30, and 19, 109–17.

Kollmorgen, W. M. (1969) The woodsman's assaults on the domain of the cattleman, *Ann. Ass. Am. Geog.*, 59, 215–39.

Kollmorgen, W. M. and **Jenks, G. F.** (1958) Suitcase farming in Sully County, South Dakota, *Ann. Ass. Am. Geog.*, 48, 27–40.

Kollmorgen, W. F. and **Simonett, D. S.** (1965) Grazing operations in the Flint Hills-Bluestem Pastures of Chase County, Kansas, *Ann. Ass. Am. Geog.*, 55, 260–90.

Kornhauser, D. H. (1982) *Japan.* London and New York : Longman.

Kostrowicki, J. (1970) Data requirements for land use survey maps. In I. H. Cox (ed.) *New possibilities and techniques for land use and related surveys.* Berkhamsted : Geographical Publications, pp.73–84.

Kunnecke, B. H. (1974) Sozialbrache – a phenomenon in the rural landscape of Germany, *Prof. Geog.*, 26, 412–5.

Kuru, A. (1978) The environmental impact of agriculture in Ethiopia, *Environ. Conserv.*, 5, 213–21.

Laband, D. N. and **Lentz, B. F.** (1983) Occupational inheritance in agriculture, *Am. J. Agric. Econ.*, 65, 311–4.

Laffan, M. D. (1979) Slope stability in the Charleston-Punakaiki region, South Island, New Zealand, *N.Z. J. Sci.*, 22, 193–201.

Lancelle, M. and **Rodefield, R. D.** (1980) The influence of social origins on the ability to attain ownership of large farms, *Rural Sociol.* 45, 381–95.

Land Use Consultants/Countryside Commission for Scotland (1971)

A planning classification of Scottish landscape resources. Perth : C.C.S., Occ. Pap. 1.

Lane, A. B. (1983) Benefits and hazards of new crops : oilseed rape in the UK, *Agric. Ecosys. & Environ.*, **10**, 299–309.

Lapping, M. B. (1975) Preserving agricultural lands : the New York experience, *Town Country Plan.* **43**, 394–7.

Lapping, M. B. (1977) Policy alternatives for the preservation of agricultural land use, *J. Environ. Manag.*, **5**, 275–87.

Laut, P. (1979) Developing a state land resources inventory : an example from South Australia, *Aust. Geog.*, **14**, 237–43.

Law, F. (1956) The effect of afforestation upon the yields of water catchment areas, *J. Brit. Waterworks Ass.*, **38**, 484–94.

Layton, R. L. (1978) The operational structure of the hobby farm, *Area*, **10**, 242–6.

Leach, G. (1976) *Energy and food production.* Guildford : IPC Press.

Lee, L. K. (1980) The impact of landownership factors on soil conservation, *Am. J. Agric. Econ.*, **62**, 1070–6.

Lee, L. K. and **Stewart, W. H.** (1983) Landownership and the adoption of minimum tillage, *Am. J. Agric. Econ.*, **65**, 256–64.

Leeming, F. (1977) State land layouts in traditional China : evidence from topographical maps, *Area*, **9**, 229–34.

Lemon, J. T. (1966) The agricultural practices of national groups in eighteenth century southeastern Pennsylvania, *Geog. Rev.*, **56**, 467–96.

Leonard, P. (1983) Management agreements : a tool for conservation, *J. Agric. Econ.*, **33**, 351–60.

Leopold, A. (1949) *A Sand County Almanac.* London : Oxford U.P.

Leopold, A. S. *et al.* (1963) Wildlife management in the national parks, *Am. For.*, **69**, 32–5 and 61–3.

Leopold, L. B. (1956) Land use and sediment yield. In W. L. Thomas Jr. (ed.) *Man's role in changing the face of the Earth* (2), Chicago : University of Chicago Press, pp.639–47.

Lewis, J. A. (1976) White and minority small farm operators in the South, *USDA Agric. Econ. Rep.* 353.

Libby, L. W. (1974) Land use policy : implications for commercial agriculture, *Am. J. Agric. Econ.*, **56**, 1143–52.

Liddle, M. J. (1975) A theoretical relationship between the primary productivity of vegetation and its ability to tolerate trampling, *Biol. Conserv.*, **8**, 251–6.

Lidman, R. and **Bawden, D. L.** (1974) The impact of government programs on wheat acreage, *Land Economics,* **50**, 327–35.

Likens, G. E., Bormann, F. H., Pierce, R. S. and **Reiness, W. A.** (1978) Recovery of a deforested ecosystem, *Science*, **199**, 492–6.

Lindblom, C. E. (1959) The science of 'muddling through', *Publ. Admin. Rev.*, **19**, 79–88.

Linton, D. L. (1968) The assessment of scenery as a natural resource, *Scott. Geog. Mag.*, **84**, 219–39.

Lionberger, H. L. (1960) *Adoption of new ideas and practices.* Ames, Iowa : Iowa State U.P.

Loehr, R. C. (1970) Changing patterns in agriculture and their effect on the environment, *CRC Crit. Rev. Environ. Control*, **1**, 69–99.

Lowe, P. and **Goyder, J.** (1983) *Environmental groups in politics.* London : George Allen and Unwin.

Lucas, R. C. (1978) Impact on human pressure on parks, wilderness and other recreational lands. In K. A. Hammond *et al.* (eds), *op.cit.*, pp.221–40.

Lund, P. J. and **Slater, J. M.** (1979) Agricultural land : its ownership, price and rent – a guide to sources of statistical information, *Econ. Trends*, **314**, 97–110.

McCashion, J. D. and **Rice, R. M.** (1981) Erosion on logging roads in northwestern California : how much is avoidable? *J. For.*, **81**, 23–6.

McConnell, G. (1954) The conservation movement – past and present, *West. Polit. Quart.*, **7**, 463–78.

McConnell, K. E. (1983) An economic model of soil conservation, *Am. J. Agric. Econ.*, **65**, 83–9.

McCormack, R. J. (1971) The Canada land-use inventory : a basis for land-use planning, *J. Soil Water Conserv.*, **26**, 141–6.

McCormack, R. J. (1975) Demands for land in Canada. In *Proc. 1975 Workshop of the Canadian Agricultural Economics Society,* Banff, Alberta, pp.20–32.

McCormack, D. E. and **Young, K. K.** (1981) Technical and societal implications of soil loss tolerance. In R. P. C. Morgan (ed.) *Soil conservation : problems and prospects.* Chichester : John Wiley, pp.365–76.

MacEwen, M. and **MacEwen, A.** (1981) *National parks : conservation or cosmetics?* London : George Allen and Unwin.

Mackney, D. (1974) Land use capability classification in the United Kingdom. In *Land capability classification.* Ministry of Agriculture, Fisheries & Food Tech. Bull. 30, pp.4–11.

MacLachlan, R. J. (1966) Land administration in New Zealand. In J. B. Brown (ed.) *Rural land administration in New Zealand.* Studies in Public Administration No. 12. Wellington, N.Z. : Inst. Publ. Admin., pp.15–36.

McQuillan, D. A. (1978) Farm size and work ethic : measuring the success of immigrant farmers on the American grassland 1875–1925, *J. Hist. Geog.*, **4**, 57–76.

McRae, S. G. and **Burnham, C. P.** (1981) *Land evaluation.* Oxford : Clarendon.

MAFF (1976) Agricultural land classification in England and Wales : the definition and identification of sub-grades within Grade 3, *Ministry of Agriculture, Fisheries & Food Tech. Rep. 11/1.*

Magleby, R. and **Gadsby, D.** (1979) Environmental regulations : impacts on farm structure, *USDA Agric. Econ. Rep.* **438**, 195–200.

Manners, I. R. (1974) The environmental impact of modern agricultural technologies. In I. R. Manners and M. W. Mikesell (eds) *Perspectives on the environment.* Washington : Ass. Am. Geog., pp.181–212.

Manners, I. R. (1978) Agricultural activities and environmental stress. In K. A. Hammond *et al.* (eds) *op.cit.,* pp.263–80.

Manners, I. R. (1979) The persistent problem of the boll weevil : pest control in principle and practice, *Geog. Rev.,* **69**, 25–42.

Manning, E. W. and **McCuaig, J. D.** (1981) The loss of Canadian agricultural land : a national perspective, *Ontario Geog.,* **18**, 25–45.

Marsh, G. P. (1864) *Man and nature : or physical geography as modified by human action.* Cambridge, Mass. : Harvard University Press (1965 reprint).

Martel, Y. A. and **Mackenzie, A. F.** (1980) Long-term effects of cultivation and land use on soil quality in Quebec, *Can. J. Soil Sci.,* **60**, 411–20.

Mason, R. and **Halter, A. N.** (1980) Risk attitudes and the forced discontinuance of agricultural practices, *Rural Sociol.,* **45**, 435–47.

Massey, D. and **Catalano, A.** (1978) *Capital and land : landownership by capital in Great Britain.* London : Edward Arnold.

Mather, A. S. (1978a) Patterns of afforestation in Britain since 1945, *Geography,* **63**, 157–66.

Mather, A. S. (1978b) *State-aided land settlement in Scotland.* University of Aberdeen O'Dell Mem. Monogr. 6.

Mather, A. S. (1978c) The alleged deterioration in hill grazings in the Scottish Highlands, *Biol. Conserv.,* **14**, 181–95.

Mather, A. S. (1982) The changing perception of soil erosion in New Zealand, *Geog. J.,* **148**, 207–18.

Mather, A. S. (1983) The desertification of Central Otago, New Zealand, *Environ. Conserv.,* **9**, 209–16.

Mattingley, P. F. (1972) Intensity of agricultural land use near cities : a case study, *Prof. Geog.,* **24**, 7–10.

Megahan, W. F. and **Kidd, W. J.** (1972) Effects of logging and logging roads on erosion and sediment deposition from steep terrain, *J. For.,* **70**, 136–41.

Mercer, D. (1979) Victoria's Land Conservation Council and the Alpine Region, *Aust. Geog. Stud.,* **17**, 107–30.

Merlo, M. (1979) Peri-urban agriculture of the province of Padua. In OECD (1979) *op.cit.,* pp.265–308.

Miles, J. and **Young, W. F.** (1980) The effects on heathland and moorland soils in Scotland and Northern England following colonisation by birch (*Betula* spp), *Bull. Ecol.*, **11**, 233–42.

Ministry of Town and Country Planning (1947) *Conservation of nature in England and Wales.* Cmd. 7122. London : HMSO.

Misek, M. and **Lapping, M. B.** (1984) Making land policy : PEI's attempts to control individual corporate land ownership, *Plan Canada*, **24**, 55–62.

Mitchell, B. (1979) *Geography and resource management.* London : Longman.

Mogoluf, M. B. (1975) *Saving the coast : California's experiment in intergovernmental land use regulation.* Lexington : Lexington Books.

Moldenhauer, W. C. (1979) Erosion control obtainable under conservation practices. In *Universal Soil Loss Equation : Past, present and future.* SSSA Spec. Publ. 8. Madison, Wisconsin : Soil Sci. Soc. Am., pp.33–44.

Moore, N. W. (1969) Experience with pesticides and the theory of conservation, *Biol. Conserv.*, **1**, 201–9.

Moore, P. W. (1975) *Public decision-making and resource management : a review.* Univ. Toronto Dept. Geog., Disc. Pap. 17.

Moore, T. R. (1979) Land use and erosion in the Machakos Hills, *Ann. Ass. Am. Geog.*, **69**, 419–31.

Moore, I. C., Sharp, B. M. H., Berkowitz, S. J. and **Schneider, R. R.** (1979) Financial incentives to control agricultural nonpoint-source pollution, *J. Soil Water Conserv.*, **34**, 60–4.

Moran, W. (1978) Land value, distance and productivity on the Auckland urban periphery, *N.Z. Geog.*, **34**, 85–96.

Moran, W. (1979) Spatial patterns of agriculture on the urban periphery : the Auckland case, *Tidj. Econ. Soc. Geog.*, **70**, 164–76.

Moran, W. (1980) Mechanisms of land use allocation on the urban periphery : the Auckland case. In A. G. Anderson (ed.) *The land our future.* Auckland : Longman Paul and N.Z. Geog. Soc., pp.223–38.

Moran, W. and **Mason, S. J.** (1981) Spatio-temporal localisations of New Zealand dairying, *Aust. Geog. Stud.*, **19**, 47–66.

Morgan, J. P. (1974) ADAS (Lands) Physical agricultural land classification. In *Land capability classification.* Ministry of Agriculture Fisheries & Food, Tech. Bull. 30, pp.80–89.

Morgan, R. P. C. (1980) Soil erosion and conservation in Britain, *Prog. Phys. Geog.*, **4**, 24–47.

Morrison, F. L. and **Krause, K. R.** (1975) State and federal legal regulation of alien and corporate land ownership and farm operation, *USDA Agric. Econ. Rep.* 284.

Mortimore, M. J. (1969) Landownership and urban growth in Bradford and its environs in the West Riding conurbation, 1850–1950, *Trans. Inst. Brit. Geog.*, **46**, 99–113.

Morzuch, B. J., Weaver, R. D. and **Helmberger, P. G.** (1980) Wheat acreage supply response under changing farm programs, *Am. J. Agric. Econ.*, **62**, 29–37.

Moss, B. (1979) An ecosystem out of phase, *Geog. Mag.*, **52**, 47–50.

Moss, D. (1978) Even-aged plantations as a habitat for birds. In Ford, E. D. *et al.* (eds) *op.cit.*, pp.413–27.

Mrohs, E. (1979) Peri-urban agriculture in the Rhein-Ruhr region (Duisburg-Dortmund, Bonn and Cologne). In OECD (1979), *op.cit.*, pp.165–212.

Muggen, G. (1969) Human factors and farm management : a review of the literature, *World Agric. Econ. Rur. Sociol. Abs.*, **11**(2), 1–11.

Mumford, J. D. (1981) Pest control decision making : sugar beet in England, *J. Agric. Econ.*, **32**, 31–41.

Munton, R. J. C. (1974) Farming on the urban fringe. In J. H. Johnson (ed.) *Suburban growth : geographical processes at the edge of the western city.* London : John Wiley, pp.201–23.

Munton, R. J. C. (1976) An analysis of price trends in the agricultural land market of England and Wales, *Tijd. Econ. Soc. Geog.*, **67**, 202–12.

Munton, R. J. C. (1977) Financial institutions : their ownership of agricultural land in Great Britain, *Area*, **9**, 29–37.

Munton, R. J. C. (1983a) *London's Green Belt : containment in practice.* London Research Series in Geography 3, London : George Allen and Unwin.

Munton, R. J. C. (1983b) Agriculture and conservation: what room for compromise? In A. Warren and F. B. Goldsmith (eds) *op.cit.*, pp.353–73.

Murdoch, W. W. (1975) Diversity, complexity, stability and pest control, *J. Appl. Ecol.*, **12**, 795–807.

NALS (1981) *National Agricultural Lands Study : Final Report.* Washington : Soil Conservation Service, USDA.

Napier, T. L. and **Forster, D. L.** (1982) Farmer attitudes and behaviour associated with soil erosion control. In H. G. Halcrow *et al.* (eds) *op. cit.*, pp.137–50.

Nash, R. (1976) *The American environment – readings in the history of conservation* (2nd edn). Reading, Mass. : Addison-Wesley.

National Academy of Sciences (1970) *Land use and wildlife resources.* Washington, D. C. : NAS.

Nature Conservancy Council (NCC) (1977) *Nature conservation and agriculture.* London : NCC.

Nature Conservancy Council (1984) *Nature Conservation in Great Britain.* London : NCC.

Nelson, F. J. and **Cochrane, W. W.** (1976) Economic consequences of federal farm commodity programs 1953–72, *Agric. Econ. Res.,* **28,** 52–64.

Nelson, J. G. (1978) Canadian national parks and related reserves : development, research needs and management. In J. G. Nelson *et al.* (eds). *op.cit.,* pp.43–90.

Nelson, J. G., Needham, R. D. and **Mann, D. L.** (eds). (1978) *International experience with national parks and related reserves.* Univ. Waterloo Dept. Geog., Publ. Series No. 12.

Nelson, R. H. (1977) *Zoning and property rights : an analysis of the American system of land-use regulation.* Cambridge, Mass. : MIT Press.

Newby, H., Bell, C., Rose, D. and **Saunders, P.** (1978) *Property, paternalism and power: class and control in rural England.* London: Hutchinson.

Newby, H., Bell, C., Saunders, P. and **Rose, D.** (1977) Farmers' attitudes to conservation, *Countryside Recreation Rev.,* **2,** 23–30.

Nicholls, D. C. (1969) Use of land for forestry within the proprietary land unit, *For. Comm. Bull. 39.*

Northfield, Lord (1979) *Report of the committee of inquiry into the acquisition and occupancy of agricultural land.* Cmnd 7599. London : HMSO.

Nylund, L., Nylund, M., Kellomäki, S. and **Haapenen, A.** (1980) Radial growth of Scots pine and soil conditions at some camping sites in southern Finland, *Silva Fennica,* **14,** 1–13.

O'Connor, K. F. (1980) The use of mountains : a review of New Zealand experience. In A. G. Anderson (ed.) *The Land our future : essays on land use and conservation in New Zealand.* Auckland : Longman Paul/N. Z. Geog. Soc., pp.193–222.

O'Connor, K. F. and **Kerr, I. G. C.** (1978) The history and present pattern of pastoral range production in N.Z., *Proc. 1st Int. Rangelands Conf.,* Denver, Colorado, pp.104–7.

OECD (1974) *Agricultural policy in the United States.* Paris : OECD.

OECD (1976) *Land use policies and agriculture.* Paris : OECD.

OECD (1979) *Agriculture in the planning and management of peri-urban areas.* Paris : OECD.

O'Laughlin, J. and **Ellefson, P. V.** (1982) Strategies for corporate timberland ownership and management, *J. For.,* **80,** 784–8.

Omernik, J. M. (1976) The influence of land use on stream nutrient levels. *US Environ. Protection Agency, Ecol. Res. Series Rep.* EPA-600/3-76-014.

O'Riordan, T. (1971) The Third American conservation movement: new implications for public policy, *J. Am. Stud.*, **5**, 155–71.

O'Riordan, T. (1982) Institutions affecting environmental policy. In R. Flowerdew (ed.) *Institutions and geographical patterns.* London and Canberra : Croom Helm, pp.103–40.

Osborn, H. B., Simanton, J. R. and **Renard, K. G.** (1977) Use of the universal soil loss equation in the semi arid southwest. In *Soil erosion : prediction and control. Proc. Nat. Conf. Soil Erosion, Purdue University.* Akeny, Iowa : Soil Conserv. Soc. Am., pp.41–49.

Painter, R. B. *et al.* (1974) The effect of afforestation on erosion processes and sediment yield. In *Symp. Effects of man on the interface of the hydrological cycle with the physical environment.* IAHS Publication No. 113, pp.62–67.

Pampel, F. and **van Es, J. C.** (1977) Environmental quality and issues in adoption research, *Rural Sociol.*, **42**, 57–71.

Paran, U. (1970) Kibbutzim in Israel : their development and distribution, *Jerusalem Stud. Geog.*, **1**, 1–36.

Passmore, J. A. (1974) *Man's responsibility for nature.* London : Duckworth.

Patric, J. H. (1976) Soil erosion in the eastern forest, *J. For.*, **74**, 671–7.

Patric, J. H. (1980) Some environmental effects of cable logging in Appalachian forests, *USDA For. Serv. Gen. Tech. Rep.* NE55.

Patrick, G. F. and **Eisgruber, L. M.** (1968) The impact of managerial ability and capital structure on growth of the farm firm, *Am. J. Agric. Econ.*, **50**, 491–506.

Paterson, J. H. (1967) American agriculture and the decline of the agrarian ideal. In J. A. Sporck (ed.) *Mélanges de Géographie offert à M. Omer Tulippe,* **1**. Gembloux : Editions J. Duculot, pp.344–51.

Patterson, G. T. and **Mackintosh, E. E.** (1976) Relationship between soil capability class and economic returns from grain crop production in southwestern Ontario, *Can. J. Soil Sci.*, **56**, 167–74.

Patterson, T. W. (1979) *Land use planning : techniques of implementation.* New York : Van Nostrand Reinhold.

Pavelis, C. A. (1983) Conservation capital in the United States 1935–1980, *J. Soil Water Conserv.*, **38**, 455–8.

Pearce, D. G. (1979) Land tenure and tourist development : a review, *Proc. 10th NZ Geog. Conf.*, 148–50.

Pearson, G. G. (1975) Preservation of agricultural land : rationale and legislation – the BC experience. In *Proc. 1975 Workshop Can. Agric. Econ. Soc.*, Banff, Alberta, pp.64–89.

Peet, R. (1969) The spatial extension of commercial agriculture in the 19th century : a von Thünen interpretation, *Econ. Geog.*, **45**, 283–301.

Peet, R. (1972) Influences of the British market on agriculture and related economic development in Europe before 1860, *Trans. Inst. Brit. Geog.*, **56**, 1–20.

Pemberton, C. A. and Craddock, W. J. (1979) Goals and aspirations: effects on income levels of farmers in the Carman region of Manitoba, *Can. J. Agric. Econ.*, **27**, 23–34.

Penn, J. B. (1979) The structure of agriculture : an overview of the issue. In *Structural issues of American agriculture. USDA Agric. Econ. Rep.* 438.

Penning-Rowsell, E. C. (1975) Constraints on the application of landscape evaluation, *Trans. Inst. Brit. Geog.*, **66**, 149–55.

Penning-Rowsell, E. C. (1981) Fluctuating fortunes in gauging landscape value, *Prog. Human. Geog.*, **5**, 25–41.

Penning-Rowsell, E. C. (1982) A public preference evaluation of landscape quality, *Reg. Stud.*, **16**, 97–112.

Perring, F. H. (1970) The last seventy years. In F. H. Perring (ed.) *The flora of a changing Britain.* Botanical Society of Britain, Rep. 11.

Peters, T. W. (1977) Relationships of yield data to agroclimates, soil capability classification and soils of Alberta, *Can. J. Soil Sci.*, **57**, 341–7.

Phillips, R. E. *et al.* (1980) No tillage agriculture, *Science*, **208**, 1108–13.

Pick, J. H. (1942) *Australia's dying heart – soil erosion and station management in the inland.* Melbourne : Melbourne University Press.

Pidot, J. R. (1982) Maine's Land-use Regulation Commission, *J. For.*, **80**, 591–3 and 602.

Pierce, J. T. (1981) Conversion of rural land to urban : a Canadian profile, *Prof. Geog.*, **33**, 163–73.

Pierce, J. T. (1983) Resource and economic considerations in the allocation of agricultural land in peri-urban areas : a Canadian perspective, *Landscape Plan.*, **10**, 363–86.

Pigram, J. J. J. (1972) Resource reappraisal and resistance to change – an Australian example, *Prof. Geog.*, **24**, 132–6.

Pimentel, D. and Pimentel, S. (1980) Ecological aspects of agricultural policy, *Nat. Resources J.*, **20**, 555–85.

Pimentel, D. *et al.* (1976) Land degradation : effects on food and energy resources, *Science*, **194**, 149–55.

Pimentel, D. *et al.* (1980) Environmental and social costs of pesticides : a preliminary assessment, *Oikos*, **34**, 126–40.

Plamoudou, A. P. (1982) Augmentation de la concentration des sédiments en suspension suite à l'exploitation forestière et durée de l'effet, *Can. J. For. Res.*, **12**, 883–92.

Platt, R. H. (1976) *Land use control : interface of law and geography.* Washington : Assoc. Am. Geog.

Plaunt, D. H. (1973) Agricultural development policies and programs in Canada, *Am. J. Agric. Econ.*, 55, 903–12.

Plaut, T. R. (1980) Urban expansion and the loss of farmland in the U.S. : implications for the future, *Am. J. Agric. Econ.*, 62, 537–42.

Pope, R. D. and **Prescott, R.** (1980) Diversification in relation to farm size and other socio-economic characteristics, *Am. J. Agric. Econ.*, 62, 554–9.

Price, E. T. (1955) Values and concepts in conservation, *Ann. Ass. Am. Geog.*, 45, 65–84.

Prundeanu, J. and **Zwerman, P. J.** (1958) An evaluation of some economic factors and farmers' attitudes that may influence acceptance of soil conservation practices, *J. Farm Econ.*, 40, 903–14.

Prunty, M. (1952) Land occupance in the Southeast, *Geog. Rev.*, 42, 439–61.

Pyatt, D. G. and **Craven, M. M.** (1978) Soil changes under even-aged plantations. In E. D. Ford (eds) *et al.*, *op.cit.*, pp.369–86.

Raitz, K. B. and **Mather, C.** (1971) Norwegians and tobacco in Western Wisconsin, *Ann. Ass. Am. Geog.*, 61, 684–96.

Ratcliff, R. U. (1949) *Urban land economics.* New York : McGraw-Hill.

Ratcliffe, D. A. (1967) Decrease in eggshell weight in certain birds of prey, *Nature*, 215, 208–10.

Radcliffe, D. A. (1970) Changes attributable to pesticides in egg breakage frequency and eggshell thickness in some British birds, *J. Appl. Ecol.*, 7, 67–115.

Ratcliffe, D. A. (1971) Criteria for selection of nature reserves, *Adv. Sci.*, 27, 294–6.

Ratcliffe, D. A. (1976) Thoughts towards a philosophy of nature conservation, *Biol. Conserv.*, 9, 45–53.

Ratcliffe, D. A. (1977a) Nature conservation : aims, methods and achievements, *Proc. Roy. Soc. Lond. B*, 197, 11–29.

Ratcliffe, D. A. (1977b) *A Nature Conservation Review* (2 vols). Cambridge : Cambridge U. P.

Ratcliffe, D. A. (1981) The purpose of nature conservation, *Ecos : a review of conservation*, 2, 8–13.

Raup, P. M. (1982) An agricultural critique of the National Agricultural Lands Study, *Land Economics*, 58, 260–74.

Reganold, J. P. and **Singer, M. J.** (1979) Defining prime farmland by three land classification systems, *J. Soil Water Conserv.*, 34, 172–6.

Reimund, D. (1979) Form of business organisation, *USDA Agric. Econ. Rep.*, 438, 128–33.

Rennie, P. J. (1955) The uptake of nutrients by mature forest growth, *Plant and Soil*, 7, 49–95.

Rey Balmaceda, R. (1967) Modification antropogena del paisage patagonico en el ultimo siglo. In J. A. Sporck (ed.) *Mélanges de Géographie Offert à M. Omer Tulippe*, 1, Gembloux : Editions J. Duculot, pp.387–400.

Rhind, D. and Hudson, R. (1980) *Land use*. London : Methuen.

Richardson, H. W. (1974) Land prices in Edinburgh 1952–67, *Scott. J. Pol. Econ.*, 21, 67–75.

RICS (Royal Institute of Charted Surveyors) (1977) *The agriculture resources of the U.K.* London : RICS.

Robertson, C. J. (1956) The expansion of the arable area, *Scott. Geog. Mag.*, 72, 1–20.

Robinson, M. and Blyth, K. (1982) The effect of forestry drainage operations on upland sediment yields : a case study, *Earth Surface Processes and Landforms*, 7, 85–90.

Robinson, D. G., Wager, J. F., Laurie, I. C. and Traill, A. L. (eds) (1976) *Landscape evaluation : the landscape evaluation research project 1970–5*. Univ. Manchester Dept. Town and Country Planning.

Robinson, J. A. and Snyder, R. C. (1965) Decision-making in international politics. In H. Kelman (ed.) *International behaviour : a social-psychological analysis*. New York : Holt Rinehart and Winston.

Rogers, A. W. (ed.) (1978) *Urban growth, farmland losses and planning*. Wye College : Inst. Brit. Geog. Rural Geog. Study Group.

Rose, A. J. (1955) The border between Queensland and New South Wales, *Aust. Geog.*, 6, 3–18.

Rose, J. G. (1984) Farmland preservation policy and programs, *Natural Resources J.*, 24, 591–640.

Rounds, R. C. (1981) The Canadian prairies in the 1980s : problems and progress in wildlife conservation, *Manitoba Geog. Stud.*, 7, 74–105.

Rowley, G. (1975) Landownership in the spatial growth of towns : a Sheffield example, *East Midland Geog.*, 6, 200–13.

Rowntree, R. A., Heath, D. E. and Voiland, M. (1978) The United States National Park System. In J. G. Nelson *et al.* (eds), *op.cit.*, pp.91–142.

Royal Commission on Environmental Pollution (1979) *Agriculture and Pollution*. Cmnd 7644. London : HMSO.

Runte, A. (1979) *National parks : the American experience*. Lincoln and London : University of Nebraska Press.

Rutherford, J. (1970) Agricultural geography as a discipline, *Jerusalem Stud. Geog.*, 1, 37–105.

Saarinen, T. F. (1966) *Perception of the drought hazard in the Great Plains.* Univ. Chicago Dept. Geog., Res. Pap. 106.

Sahi, R. K. and **Craddock, W. J.** (1975) Estimating crop acreages in the Prairie Provinces – application of recursive programming, *Can. J. Agric. Econ.,* **23,** 1–16.

Saini, G. R. and **Grant, W. J.** (1980) Long-term effects of intensive cultivation on soil quality in the potato growing areas of New Brunswick (Canada) and Maine (USA), *Can. J. Soil Sci.,* **60,** 421–8.

Sanchez, P. A. and **Buol, S. W.** (1975) Soils of the tropics and the world food crisis, *Science,* **188,** 598–603.

Schertz, L. P. and **Wunderlich, G.** (1982) Structure of farming and landownership in the future. In H. G. Halcrow *et al.* (eds), *op.cit.,* pp.163–83.

Schmid, A. A. (1968) *Converting land from rural to urban uses.* Washington, D.C. : Resources for the Future.

Schmid, J. A. (1974) The environmental impact of urbanisation. In I. R. Manners and M. W. Mikesell, *Perspectives on environment.* Washington: Ass. Am. Geog., pp.213–51.

Scobie, J. R. (1964) *Revolution on the Pampas : a social history of Argentine wheat 1860–1960.* Austin: Univ. Texas.

Scott, R. V. (1979) Land use and American railroads in the twentieth century, *Agric. Hist.,* **53,** 683–703.

Scott Committee (1942) *Report of the Committee on land utilisation in rural areas.* Cmd 6378. London : HMSO.

Scotter, C. N. G., Wade, P. M., Marshall, E. J. P. and **Edwards, R. W.** (1977) The Monmouthshire Levels' drainage system : its ecology and relation to agriculture, *J. Environ. Manag.,* **5,** 75–86.

Seitz, W. D. and **Swanson, E. R.** (1980) Economics of soil conservation from the farmer's perspective, *Am. J. Agric. Econ.,* **62,** 1084–8.

Seitz, W. D. *et al.* (1979) Economic impacts of soil erosion control, *Land Economics,* **55,** 28–42.

Self, P. and **Storing, P.** (1962) *The state and the farmer.* London : George Allen and Unwin.

Sheail, J. (1976) *Nature in Trust : The history of nature conservation in Britain.* Glasgow : Blackie.

Sheail, J. (1982) Wild plants and the perception of land-use change in Britain : an historical perspective, *Biol. Conserv.,* **24,** 129–46.

Sheehy, S. J. (1982) Factors influencing ownership, tenancy, mobility and use of farmland in Ireland. *Information on Agriculture* No. 84.

Sherlock, R. L. (1922) *Man as a geological agent : an account of his action on inanimate nature.* London : Witherby.

Shoard, M. (1980) *The theft of the countryside.* London : Temple Smith.

Shortridge, J. R. (1976) The collapse of frontier farming in Alaska, *Ann. Ass. Am. Geog.,* **66,** 583–604.

Simmons, I. G. (1975) Towards an ecology of Mesolithic man in the uplands of Great Britain, *J. Arch. Sci.*, 2, 1–15.

Simms, D. H. (1970) *The Soil Conservation Service*. New York : Praeger.

Simon, H. A. (1957) *Models of man*. New York : John Wiley.

Sinclair, R. (1967) Von Thünen and urban sprawl, *Ann. Ass. Am. Geog.*, 57, 72–88.

Singer, M. J., Huntingdon, G. L. and Sketchley, H. R. (1977) Erosion prediction on Californian rangeland : research developments and needs. In Soil Conservation Society (1977) *op.cit.*, pp.143–51.

Skidmore, E. L., Carstenson, W. A. and Banbury, E. E. (1975) Soil changes resulting from cropping, *Proc. Soil Sci. Soc. Am.*, 39, 964–7.

Skrubbeltrang, F. (1953) *Agricultural development and rural reform in Denmark*. Rome : FAO Agricultural Studies No. 22.

Slesser, M. (1976) Energy requirements of agriculture. In J. Lenihan and W. W. Fletcher (eds) *Food, agriculture and the environment*. Glasgow : Blackie, pp.1–20.

Smith, B. D. (1980) The effects of afforestation on the trout of a small stream in southern Scotland, *Fish Manag.*, 11, 39–57.

Smith, E. G. Jr (1975) Fragmented farms in the United States, *Ann. Ass. Am. Geog.*, 65, 58–70.

Smith, R. and Smith, D. L. (1977) Farm fragmentation on Western Eyre Peninsula, South Australia, *Aust. Geog. Stud.*, 15, 158–73.

Smith, R. M. and Stamey, W. L. (1965) Determining the range of tolerable erosion, *Soil Sci.*, 100, 414–24.

Smith, P. and Sutherland, N. S. (1974) Use of a land capability classification in a survey development plan for the Island of Mull. In *Land capability classification*. Ministry of Agriculture, Fisheries & Food Tech. Bull. 30, London : HMSO, pp.90–96.

Smith, T. F., Van Genderen, J. L. and Holland, E. W. (1977) A land use study of Developed Areas in England and Wales, *Cart. J.*, 14, 23–9.

Smith, W. and Mears, A. (1975) The impact of urban sprawl : horticulture in the Port Hills, Christchurch, *N.Z. J. Geog.*, 59, 18–24.

Soil Conservation Society (1977) *Soil erosion : prediction and control. Proc. Nat. Conf. Soil Erosion, Purdue University*. Ankeny, Iowa : Soil Conservation Society of America.

Speight, M. C. D. (1973) *Ecological change and outdoor recreation*. Univ. Coll. London Dept. Geog., Disc. Pap. Conservation, 4.

Spencer, J. E. and Horvath, R. J. (1963) How does an agricultural region originate? *Ann. Ass. Am. Geog.*, 62, 283–306.

Spoor, G. and Muckle, T. B. (1974) Influence of soil type and slope on tractor and implement performance. In D. Mackney (ed.), *op.cit.*, pp.125–34.

Springett, J. (1982) Landowners and urban development : the Ramsden Estate and nineteenth century Huddersfield, *J. Hist. Geog.*, **8**, 129–44.

Stamp, L. D. (1948) *The land of Britain : its use and misuse.* London: Longman.

Steen, H. K. (1976) *The U.S. Forest Service : a history.* Seattle and London : University of Washington Press.

Storrow, T. and **Winthrop, F.** (1983) Agricultural land retention : the Massachusetts experience, *J. Soil Water Conserv.*, **38**, 472–4.

Stover, S. L. (1969) Government as farmer in New Zealand, *Econ. Geog.*, **45**, 324–38.

Strahler, A. N. (1958) Dimension analysis applied to fluvially eroded landforms, *Bull. Geol. Soc. Am.*, **69**, 279–300.

Strong, A. L. (1979) *Land banking : European reality, American prospect.* Baltimore and London : John Hopkins University Press.

Study Team (1975) *National land use classification.* London : HMSO.

Swank, W. T. and **Douglass, J. E.** (1974) Streamflow greatly reduced by converting deciduous hardwood stands to pine, *Science*, **185**, 857–9.

Swanston, D. N. and **Dyrness, C. T.** (1973) Stability of steepland, *J. For.*, **71**, 264–9.

Syrodoyev, N. (1975) *Soviet land legislation.* Moscow : Progress Publishers.

Thomas, M. F. and **Coppock, J. T.** (eds) (1980) *Land assessment in Scotland.* Proc. Roy. Scott. Geog. Soc. Symp. Aberdeen : University Press.

Thomson, K. J. (1981) *Farming in the Fringe.* Cheltenham : Countryside Commission, CCP 142.

Tittensor, R. (1981) *A sideways look at nature conservation in Britain.* Univ. Coll. London Dept. Geog., Disc. Pap. Conservation, 29.

Toleman, R. D. L. (1974) Land capability classification in the Forestry Commission. In *Land capability classification.* Ministry of Agriculture, Fisheries & Food Tech. Bull. 30, London : HMSO, pp.97–108.

Tracy, M. (1982) *Agriculture in Western Europe : challenge and response 1880–1980,* 2nd edn. London : Granada.

Traill, B. (1982) The effect of price support policies on agricultural investment, employment, farm incomes and land values in the U.K., *J. Agric. Econ.*, **33**, 369–85.

Trewartha, G. T. (1925) The Green County, Wisconsin, foreign cheese industry, *Econ. Geog.*, **1**, 296–9.

Trimble, S. W. (1983) Commentary on 'land use change in a

Piedmont county' by John Fraser Hart, *Ann. Ass. Am. Geog.*, **73**, 285–8.

Trimble, S. W. and Lund, S. W. (1982) Soil conservation and the reduction of erosion and sedimentation in the Coon Creek Basin, Wisconsin, *US Geol. Surv. Prof. Pap.* 1234.

Troeh, F. R., Hobbs, J. A. and Donohue, R. L. (1980) *Soil and water conservation for productivity and environmental protection.* Englewood Cliffs, N.J. : Prentice-Hall.

Troughton, M. J. (1976) Comparative profiles of land holding types in the rural-urban fringe of London, *Ontario Geog.*, **10**, 27–53.

Troughton, M. J. (1981) The policy and legislative response to loss of agricultural land in Canada, *Ontario Geog.*, **18**, 79–109.

Trudgill, S. T. and Briggs, D. J. (1980) Soil and land potential, *Prog. Phys. Geog.*, **4**, 262–75.

Tuma, E. H. (1965) *Twenty-six centuries of agrarian reform.* Berkeley and Los Angeles : University of California Press.

Turner, J. R. (1975) Applications of landscape evaluation : a planner's view, *Trans. Inst. Brit. Geog.*, **66**, 156–62.

US Council for Environmental Quality (1979) *Annual Report for 1978.* Washington, D.C. : CEQ.

USDA Forest Service (1977) The nation's renewable resources – an assessment 1976. *Forest Resource Report* No. 21.

USDA Forest Service (1981) An assessment of the forest and range land situation in the United States. *Forest Resource Report* No. 22.

US Environmental Protection Agency (1976) Forest harvest, residue treatment, reforestation and protection of water quality. *US Environ. Prot. Agency*, EPA 910/9-76-020.

Vale, T. R. (1979) Use of public rangelands in the American West, *Envir. Conserv.*, **6**, 53–62.

Vale, T. R. and Vale, G. R. (1976) Suburban bird populations in west-central California, *J. Biogeog.*, **3**, 157–65.

Vamplew, W. (1980) The protection of English cereal producers: the Corn Laws reassessed, *Econ. Hist. Rev.*, **33**, 382–95.

Van der Weijden, W. J., Keurs, W. J. ter and Van der Zande, A. N. (1978) Nature conservation and agricultural policy in the Netherlands, *Ecol. Quart.*, **4**, 317–35.

Van Hise, C. R. (1910) *Conservation of natural resources in the United States.* New York : Macmillan.

Van Vliet, L. J. P. and Wall, G. J. (1979) Comparison of predicted and measured sheet and rill erosion losses in Southern Ontario, *Can. J. Soil Sci.*, **59**, 211–3.

Van Vliet, L. J. P., Wall, G. J. and Dickinson, W. T. (1976) Effects of agricultural land use on potential sheet erosion losses in Southern Ontario, *Can. J. Soil Sci.*, 56, 443–51.

Vance, J. E. Jr (1971) Land assignment in pre-capitalist, capitalist and post-capitalist cities, *Econ. Geog.*, 47, 101–20.

de Viedma, M. G., Leon, F. and Coronado, R. (1976) Nature conservation in Spain : a brief account, *Biol. Conserv.*, 9, 181–90.

Vining, D. R. Jr, Plaut, T. and Bieri, K. (1977) Urban encroachment on prime agricultural land in the United States, *Int. Reg. Sci. Rev.*, 2, 143–56.

Vitousek, P. M. *et al.* (1979) Nitrate losses from disturbed ecosystems, *Science*, 204, 469–73.

Walcott, C. F. (1974) Changes in bird life in Cambridge, Massachusetts from 1860 to 1964, *The Auk*, 91, 151–60.

Wall, G. and Wright, C. (1977) *The environmental impact of outdoor recreation.* Waterloo, Ontario: Univ. Dept. Geog. Publication Series No. 11.

Wall, G. J., Dickinson, W. T. and Greud, J. W. (1983) Rainfall erosion indices for Canada east of the Rocky Mountains, *Can. J. Soil Sci.*, 63, 271–80.

Wallach, B. (1981) Sheep ranching in the dry corner of Wyoming, *Geog. Rev.*, 71, 51–63.

Walling, D. E. (1979) Hydrological processes. In K. J. Gregory and D. E. Walling (eds) *Man and environment processes.* Folkestone : Dawson, pp.57–81.

Walsh, J. A. (1975/76) Spatial-temporal variations in crop production in the Republic of Ireland, *Ir. J. Agric. Econ. Rur. Soc.*, 6, 55–74.

Ward, D. (1962) The pre-urban cadaster and the urban pattern of Leeds, *Ann. Ass. Am. Geog.*, 52, 150–66.

Warkentin, J. (1959) Mennonite agricultural settlements of Southern Manitoba, *Geog. Rev.*, 49, 342–68.

Warren, A. and Goldsmith, F. B. (eds) (1983) *Conservation in perspective.* Chichester : John Wiley.

Watson, A. (1979) Bird and mammal numbers in relation to human impact at ski-lifts on Scottish hills, *J. Appl. Ecol.*, 16, 753–64.

Weaver, T. and Dale, D. (1978) Trampling effects of hikers, motorcycles and horses in meadows and forests, *J. Appl. Ecol.*, 15, 451–7.

Webster, R. and Beckett, P. H. T. (1973) Soil and agricultural land classification in Co. Londonderry : a reappraisal, *Trans. Inst. Brit. Geog.*, 58, 125–8.

Wehrwein, G. S. (1942) The rural-urban fringe, *Econ. Geog.*, 18, 217–28.

Weiers, C. J. (1975) Soil classification and land valuation, *Town Country Plan.*, 43, 390–3.

Wenger, W. D. and Videbeck, R. (1969) Eye pupillary measurements of aesthetic responses to forest scenes, *J. Leisure Res.*, 1, 149–61.

Wert, S. and Thomas, B. R. (1981) Effects of skid roads on diameter, height and volume growth in Douglas fir, *Soil Sci. Soc. Am. J.*, 45, 629–32.

Westmacott, R. and Worthington, T. (1974) *New Agricultural Landscapes*. Cheltenham : Countryside Commission.

Westmacott, R. and Worthington, T. (1984) *Agricultural landscapes: a second look*. Cheltenham : Countryside Commission.

White, F. C. *et al.* (1981) Relationship between crop acreage and non-point-source pollution : a Georgia case study, *J. Soil Water Conserv.*, 36, 172–76.

White, G. F. (1961) The choice of use in resource management, *Nat. Resources J.*, 1, 23–40.

White, P. S. and Bratton, S. P. (1980) After preservation : philosophical and practical problems of change, *Biol. Conserv.*, 18, 241–55.

Whitehand, J. W. R. (1972) Building cycles and the spatial pattern of urban growth, *Trans. Inst. Brit. Geog.*, 56, 39–56.

Willard, B. E. and Marr, J. W. (1970) Effects of human activities on alpine tundra ecosystems in Rocky Mountain National Park, Colorado, *Biol. Conserv.*, 2, 257–65.

Willard, B. E. and Marr, J. W. (1971) Recovery of alpine tundra under protection after damage by human activities in the Rocky Mountains of Colorado, *Biol. Conserv.*, 3, 181–90.

Williams, M. (1970) Town farming in the Mallee lands of South Australia and Victoria, *Aust. Geog. Stud.*, 8, 173–91.

Williams, M. (1976) Planned and unplanned changes in the marginal lands of South Australia, *Aust. Geog.*, 13, 271–81.

Wischmeier, W. H. (1976) Use and misuse of the universal soil loss equation, *J. Soil Water Conserv.*, 31, 5–9.

Wischmeier, W. H. and Smith, D. D. (1965) Rainfall-erosion losses from cropland east of the Rocky Mountains, *USDA Agric. Handbook* No. 282.

Wischmeier, W. H. and Smith, D. D. (1978) Predicting rainfall erosion losses – a guide to conservation planning, *USDA Agric. Handbook* No. 537.

Wise, M. J. (1948) The growth of Birmingham, *Geography*, 33, 176–90.

Wolman, M. G. (1967) A cycle of sedimentation and erosion in urban river channels, *Geog. Ann.*, 49A, 385–95.

Wolpert, J. (1964) The decision process in a spatial context, *Ann. Ass. Am. Geog.*, 54, 537–58.

Wood, L. J. (1981) Energy and agriculture : some geographical implications, *Tijd. Econ. Soc. Geog.*, 72, 224–34.

Wright, H. E. (1974) Landscape development, forest fires and wilderness management, *Science,* **186,** 487–95.

Wright, L. W. (1980) Decision making and the logging industry : an example from New Zealand, *Biol. Conserv.,* **18,** 101–16.

Wunder, W. (1983) Die Forstpolitik Schwedens unter veranderten gesamtpolitischer Konzeption, *Allegemeine Forstzeitschrift,* **43,** 1171–2.

Wunderlich, G. (1975) Land along the Blue Ridge : ownership and use of land in Rappahannock County, Va., *USDA Agric. Econ. Rep. 299.*

Yeates, M. H. (1965) Some factors affecting the spatial distribution of Chicago land values 1910–1960, *Econ. Geog.,* **41,** 57–70.

Ziemetz, K. A., Dillon, E., Hardy, E. E. and **Otte, R. C.** (1976) Dynamics of land use in fast growth areas, *USDA Agric. Econ. Rep. 325.*

Zube, E. H. (1974) Cross-disciplinary and intermode agreement on the description and evaluation of landscape resources, *Environ. Behav.,* **6,** 69–89.

Zube, E. H., Pitt, D. G. and **Anderson, T. W.** (1975) Perception and prediction of scenic resource values of the Northeast. In E. H. Zube, R. O. Brush and J. G. Fabos (eds) *Landscape assessment : values, perceptions and resources.* Stroudsburg, Penn. : Bowden, Hutchison and Ross, pp.151–67.

Index